The Unassumed Is the Unhealed

The UNASSUMED Is the UNHEALED

The Humanity of Christ
in the Theology of T. F. Torrance

KEVIN CHIAROT

◥PICKWICK Publications · Eugene, Oregon

THE UNASSUMED IS THE UNHEALED
The Humanity of Christ in the Theology of T. F. Torrance

Copyright © 2013 Kevin Chiarot. All rights reserved. Except for brief quotations in critical publications or reviews, no part of this book may be reproduced in any manner without prior written permission from the publisher. Write: Permissions. Wipf and Stock Publishers, 199 W. 8th Ave., Suite 3, Eugene, OR 97401.

Pickwick Publications
An Imprint of Wipf and Stock Publishers
199 W. 8th Ave., Suite 3
Eugene, OR 97401

www.wipfandstock.com

ISBN 13: 978-1-62564-072-7

Cataloguing-in-Publication Data

Chiarot, Kevin

The unassumed is the unhealed : the humanity of Christ in the theology of T. F. Torrance / Kevin Chiarot

viii + 236 p. ; 23 cm. Includes bibliographical references.

ISBN 13: 978-1-62564-072-7

1. Torrance, Thomas F. (Forsyth), 1913–2007. 2. Incarnation. 3. Jesus Christ—Humanity. I.

BT220 C451 2013

Manufactured in the U.S.A.

CONTENTS

Acknowledgments | vii

1 INTRODUCTION | 1

2 ISRAEL
  The Womb Of The Incarnation | 23

3 ONCE AND FOR ALL UNION
  The Word Made Flesh | 87

4 THE CONTINUOUS UNION
  Theological Foundations | 103

5 THE CONTINUOUS UNION
  The Life Of Perfect Faithfulness | 165

6 THE CROSS OF CHRIST | 204

7 CONCLUSION | 224

Bibliography | 227

ACKNOWLEDGMENTS

I WISH TO EXPRESS my gratitude to a number of people without whom this work would not have been possible. Dr. John Vance, pastor of Westminster Presbyterian Church in Rock Tavern, New York, has been my father in a genuinely Reformed and catholic approach to theology and the pastoral ministry. Dr. Vance introduced me to the work of T. F. Torrance some twenty years ago. My debt to him is immense. The session of Covenant Presbyterian Church in Jackson, Tennessee, my current charge, has been unwaveringly gracious and supportive of this work. They have needed no prodding to see that high Christological doctrine is highly relevant to the ongoing life of the church. My good friend, Mr. Subra Balan, has generously provided the practical support to enable this study. His friendship and encouragement have enriched my life immeasurably. Finally, my incomparable wife, Cheryl, has endured the years of labor needed for this research and writing with her usual good cheer, hope, and steadfast love. She is a veritable sacrament of the goodness of God, and nothing would be possible without her.

1

INTRODUCTION

THE THEOLOGY OF T. F. Torrance is a complex integrated whole. The various loci interpenetrate each other with a remarkable coherence. His work spans a wide range of fields including the intersection of science and theology, epistemology and the philosophy of language, patristic studies, Calvin and Reformation studies, Barth reception and interpretation, as well as ecumenical theological engagement. Nevertheless, Torrance is always a Christian dogmatician working from an integrating center in the incarnate Word. From this center his thought moves upstream to a fully Trinitarian theology and downstream to the doctrines of the church, the sacraments, and the Christian life.[1] Thus, when looking at any narrow aspect of his theology the whole must ever be kept in mind.[2]

Our purpose is to trace the theme of Christ's assumption of our fallen humanity throughout Torrance's Christology. This Christological focus will, of necessity, enable us to illustrate how the doctrine impacts various aspects of his dogmatic thought such as his bibliology, his conception of our knowledge of God, faith, reception of the Spirit, and our human response in general. Nevertheless, our controlling concern will be Christological.

---

1. The best single volume on the whole of Torrance's thought is Colyer, *How To Read T. F. Torrance*. A good shorter summary is Palma, "Thomas F. Torrance's Reformed Theology."

2. In Polanyian terms, we might say our consideration of the subsidiary aspect of Christ's fallen humanity needs to give constant attention to a focal awareness of the whole of Torrance's theology. In our case, this will mean the whole of his Christology. See T. F. Torrance, *Belief in Science and in Christian Life*, 137.

Torrance not only affirms that Christ assumed our fallen humanity, but, as we shall see, it is a pervasive and decisive component of his "Christological science."[3] In addition to the pervasive nature of the doctrine, we contend that, as it is worked out in Torrance's thought, one encounters a weighty biblical-theological *argument* for Christ's assumption of our fallen humanity. That is, while never gathered together by Torrance himself in the service of the doctrine, the accumulation of biblical texts and dogmatic exposition results in an architecture, which constitutes the doctrine's most compelling rationale.

One result of Torrance's tightly interlocked thought is that in the published literature on his theology, regardless of the particular concerns of the author, there is a good deal of surveying the same ground. Nonetheless, we feel that the literature can be divided broadly into two classes. The first, and larger of the two categories, are works that deal primarily with the scientific and philosophical aspects of Torrance's thought, including works on his theological method.[4] The second category, smaller but growing, covers the dogmatic side of his thought. Our topic necessitates that we concentrate on this body of literature.

Before we look directly at the full-length works on Torrance that bear upon our topic, we must briefly survey some of the historical background and general literature that provide the context for Torrance's doctrine of Christ's humanity. Thus, we shall divide this chapter into four parts. *First*, we shall address the historical backdrop to Torrance's thought on the humanity of Christ. Here we shall briefly address the classical orthodox background with its consensus that Christ did *not* assume our fallen humanity. It is in this context that we shall note Torrance's historical scholarship and the dissent from the prevailing orthodoxy it underwrites. Then we shall trace the more immediate near term genealogy of his thought, where our concern will be with nineteenth- and twentieth-century theologians who provide some context and precedent for Torrance's views. *Second*, we shall look at broader, more recent works that address the question of Christ's assumption of fallen humanity and that are of interest in engaging Torrance's construction of the issue. *Third*, we shall look at the full-length works that address the relevant

---

3. Torrance sees his theology as a "science" in the sense that it is an obedient unfolding of the given reality of the "Object" of investigation, namely, the revelation of the Triune God in Christ. See T. F. Torrance, *Theological Science*.

4. A few examples among many will suffice. Dealing with the natural sciences is Luoma, *Incarnation and Physics*. On theological method see Colyer, *The Nature of Doctrine*. Rankin lists a dozen more works on science and theological method in Rankin, "Carnal Union," 6–7.

dogmatic side of Torrance's thought. *Fourth*, and finally, we shall state our thesis and provide an overview of its chapters.

THE HISTORICAL BACKGROUND

Classical and Reformed Orthodoxy

Classical Christology holds that Jesus Christ assumed a humanity free from original sin.[5] Ludwig Ott summarizes the traditional doctrine as resting on the nature of the virgin birth[6] and the hypostatic union.[7] This freedom from original sin entails the consequent freedom from concupiscence.[8] Ott cites the Fifth Ecumenical Council of Constantinople (553) which rejected the teaching of Theodore of Mopsuestia that Christ "was burdened with the passions of the soul and with the desires of the flesh."[9] Thus, Christ's humanity was perfectly holy even as Adam's was in the original pre-fall situation.

This pre-Reformation consensus was affirmed at the fountainhead of Reformed theology by John Calvin.[10] Calvin holds that Christ was "exempted from the common rule, which includes under sin all of Adam's offspring without exception."[11] This is the view that becomes codified in the Re-

---

5. This holds in spite of the differences across traditions as to the nature of original sin. Writing from a traditional Roman Catholic perspective, where original sin is construed as the deprivation of sanctifying grace, Ludwig Ott states that it is a *de fide* matter that Christ was free from original sin. Ott, *Fundamentals of Catholic Dogma*, 110, 168.

6. Ott, *Fundamentals of Catholic Dogma*, 168. "As original sin is propagated by natural generation, and since Christ entered life in a supernatural manner through the conception of the Holy Ghost, it follows that He was not subject to the general law of original sin." Here Ott cites Augustine, *Enchridion* 13:41: "Christ was generated or conceived without any concupiscence of the flesh, and thus remained free from every stain of original sin."

7. Ott, *Fundamentals of Catholic Dogma*, 168, 170. "The Fathers and the theologians infer Christ's freedom from original sin from the Hypostatic Union, which being a most intimate connection with God, excludes the condition of separation from God implied by original sin." Also, "by reason of the Hypostatic Union, Christ's human nature, through the Uncreated Holiness of the Word, is substantially holy."

8. Ott, *Fundamentals of Catholic Dogma*, 168.

9. Ibid., 168–69.

10. Calvin, *The Institutes of the Christian Religion*, 2.1.8. Here original sin is not merely privation of grace but "a hereditary depravity and corruption of our nature, diffused into all parts of the soul, which first makes us liable to God's wrath, then also brings forth in us those works which Scripture calls 'works of the flesh' (Gal. 5:19)."

11. Calvin, *The Institutes of the Christian Religion*, 2.13.4. After citing a number of Pauline passages, including Romans 8:3–4, Calvin concludes of the apostle, "thus, so skillfully does he distinguish Christ from the common lot that he is true man but

formed confessions. For example, the Westminster Confession of Faith and Catechisms, with their bi-covenantal structure and two-Adam Christology[12] strongly rely on, and thus affirm, the traditional position. Here Christ's being "without sin" is also tied to his virginal conception[13] and the hypostatic union.[14] Even clearer is the exclusion of any battle with concupiscence or our fallen humanity in the description of Christ's humiliation.[15] This view has been the dominant Reformed position down to our day.[16]

T. F. Torrance and the Historical Consensus

Against the backdrop of this history, T. F. Torrance's view that Christ assumed our fallen humanity appears as a voice of dissent. Yet, as Harry Johnson has shown,[17] it is not a position without precedence. Johnson surveys the minority witnesses to the doctrine throughout church history.[18] In Johnson's examination of the witnesses, the ante-Nicene and Nicene fathers, which are crucial for Torrance, are given scant notice and are cited as contributing to the comparative historical neglect of the doctrine.[19]

---

without fault and corruption." McCormack, while admitting that if the question were put to Calvin as to the flesh of Christ being fallen or unfallen he would have undoubtedly answered unfallen, thinks there are elements at the boundaries of Calvin's thought which point in the other direction. McCormack, "For Us and Our Salvation," 295. Matters of consistency aside, the Reformed tradition has enshrined Calvin's central and explicitly stated position.

12. *The Westminster Confession of Faith*, 7.2–3; *The Westminster Shorter Catechism*, 12, 20; *The Westminster Larger Catechism*, 20, 30, 31.

13. *The Westminster Shorter Catechism*, 22; *The Westminster Larger Catechism*, 37.

14. *The Westminster Confession of Faith*, 8.2–3. Consequent to the hypostatic union, Christ's purity is linked to his being anointed with the Holy Spirit as well. This corresponds to what Ott calls Christ's "accidental holiness" which is due to "the fullness of created grace." Ott, *Fundamentals of Catholic Dogma*, 170.

15. *The Westminster Shorter Catechism*, 27; *The Westminster Larger Catechism*, 39, 46–50. Here it should be noted that a robust description of all the *effects* of the fall, short of the assumption of fallen humanity itself, are affirmed.

16. Three examples from the multitude are Berkhof, *Systematic Theology*, 318; Berkouwer, *Person of Christ*, 256–57; Macleod, *Person of Christ*, 221–30.

17. Johnson, *Humanity of the Savior*.

18. The list contains Gregory of Nyssa, the Spanish Adoptionists, Antoinette Bourignon, Peter Poiret, Christian Fende, Johann Conrad Dippel, Gottfried Menken, Edward Irving, Erskine of Linlathen, Hermann Friedrich Kohlbrugge, Johann Christian Konrad von Hoffmann, Eduard Bohl, Hermann Bezzel. Johnson, *Humanity of the Savior*, 129–77.

19. Johnson, *Humanity of the Savior*, 195–97.

This stands in marked contrast to Torrance's reading of, and rigorous engagement with, the patristic evidence.[20] For Torrance, the Fathers show that the doctrine of Christ assuming our fallen humanity, far from being novel, has broad ancient support. Thus, it is urgent that the church recover what it has long forgotten: "perhaps the most fundamental truth which we have to learn in the Christian Church, or rather relearn since we have suppressed it, is that the Incarnation was the coming of God to save us in the heart of our *fallen* and *depraved* humanity."[21] This revealing statement shows the urgency and passion Torrance has for our topic. He claims "this is a doctrine found everywhere in the early Church in the first five centuries, expressed again and again in the terms that the whole man had to be assumed by Christ if the whole man is to be saved, that the unassumed is the unhealed, or that what God has not taken up in Christ is not saved."[22]

In *The Trinitarian Faith* Torrance mounts his most sustained argument from the Fathers. The heart of his contention is that, for the Fathers, the reality of the incarnation itself necessitates Christ's assuming our actual condition. "It is to be noted that the defense of the complete reality and integrity of the historical humanity of Christ by the Nicene theologians was offered mainly on *soteriological grounds*. It was the *whole man* that the Son of God came to redeem by becoming man himself and effecting our salvation in and through the very humanity that he appropriated from us."[23]

---

20. The fullest engagement with the patristic data relevant to our topic is in T. F. Torrance, *The Trinitarian Faith*, 146–90. Two chapters in T. F. Torrance, *Theology in Reconciliation* are also crucial: chapter 4 "The Mind of Christ in Worship: The Problem of Apollinarianism in the Liturgy," and chapter 5, "Athanasius: A Study in the Foundations of Classical Theology." Additional patristic background is found in the essays T. F. Torrance, "Dramatic Proclamation"; T. F. Torrance, "The Kerygmatic Proclamation of the Gospel"; These last two essays were published in T. F. Torrance, *Divine Meaning: Studies in Patristic Hermeneutics*. Also, T. F. Torrance, "Athanasius: A Reassessment"; "The Relation of the Incarnation to Space"; T. F. Torrance, "Karl Barth and Patristic Theology"; T. F. Torrance, "Alexandrian Theology." Torrance's doctoral work provides important background as well: T. F. Torrance, *The Doctrine of Grace*.

21. T. F. Torrance, *The Mediation of Christ*, 39.

22. Ibid.

23. T. F. Torrance, *The Trinitarian Faith*, 152.

Torrance piles up citations from, among others, Basil,[24] Nyssa,[25] Athanasius,[26] Hilary,[27] and Nanzianzen[28] who "provides the principle with its most epigrammatic expression in a trenchant refutation of Apollinarian denial that Christ had a human soul or mind. 'The unassumed is the unhealed; but what is united to God is saved. If only half Adam fell, then what Christ assumes and saves may be half also; but if the whole of his nature fell, it must be united to the whole nature of him who was begotten, and so be saved as a whole.'"[29]

Torrance amasses a great deal of patristic evidence for his case throughout his work. Yet, the correctness of his historical reading will not concern us. It is enough to note that Torrance is confident that what we have called classical orthodoxy is wrong on the nature of Christ's incarnate humanity. Torrance has his own "counter-genealogy" that cuts through the (mainly Eastern) fathers, Calvin and the early reformers, a handful of Scottish post-Reformation divines, and, finally, terminates on Karl Barth.

With respect to the Reformation, Torrance often cites certain features of Calvin's thought that can leave the impression that the reformer, and Reformed theology in general, held to Christ's assumption of our fallen humanity. The difficulty of this assertion is acknowledged by Torrance with reference to Calvin's *Geneva Catechism*, question 55: "Why do you go immediately from His birth to His death, passing over the whole history of

---

24. "Basil insisted, that the Pauline expression 'form of a servant' should be taken to mean, not some 'likeness' or 'resemblance' assumed by Christ in his incarnation, but the actual form of existence which he took over from 'the lump of Adam'—it was a 'real incarnation.'" T. F. Torrance, *The Trinitarian Faith*, 153.

25. Thus Gregory Nyssen exclaimed: "Why did the divine being descend to such humiliation? Our faith staggers at the thought that God, the infinite, inconceivable, ineffable reality, who transcends all glory and majesty, should be clothed with the defiled nature of man, so that his sublime activities are abased through being united with what is so degraded." Ibid.

26. "If sinlessness had not been seen in the nature which had sinned, how could sin have been condemned in the flesh, when that flesh had no capacity for action, and the Godhead knew not sin?" Ibid., 161–62.

27. "For God took upon himself the flesh in which we have sinned that by wearing our flesh he might forgive sins; a flesh which he shares with us by wearing it not by sinning in it." Torrance adds an important qualifier here: "However, Hilary had a habit of qualifying what he said in this connection which appears to leave his conception of God's self-identification with sinful humanity somewhat ambiguous." Ibid., 162.

28. "Just as he was called a curse for the sake of our salvation, who cancels my curse, and was called sin, who takes away the sin of the world, and instead of the old Adam is made a new Adam—in the same way he makes my rebellion his own as the Head of the whole Body. As long, therefore, as I am disobedient and rebellious by the denial of God and by my passions, Christ also is called disobedient on my account." Ibid.

29. Ibid., 164. See T. F. Torrance, *Theology in Reconciliation*, 154.

His life? Because nothing is said here about what belongs properly to the substance of our redemption."[30] Torrance, citing G. S. Hendry, claims that Calvin was not satisfied with this answer and that certain aspects in his thought point in the other direction. These include the fact that, for Calvin, the whole of Christ's life was "a perpetual cross," that He made atonement by "the whole course of His obedience," and that the teaching office of Christ belongs to His saving work.[31] To this list Torrance adds Calvin's repeated use of the phrase "Christ clothed with His gospel." This "clothing" Torrance takes to refer to Christ's ontic and noetic penetration into our fallen condition.[32]

In addition, Torrance often cites what Calvin calls the "wonderful exchange" embedded in the incarnation, which he sees as an exchange between God and sinful humanity and, thus, as an atoning exchange.[33] Finally, we must mention Torrance's fondness for Calvin's statement that "from the moment He took the form of a servant, He began to pay the price of our liberation,"[34] which he interprets as entailing a life of atoning obedience from within our sinful humanity.[35]

While these aspects of Calvin's thought are congenial to Torrance's project, it appears that he acknowledges that Calvin stopped short of affirming Christ's assumption of our fallen humanity. With regard to the saving significance of Christ's humanity, Torrance says "Calvin did not work that out in the detail that we would like."[36] In an illuminating remark on the Latin rejection of "the unassumed is the unhealed" he says: "Strange to say, almost all Protestant theology, not least in its evangelical forms, has followed

---

30. T. F. Torrance, *The School of Faith: The Catechisms of the Reformed Church*, lxxx–lxxxi. Torrance could have added the answer to question 53 as well which asserts that the virgin birth "preserves our Lord from all corruption."

31. Ibid., lxxxi. Hendry's work is Hendry, *Incarnation*. The difference with McCormack seems to be that, while McCormack sees these aspects on the boundaries of Calvin's thought, Torrance conceives of them as closer to the center.

32. Ibid., lxxxi–lxxxv. While this is an early work (1959), the same assertions about aspects of Calvin's thought vis-a-vis the tradition can be found in later works such as T. F. Torrance, "The Distinctive Character," 6–7; T. F. Torrance, *Karl Barth: Biblical and Evangelical Theologian*, 206–7; T. F. Torrance, "Karl Barth and the Latin Heresy," 470; T. F. Torrance, *Scottish Theology: From John Knox to John McLeod Campbell*, passim.

33. T. F. Torrance, *The Trinitarian Faith*, 179. The primary citation from Calvin is from *Institutes* 4.17.2.

34. The citation, from *Institutes* 2.16.5, is referred to in T. F. Torrance, *The School of Faith: The Catechisms of the Reformed Church*, lxxxi; T. F. Torrance, *Theology in Reconstruction*, 155; T. F. Torrance, *Incarnation*, 81; T. F. Torrance, *Scottish Theology: From John Knox to John McLeod Campbell*, 19, 49, 103, 138–39.

35. T. F. Torrance, *Theology in Reconstruction*, 155.

36. T. F. Torrance, *The School of Faith: The Catechisms of the Reformed Church*, lxxxii.

Latin theology down this road—although here too there have been notable exceptions such as Martin Luther and H. R. Mackintosh."[37] The ambiguity of the situation in Torrance's eyes is nicely summarized as follows: "In his doctrine of the Mediator, however, which he allied closely to the priestly office of Christ, Calvin operated with a more Western conception of atoning satisfaction, but with greater stress upon the whole course of Christ's vicarious obedience, as satisfying divine judgment and paying the penalty for the sin and guilt of mankind."[38]

Turning to the matter of post-Reformation dogmatics, we can do no better than Alasdair Heron's summary of Torrance's *Scottish Theology*:

> The dominant line of the tradition through the centuries is chiefly subjected to highly critical examination and called to judgment for far-reaching theological and pastoral defects. The theologians positively regarded and warmly recommended are rather those outside or in conflict with the mainstream, the tradition among others of the Erskines and the other Marrowmen (and of what came to be known as the Original Secession) in the eighteenth century, of Thomas Erskine of Linlathen, Edward Irving, and above all John McLeod Campbell in the first half of the nineteenth.[39]

Heron bluntly summarizes Torrance's reading: "'The whole Reformed tradition from John Calvin to Karl Barth' seems at points at least to mean rather 'the Reformed tradition initiated by Calvin, subsequently distorted beyond recognition by the Calvinists, but then recovered and deepened—particularly by Barth.'"[40] As with the patristic material, Torrance's handling of the sources provides an alternative genealogy that underwrites his confidence in the main contours of his dogmatic work and, thus, in the truth of Christ's assumption of sinful flesh.

---

37. T. F. Torrance, "Karl Barth and the Latin Heresy," 477. The absence of Calvin is significant.

38. T. F. Torrance, *Scottish Theology: From John Knox to John McLeod Campbell*, 95.

39. Heron, "Relation to Reformed Theology," 39. For another critical review of Torrance's reading of Scottish historical theology see Macleod, "T. F. Torrance and Scottish Theology."

40. Heron, "Relation to Reformed Theology," 41. For another critical appraisal of Torrance's reading of the tradition from the perspective of its culmination in Barth, see Muller, "The Barth Legacy," 684, 700.

The Near Term Genealogy of Torrance's Thought

We start our near-term genealogy with the work of Edward Irving. Like Torrance, Irving was a Church of Scotland minister. Irving is important because he is a Scotsman who taught that Christ assumed our fallen humanity a century before Torrance. He was charged with heresy and deposed from the ministry in 1833.[41] Irving laid great stress on the role of the Spirit in maintaining Christ's purity, a position which, over time, was integrated into Torrance's doctrine as well.[42]

The work of John McLeod Campbell, another Church of Scotland minister, who was deposed in 1831 for teaching universal atonement and the assurance of salvation as belonging to the essence of faith, clearly has influenced Torrance's thought.[43] Here we have in mind Campbell's integration of incarnation and atonement, his focus on the humanity of Christ, and particularly the notion of Jesus' vicarious repentance on our behalf.[44] Although we think he was less influential than Campbell on Torrance, Thomas Erskine also deserves mention. Though lesser known, he clearly belongs to the list of nineteenth century Scottish theologians who taught the doctrine of our Lord's assumption of our fallen human flesh.[45]

Mention must also be made of Torrance's beloved teacher at New College, H. R. Mackintosh. Torrance's relationship with Mackintosh was cut short by Mackintosh's death in 1936, but it is clear his Christ-centered evangelical theology, his emphasis on the homoousion, his use of ontological

---

41. The keys works are Irving, *Orthodox and Catholic Doctrine*, which sets out his teaching plainly, and Irving, *Christ's Holiness*, which is a refutation of the charge that he denied the sinlessness of Christ. Also see Dorries, "Nineteenth-Century British Christological Controversy." Dorries argues at length for the patristic foundation of Irving's doctrine. For a nineteenth-century criticism see Bruce, *The Humiliation of Christ*, 249–56. Bruce's work defends the traditional view. More recent appraisals include Strachan, *Pentecostal Theology*; Gunton, "Two Dogmas."

42. Torrance interacts critically with Irving in T. F. Torrance, *The Doctrine of Jesus Christ*, 122. This work stems from his lectures at Auburn Seminary in New York given in 1938–39.

43. The key work is Campbell, *Atonement*. See Torrance's sympathetic treatment of Campbell in *Scottish Theology: From John Knox to John McLeod Campbell*, 287–317. Campbell's affirmation of Christ's wearing our fallen nature is expounded on pp. 294, 301. See J. B. Torrance, "The Contribution of John McLeod Campbell."

44. Campbell, *Atonement*, 305–8. See Kettler, *Vicarious Humanity*, 187–204 for a good discussion of vicarious repentance in Campbell. Also, Redding, *Prayer and the Priesthood*, 189–220 discusses the impact of Campbell's view of the atonement on prayer and worship.

45. For Torrance's positive assessment of Erskine see T. F. Torrance, *Scottish Theology: From John Knox to John McLeod Campbell*, 263–77.

categories, not to mention his personal piety, left a substantial impression on Torrance.[46]

No discussion of the "genealogy" of this issue can be complete without paying attention to the towering figure of another of Torrance's teachers, his doctoral adviser, Karl Barth. Barth's overall theology, particularly his dynamic doctrine of God, his riveting focus on the centrality of Christ, his insistence that God is the content of His revelation, along with his concomitant interlocking of revelation and reconciliation, all had an immense impact on Torrance.[47]

Barth, with great passion, holds that Christ assumed our actual condition—our fallen humanity.[48] Here we have a direct, powerful, and formative influence on Torrance's doctrine. Barth is repeatedly emphatic: "the Word is not only the eternal Word of God but 'flesh' as well, i.e., all that we are and exactly like us even in our opposition to Him."[49] As with Torrance, Barth sees this as crucial to the doctrine of revelation. "He would not be revelation if He were not man. And He would not be man if were not 'flesh' in this definite sense."[50] Like all adherents of this doctrine, Barth holds that Christ was personally sinless: "He bore innocently what Adam and all of us in Adam have been guilty of."[51]

---

46. See the warm recollections in T. F. Torrance, "Hugh Ross Mackintosh." For a brief discussion of the relationship between Torrance and his teacher see McGrath, *Intellectual Biography*, 29–33. It was Mackintosh who first introduced Torrance to the work of Barth.

47. T. F. Torrance, *Karl Barth: An Introduction*; T. F. Torrance, *Karl Barth: Biblical and Evangelical Theologian*; T. F. Torrance, "The Place of Christology"; T. F. Torrance, "Karl Barth and Patristic Theology"; T. F. Torrance, "Karl Barth and the Latin Heresy"; T. F. Torrance, "Karl Barth"; T. F. Torrance, "The Legacy of Karl Barth (1886–1968)"; T. F. Torrance, *Transformation and Convergence*, 285–301. T. F. Torrance, "My Interaction with Karl Barth," 52–64.

48. See Torrance's exposition of Barth on this matter in T. F. Torrance, "Karl Barth and the Latin Heresy," 473–77; T. F. Torrance, *Karl Barth: Biblical and Evangelical Theologian*, 202–5; T. F. Torrance, "The Legacy of Karl Barth (1886–1968)," 305–6; T. F. Torrance, *Karl Barth: An Introduction*, 115–16.

49. Barth, *CD*, I.2, 151. Numerous similar statements are found in Barth, *CD*, II.1, 151, 397–98.

50. Barth, *CD*, I.2, 152. Here Barth uses many of the texts that are staples of Torrance's argument: Romans 8:3, 2 Corinthians 5:21, the Synoptic accounts of the baptism of Jesus, and Hebrews 2:18, 4:15. Note the integration of revelation and reconciliation which the assumption of our fallen humanity facilitates. "He exists in our place where we are, in all the remoteness not merely of the creature from the Creator, but of the sinful creature from the Holy Creator. Otherwise His action would not be a revealing, a reconciling action. He would always be for us an alien word. He would not find us or touch us." Barth, *CD*, I.2, 155.

51. Barth, *CD*, I.2, 152.

With regard to the Fathers, Barth apparently recognizes counter-evidence to the thesis Torrance would later develop, yet his sympathies would clearly lie with his student:

> The early church and its theology often went too far in its well-intentioned effort to equate these statements [of Christ's full solidarity with us] with those about the sinlessness of Jesus. But there must be no weakening or obscuring of the saving truth that the nature which God assumed in Christ is identical with our nature as we see it in the light of the fall. If it were otherwise, how could Christ really be like us? What concern would we have with Him?[52]

Calvin also receives sharp criticism from Barth for his perceived ambiguity on this matter.[53] Barth summarizes the historical situation as one in which "all earlier theology, up to and including the Reformers and their successors, exercised at this point a very understandable reserve, calculated to dilute the offense, but also to weaken the high positive meaning of passages like 2 Cor. 5:21, Gal. 3:13."[54]

BROAD BACKGROUND WORKS

Let us look now at broader, more recent works which provide context for Torrance's theology as it bears upon the humanity of Christ. Prominent in this regard is the aforementioned work of Harry Johnson.[55] Johnson's is the earliest work in this category that affirms Christ's assumption of our sinful flesh. While he has a good overview of the New Testament evidence, there is no treatment of Israel whose ordeal figures prominently in Torrance's architecture of the doctrine. In addition to his rather thin engagement with the

---

52. Barth, *CD*, I.2, 153.

53. Barth, *CD*, I.2, 152–53. Here Barth affirms Calvin's initial exposition of "flesh" as derogatory in John 1:14, but after Calvin qualifies it as meaning mortality, and not corruption, he writes: "How far, then, was it a *vilis et abjecta conditio* to which the Son of God condescended?" See Calvin, *The Gospel According to John 1–10*, 20.

54. Barth, *CD*, I.2, 153–54. Here we might state the difference between Torrance and Barth on Christ's assumption of sinful flesh as follows: Barth thinks the Fathers and reformers understandably, yet inconsistently, integrated texts on the solidarity of Christ with us with texts on His sinlessness. Torrance thinks the pre-Nicene fathers (and a few others) taught the doctrine and, for historical reasons, it dropped out of the church's consciousness.

55. Johnson, *Humanity of the Savior*.

Fathers, Johnson has a section on modern expositors of the doctrine which covers Torrance in three pages.[56]

Thomas Weinandy's more recent work[57] also contains a historical overview and a survey of the New Testament evidence. This book suffers from an ambiguity between the assumption of sinful flesh and the assumption of all the effects of human sin. While apparently holding that Jesus came in sinful flesh, he denies any inner propensity to sin or concupiscence.[58] Thus, Weinandy contends that the doctrine is not only compatible with the Catholic tradition within which he writes, but also with the Immaculate Conception of Mary. He mentions Torrance only once in a footnote.[59]

Two published dissertations are important which, while not wholly devoted to Torrance, feature his thought at some length. Christian Kettler in *The Vicarious Humanity of Christ and the Reality of Salvation* has a chapter devoted to Torrance.[60] While this work ranges over a wide swath of thinkers, in taking up the vicarious humanity of Christ it does touch a theme very close to ours. By vicarious humanity Torrance means, minimally, that Christ's humanity substitutes for us at every point. His incarnate humanity displaces our fallen humanity, not just at Calvary, but throughout the whole incarnate economy. We might say that our topic, the assumption of our fallen estate, is one of the crucial presuppositions behind the vicarious humanity of Christ. Kettler, in accord with his purposes, presupposes the assumption of our fallen nature rather than examining it in any depth. He then proceeds briefly to delineate the implications of the vicarious humanity across the various theological disciplines.

The second work in which Torrance figures largely is Graham Redding's *Prayer and the Priesthood of Christ in the Reformed Tradition*.[61] While the concern here is primarily liturgical, Redding also engages the Fathers on the nature of Christ's humanity. In particular the different readings of Athanasius given by Torrance on the one hand, and Grillmeier and Wiles on the other, receive attention.[62] Redding follows what he calls the

---

56. The list contains Karl Barth, J. A. T. Robinson, T. F. Torrance, Nels F. S. Ferre, C. E. B. Cranfield, Harold Roberts, and Lesslie Newbigin. Johnson, *Humanity of the Savior*, 167–77. One indication of the complexity here is the different lists presented by different authors of who "held" the doctrine.

57. Weinandy, *In the Likeness*.

58. Ibid., 18. See the critique of Weinandy in Hart, review of *In the Likeness*.

59. Weinandy, *In the Likeness*, 30.

60. Kettler, *Vicarious Humanity*. See chapter 6, "The Vicarious Humanity as Theological Reality: T. F. Torrance," 121–154.

61. Redding, *Prayer and the Priesthood*.

62. Ibid., 26–46. The relevant works are: Grillmeier, *Christ in the Christian Tradition*

Jungmann-Torrance thesis[63] in maintaining that the full humanity of Christ, particularly His assumption of our alienated mind, tended to drop out of view in the life of the church from the Nicene period onward resulting in a kind of "liturgical Apollinarianism."[64] Here the fallen humanity, while acknowledged, is simply subsumed under the concept of vicarious humanity which is then seen to have far-reaching implications for Reformed worship.

There have been a number of collections of essays published that deal with Torrance's theology or the key themes related to his work. Torrance edited a volume on the Incarnation[65] that provides important context for our topic. Of particular interest here are the essays on the homoousion,[66] the virgin birth,[67] the vicarious humanity of Christ,[68] and the incarnation in its relation to the atonement.[69]

Gerrit Scott Dawson has edited a volume[70] which, while dealing with the Torrance circle and not T. F. Torrance exclusively, also has a number of relevant contributions. Andrew Purves deals with the person of the incarnate Son,[71] and Elmer Colyer takes up incarnate atonement.[72] More directly to our topic is Dawson's own contribution on Christ's assuming a fallen humanity.[73] While this is a bird's eye view of the topic, it does touch briefly on a number of important theological, biblical and patristic themes which Torrance marshals in support of his view. Daniel Thimell and Trevor Hart edit a volume in honor of Torrance's brother, James, which is also of note.[74] Hart's contribution is important in handling common objections to

---

(Vol.1): *From the Apostolic Age to Chalcedon (AD 451)*, 308–10; Wiles, "Nature of the Early Debate," 139–51; Anatolios, "The Soteriological Significance of Christ's Humanity in St. Athanasius," 265–86. A summary of the Torrance-Grillmeier debate, with a decided preference for Torrance's reading, is found in Twombly, "Nature of Christ's Humanity," 227–41.

63. See Jungmann, *Liturgical Prayer*.

64. The reference is to Torrance's essay, "The Mind of Christ in Worship: The Problem of Apollinarianism in Worship," in *Theology in Reconciliation*, 139–214.

65. T. F. Torrance, *The Incarnation: Ecumenical Studies*.

66. Methodios, "The Homoousion." Heron, "Homoousios."

67. Houssiau, "Homoousios."

68. J. B. Torrance, "Vicarious Humanity."

69. Walgrave, "Incarnation and Atonement."

70. Dawson, *An Introduction to Torrance Theology*.

71. Purves, "Who is the Incarnate Saviour of the World?," 23–32.

72. Colyer, "The Incarnate Saviour: T. F. Torrance on the Atonement," 33–54.

73. Dawson, "Far as the Curse is Found: The Significance of Christ's Assuming a Fallen Human Nature in Torrance Theology."

74. Thimell and Hart, *Christ in Our Place*.

the patristic view, shared by Torrance, that the incarnation itself is of saving significance and not merely instrumentally ordered to the atonement.[75] Finally, in this genre, we should note the volume edited by Colyer, *The Promise of Trinitarian Theology*.[76] Here Purves contributes an essay on Torrance's Christology,[77] Deddo addresses his pneumatology,[78] and Richardson takes up his doctrine of Scripture.[79]

A rash of scholarly articles in recent years address the question of Christ's human nature and the possibility of its being fallen. John Meyendorff argues for Christ's assumption of fallen humanity from an Orthodox perspective.[80] Bruce McCormack's previously mentioned work[81] addresses our question directly while acknowledging that in modern times "the question in the form we have posed it here has a degree of precision which was lacking before the nineteenth century."[82] Kelly M. Kapic issues a much needed call for clarity on this controversial question.[83] He surveys the conflicting historical assessments of the data, and, without pronouncing on the matter, claims "it appears that the Dorries-Torrance thesis at present seems most viable with its massive compilation of evidence."[84] Rather, his purpose is a call for clarifying how Jesus can maintain his *personal* sinlessness with a fallen *nature*. In particular, the question of original sin and its relation to the assumption of a fallen nature needs greater attention. Oliver Crisp asks "Did Christ Have a Fallen Nature?"[85] Crisp argues that the assertion that Jesus assumed a fallen nature is difficult to square with a traditional understanding of original sin. After exploring this nexus, he proposes a possible solution, but concludes that it faces insuperable logical obstacles. Ivor J. Davidson ponders the complexity of the scriptural portrait of Jesus and the problems it raises for claims of his sinlessness.[86] While his concern is to strip

---

75. Hart, "Irenaeus."

76. Colyer, *The Promise of Trinitarian Theology*.

77. Purves, "Christology."

78. Deddo, "Holy Spirit."

79. Richardson, "Revelation, Scripture, and Mystical Apprehension," 185–204. Torrance's doctrine of Scripture depends upon the assumption of our fallen humanity in Christ. Richardson briefly mentions this.

80. Meyendorff, "Christ's Humanity: The Pascal Mystery."

81. McCormack, "For Us and Our Salvation," 281–316.

82. Ibid., 295.

83. Kapic, "The Son's Assumption of a Human Nature," 154–66.

84. Ibid., 159.

85. Crisp, "Fallen Nature," 270–88; Crisp, *Divinity and Humanity*, 90–119.

86. Davidson, "Pondering the Sinlessness," 372–98. For a related look at the humanity of Christ and the anhypostatic-enhypostatic couplet see Davidson, "Theologizing

sinlessness of its idealistic strains, he nonetheless feels that the advocates of the fallen view are often too simplistic in their opposition to the classical orthodoxy.[87] Ian McFarland looks into the relation of nature and hypostasis in relation to the question of Christ's assumption of human flesh.[88] He claims that Christ's taking a fallen human nature can be defended by distinguishing between fallenness and sinfulness as properties of nature and hypostasis, respectively. Even a fallen human will (a property of the nature) does not entail sinfulness, since sinfulness is a property of the "I," the hypostasis.[89] This essay is important for its deep interaction with the tradition and for its engaging in what might be called a "Chalcedonian" clarification of what precisely is meant by assuming a fallen nature.[90] The number of articles on this question show us that we are dealing with an issue which is still a live topic in contemporary theological discussion.

FULL-LENGTH WORKS ON TORRANCE'S DOGMATIC THOUGHT

Turning to works that deal exclusively with Torrance, let us begin with dissertations which are adjacent, and thus relevant, to our thesis. Robert J. Stamps takes up Torrance's eucharistic theology.[91] While he does deal with the Christological foundations of the sacrament, this work is relatively narrow in focus, excluding large tracts of Torrance's dogmatic work, and without substantial attention to the fallen humanity. Next, we mention two works that straddle Torrance's work on science and his dogmatic concerns. First, Richard Kirby takes up the issue of cosmic disorder in Torrance's thought.[92]

---

the Human Jesus," 129–53.

87. Davidson, "Pondering the Sinlessness," 397. Torrance, along with Johnson and Weinandy, is singled out here. For related explorations on sinlessness with connections to Torrance, see Owen, "Soul and Person," 119–28. Also, Hart, "Sinlessness and Moral Responsibility," 37–54.

88. McFarland, "Fallen or Unfallen?," 399–415.

89. Ibid., 412.

90. McFarland finds the language of the Fathers ambiguous enough to make it unclear how it would map onto the later controversy. "Inattention to this lack of fit between the rhetoric of the Fathers and the character of later controversies renders unpersuasive Thomas Weinandy's attempts to show that Christ's assumption of a fallen human nature was a matter of consensus in the patristic period. The same reservations apply to T. F. Torrance's more nuanced analysis in *The Trinitarian Faith*." McFarland, "Fallen or Unfallen?," 402.

91. Stamps, *Sacrament of the Word Made Flesh*. The dissertation upon which this book is based dates from 1988. See also Agnew, "The Concept of Sacrifice."

92. Kirby, "Cosmic Disorder."

Here the main thrust has to do with cosmology and creation, though Kirby's discussion of evil and entropy in Torrance is of some relevance to us. He discusses the issue of incarnational union only briefly.[93] In the second work, Douglas Trook engages in an ambitious scientific-theological quest for what he calls "the unified Christocentric field."[94] Here the center of gravity is Torrance's theology of relation. While Trook engages Torrance's Christology,[95] this is a rather eclectic work which deals with Torrance's quest for a theological science, thus engaging his epistemology and the scientific side of his thought as well. There is no sustained discussion of the assumption of our fallen humanity.

Inasmuch as the nature of personhood in Torrance's thought is important for untangling what it means to say that Christ assumed our fallen nature, two works are worthy of our attention. First, Robert Lucas does a comparative study on personhood and sanctification in Torrance and Hans Urs von Balthasar.[96] He deals with Torrance's basic anthropology, his theology of evil, and his conception of the fallen creation.[97] Lucas has a chapter on Torrance called "The Christological and Trinitarian Ground of Salvation."[98] Here he has ten pages on the all important context which Israel provides for the vicarious humanity of Christ. Lucas also speaks of the assumption of the whole fallen man and mentions the importance of this in Torrance's thought. He briefly describes the characteristic elements of the nature Christ has assumed. All of this is done, however, with a view toward Torrance's doctrine of sanctification. The second work in the area of personhood is by Andrew Bevan.[99] Bevan surveys Torrance's critique of dualism and its effects on the human person. He sets forth Torrance's incarnational critical realism as the remedy. While there is a survey of his Christology, nothing more than passing reference is made to the assumption of our actual humanity. Bevan's concern is that Torrance's Christology "provides an ontic-noetic foundation for human personhood."[100]

Michael Habets examines nearly all the loci of Torrance's thought with respect to his singular concern, the doctrine of theosis.[101] We hear again of

---

93. Ibid., 246–49.
94. Trook, "The Unified Christocentric Field."
95. Ibid., 53–96.
96. Lucas, "The Whole Christ for the Whole Person."
97. Ibid., 52–83.
98. Ibid., 147–213.
99. Bevan, "Nature of Human Participation."
100. Ibid., 79.
101. Habets, "The Danger of Vertigo."

the ontological nature of atonement which, for Torrance, takes place in the incarnate constitution of the Mediator.[102] Christ's humanity which, with respect to the hypostasis, is sinless, nevertheless, entails the assumption of our fallen nature.[103] Yet, our theme is not worked out at length. Habets' concern is that theosis is an internal work of God on our humanity wrought out in Christ.[104] Joel Scandrett looks at the challenges to the traditional notion of impassability in Torrance's thought.[105] Here Israel is seen as the workshop in which the suffering of God with His people which was to be fully wrought in the Incarnation is prepared.[106] The vicarious humanity, and the fact that it is fallen, is also affirmed.[107] Scandrett's larger point is that Christ suffers in our humanity in the unity of His person, and thus we must insist that, in some sense, the divine nature suffers.

Let us turn now to works which deal largely, if not exclusively, with Torrance's Christology.

We start with the earliest dissertation on his thought, Joannes Guthridge's work *The Christology of T. F. Torrance: Revelation and Reconciliation in Christ.*[108] This work, in the nature of the case, cannot interact with large portions of Torrance's mature thought. However, it is a cogent and clear account of his thought into the 1960's. Guthridge highlights Torrance's "thinking together" of Christology and Soteriology, his desire to state the hypostatic union, and thus traditional Chalcedonian Christology, not just in static, structural terms concerning the "composition" of Christ, but as dynamically at work both in revelation and reconciliation. He acknowledges that it is fallen humanity that Christ came to save and gives due place to the role of Israel in preparing the way for the incarnation. However, there is no tracing of the fallen humanity through the various strata of Torrance's Christology.[109]

102. Ibid., 154.

103. Ibid., 136–39.

104. We should note that Habets, like many others, deals with some of the standard criticisms leveled against Torrance's conception of the vicarious humanity of Christ. Namely, that it smacks of physical redemption, that it does not leave much room for pneumatology, and that the role of human response is muted. He brings some helpful clarification to the issue of our human response from Athanasius. Ibid., 148–49. See Anatolios, *Athanasius*, 158–61.

105. Scandrett, "Suffering Servant."

106. Ibid., 32–65.

107. Ibid., 74–89. Yet, the discussion of the fallenness of this humanity occupies only pp. 84–89.

108. Guthridge, "Christology."

109. This early work shows that the major features of Torrance's Christology are present quite early. While there has been development, there have been no epochal

18   The Unassumed Is the Unhealed

In the 1983 work of P. S. Kang,[110] the vicarious humanity of Christ is traced through the mediation of Israel, into Torrance's Christology, and downstream through our participation in his vicarious response via faith, conversion, worship, the sacraments, evangelism and Christian service. What is noteworthy, however, is that in a work of nearly 500 pages devoted to Christ's humanity, there are roughly fifteen pages devoted to the fallen humanity.[111] In addition, Kang provides no critical interaction with Torrance's theological and biblical arguments for the assumption of sinful flesh. Next, we note C. Baxter Kruger's thorough and clearly written dissertation.[112] Here, as the title indicates, we are concerned with how we know God. For Torrance, this is participation in God's self-knowledge through our partaking in Christ's vicarious humanity by the Spirit. Kruger has an excellent discussion of the role of Israel as the womb of the incarnation,[113] and fully acknowledges the importance of, and need for, Christ's assumption of our fallen humanity in Torrance's thought.[114] The doctrine, he asserts, "appears in explicit form at least sixty-six times in his writings and in at least nineteen different publications."[115] However, the concern here is strictly epistemological. To the extent that the fallen humanity of Christ is important to these questions it is addressed. It is not traced as a pervasive theme in its own right and no critical interaction with it is given.

L. G. Robertson's thesis is on the relationship between incarnation and atonement in Torrance's thought.[116] This is a critical work which raises some important and common questions against Torrance's views of incarnation

---

changes.

110. Kang, "Vicarious Humanity."

111. Ibid., 260–74.

112. Kruger, "Participation in the Self-Knowledge of God."

113. Ibid., 22–73.

114. Ibid., 146–64.

115. Ibid., 147. We can say that the numbers are now larger than this 1989 statement. Since then a number of key items have been published which take up the theme directly. A new enlarged version of T. F. Torrance, *The Mediation of Christ*, the Auburn Lectures, T. F. Torrance, *The Doctrine of Jesus Christ*, and the two volumes of Torrance's Edinburgh lectures, T. F. Torrance, *Incarnation* and T. F. Torrance, *Atonement*, all address the topic in detail. In addition, some key works which provide context and related analysis have appeared, for example, T. F. Torrance, *Karl Barth: Biblical and Evangelical Theologian*, 166–79. The doctrine is addressed in its wider Trinitarian frame in his magnum opus: T. F. Torrance, *The Christian Doctrine of God*, 142–44, 214, 251. It is given a more popular and pastoral treatment in T. F. Torrance, *Preaching Christ Today*, 12–13, 28–38, 58–60, and it is seen in the perspective of the history of Scottish theology throughout T. F. Torrance, *Scottish Theology: From John Knox to John McLeod Campbell*.

116. Robertson, "Incarnation and Atonement."

and atonement. Namely, is he not steering close to a physical theory of redemption?[117] Is his notion of solidarity and the ontological relation between Christ's humanity and ours clearly worked out?[118] Does he leave any place for faith?[119] Is his Christocentrism a denigration of Old Testament revelation?[120] These are all good questions, but this work does not flesh out either the logic or the extent of Torrance's view of Christ's assumption of fallen flesh.

Hing Kau Yeung's work deals largely with methodological and epistemological questions which arise out of Torrance's Christology.[121] He mentions the fallen humanity only briefly.[122] Timothy Gill's dissertation on revelation in Torrance deals largely with the question of natural theology,[123] though he does have scattered references to Christ's assuming fallen humanity.[124]

Man Kei Ho's study looks at Torrance's theology of the incarnation.[125] This work is broader than the fallen humanity which, surprisingly, receives only nine pages. We feel that this is an uneven work containing a number of critical remarks, some of which could be cleared up with a deeper penetration into Torrance's thought, some of which are simply wrong, and a few of which are legitimate.[126]

Another work with close ties to our subject is Kye Won Lee's *Living in Union With Christ*.[127] This is a thorough work which, after dealing with some methodological prolegomena, looks at Christ's incarnational union with us and our participation in that union in the life of the church. The crucial point is that the way of our union with Christ is the way of his prior ontological union with us. Lee, curiously, deals only briefly with Israel's

---

117. Robertson, "Incarnation and Atonement," 36.

118. Ibid., 98–120.

119. Ibid., 114.

120. Ibid., 83–86.

121. Yeung, "Being and Knowing."

122. Ibid., 185–86, 266–67. A short section on the authentic humanity of Christ makes no mention of his assuming fallen nature. Yeung, "Being and Knowing," 204–7.

123. Gill, "The Doctrine of Revelation."

124. Ibid., 33–35, 48, 52–56, 80, 100–1.

125. Ho, *A Critical Study on T. F. Torrance's Theology of Incarnation*.

126. An example of a legitimate issue is Ho's contention that, since Jesus' uniqueness (he was male and of a particular race, he did not have a human father, etc.) does not prohibit his identification with all men, neither is the fallen humanity necessary for full identification. Ho, *A Critical Study on T. F. Torrance's Theology of Incarnation*, 75–76.

127. Lee, *Living in Union with Christ*. This is a slightly revised version of Lee's dissertation written under T. F. Torrance's son, Iain.

crucial role.[128] He has about twenty pages on Christ's vicarious humanity as our only proper response to God.[129] Lee acknowledges the assumption of our fallen humanity and its importance throughout the various loci of Torrance's thought, but the theme is given no independent treatment.

Torrance's incarnational theology of union is also taken up by Duncan Rankin.[130] The contention here is that Torrance's notion of "carnal union" (essentially synonymous with ontic-incarnational union with all men) in its deployment of the anhypostatic-enhypostatic couplet, particularly the notion of anhypostatic solidarity, has some crucial ambiguities.[131] What needs clarification is the role and relevance of the Holy Spirit and human response in Torrance's Christology.[132] In addition, Rankin feels that Torrance's handling of anhypostatic solidarity adds an element of contingent necessity to the nature of the atonement.[133] While the fallen humanity is touched on briefly,[134] it is not developed in its own right. In his conclusion, Rankin does question whether Torrance's handling of anhypostatic solidarity demands concupiscence in the Savior.[135]

The final work for us to discuss is one which, from its title, appears closest to our topic. Peter Cass's work,[136] while certainly affirming the importance of Christ's assumption of our fallen humanity, does not trace the idea systematically through Torrance's whole theology. A large portion of the work deals with the Scottish tradition[137] and the rise of the Federal Theology (and Torrance's distaste for it). A final section deals with the ecumenical implications of Torrance's soteriology and compares him with Leon Morris, Walter Kasper and Vladimir Lossky. In the middle section, dealing with the fallen humanity, there is no exposition of the role of Israel, and no critical engagement with Torrance's account of the fallen humanity.

We are ready to draw some conclusions. First, there is no full-length work which deals solely with the fallen humanity of Christ in the thought

---

128. Ibid., 106–9, though it is referred to in passing elsewhere.

129. Ibid., 159.

130. Rankin, "Carnal Union."

131. Ibid. 18.

132. Ibid. 285–89.

133. Ibid. 289–94.

134. See, for example, ibid., 141.

135. Ibid., 294. Rankin notes that in the early Auburn lectures Torrance appears to steer away from this, and that his later thought clearly embraces the idea of internal struggle in the Savior.

136. Cass, "Christ Condemned Sin in the Flesh."

137. Basically an overview of T. F. Torrance, *Scottish Theology: From John Knox to John McLeod Campbell*.

of T. F. Torrance. Due to its pervasive place in his theology it is virtually impossible to avoid it in any work on Torrance's dogmatics. Thus, many works touch it briefly or indirectly, generally seeing it as an integral sub-theme of a larger concern such as personhood, vicarious humanity, knowledge of God, union with Christ, or theosis. What has not been done is a study of the theme throughout the whole of Torrance's "Christological science."

THESIS STATEMENT AND OVERVIEW

We shall provide a comprehensive study of Torrance's Christology with an exclusive focus on Christ's assuming of our sinful flesh. While this is unique in itself, our approach will also have a large narrative component which is often missing in works on Torrance's dogmatic thought. That is, we shall trace the narrative contours of Israel's history, as well as the narrative of the life of Christ from his virgin birth, through his baptism and earthly ministry, to its culmination in the cross. This, in addition to the standard theological analysis, will enable us to see with greater clarity and depth the role of our fallen flesh within Torrance's *dynamic* conception of atoning union. We shall demonstrate three things. First, the assumption of our fallen humanity is a critical, pervasive, and foundational feature of the whole of Torrance's Christological enterprise. Second, this will allow us to see that it is often conjoined to, if not conceptually behind, other debated aspects of Torrance's thought such as the nature of our union with Christ and the place of our human response. Third, we will contend that there are critical problems in Torrance's presentation of the doctrine that call into question its intelligibility. While we raise a number of concerns, we can summarize the most telling ones under two headings. First, there is the ambiguous status of the humanity that Christ assumes. We shall highlight this by contending that the human will of Christ, as Torrance conceives it, cannot be viewed as a coherent entity. Second, we shall point out a split between anhypostasia and enhypostasia that arises from, and in turn undermines, the assumption of our fallen flesh. This works itself out in a split in the way the hypostatic union works *within* the person of the mediator and the way it works in Christ's personal interactions with others.

In chapter 2, we shall examine the history of Israel at length. We shall contend that this history is not only "Christology in advance," but a Christology which both shapes, and is shaped by, the assumption of our fallen flesh in the incarnation. Many of the critical features entailed in the Word's assumption of our sinful flesh arise out of Torrance's reading of Israel's history as the pre-history of the incarnation. In chapter 3, we shall examine the "womb" prepared in Israel as it culminates in the virgin birth of Christ. Here we have what Torrance calls "the once for all union of God and man." In chapter 4, we shall provide a set of theological foundations which are necessary for examining this union as it works itself out dynamically in the life of Christ. Accordingly, we shall deal with the homoousion, the hypostatic union, and the anhypostasia-enhypostasia couplet. In chapter 5, we shall proceed to what Torrance calls "the continuous union of God and man." We shall explore the critical concept of "condemning sin in the flesh" which is a feature of the whole historical life of Christ. Then we shall proceed to examine crucial events and features of the life of Christ as Torrance narrates it from the Gospels. Finally, in chapter 6, we shall see the various lines of Torrance's though converge on the cross of Christ. We shall look at the judgment of the cross and the extent of the atonement.

2

ISRAEL
The Womb of The Incarnation

IN TORRANCE'S EXPOSITION OF the history of the covenant we have "an extremely sophisticated form of the Christological exegesis of the Old Testament that we find in the early church and in Luther, for example."[1] In this chapter we intend to look at this provocative reading for the light it sheds on our thesis. We shall see that, given Torrance's reading of the Old Testament, it is absolutely necessary that Christ, who comes to fulfill the whole movement, assumes our fallen humanity. Indeed, Israel is the pre-history of that assumption.

We shall look first at the election of Israel. Here we shall examine the broad parameters Torrance lays down for the understanding of God's purposes with his ancient people. We shall also set forth Torrance's understanding of the covenant of grace and Israel's role in it as the womb of the incarnation.

We shall then examine the movement of divine revelation in and through Israel's historical life. This movement of the Word of God intersects with her physical and spiritual reality and creates what Torrance calls "permanent structures of thought and speech" that are crucial in grasping the mystery of Christ. In addition, divine revelation creates what Torrance calls a "community of reciprocity" between Israel and God. We shall examine this with respect to both its corporate reality and the nature of the

---

1. Colyer, *How To Read T. F. Torrance*, 67.

reciprocity involved. The movement of the Word of God in and through this community creates a "spiral" in which the Word of God *to* Israel elicits and assimilates responses *from* Israel to itself. We shall examine this historical spiraling movement to uncover its inner dynamic. This will take us into the heart of Torrance's theology of revelation.

Next, we shall survey Israel's role as the mediator of reconciliation. We shall look first at the complex and interlocked relation which revelation and reconciliation have in Torrance's thought. Then, we shall examine the "covenanted way of response" that God provides for obedience to his Word. This entails the idea that the covenant must be fleshed out in obedience and, nevertheless, that Israel will be unable to keep the covenant. This will lead us to see that the Word of God has a running conflict with the "carnal mind" in Israel. We will examine the conflict's historical contours culminating in an exposition of Torrance's critical doctrine of the Isaianic Servant of the Lord. Our analysis will lead us, at various points, to discussing Torrance's Christology proper, though we shall do that more fully in the subsequent chapters. Finally, we shall draw some conclusions and offer an evaluation of Torrance's doctrine of Israel.

THE ELECTION OF ISRAEL

Torrance holds that God has made one covenant of grace with the whole creation.

> This relation between God and the creature through grace Reformed theology expounded by using the conception of the "covenant of grace," which embraces not only man but the whole of creation, involving a covenanted correspondence between the creation and the Creator reposing upon the free decision of God.[2]

This universal covenant becomes particularized in the covenant with Abraham.

---

2. T. F. Torrance, *Theology in Reconstruction*, 65. See T. F. Torrance, *Christian Theology and Scientific Culture*, 132–33. Also, God's fidelity to his creation "is powerfully expressed in the Biblical Tradition in terms of the Covenant of Grace in which God has grounded his creation upon his own eternal faithfulness and with which he ceaselessly undergirds its reality and maintains its integrity before him." T. F. Torrance, "The Goodness and Dignity of Man," 313. Thus, "Redemption is no mere afterthought for in it the original creation comes to a transcendent realization and the one covenant of grace with all creation is fulfilled." T. F. Torrance, *The School of Faith: The Catechisms of the Reformed Church*, cxiii. As is evident here, Torrance denies any notion of a "covenant of works" with Adam.

Thus while the covenant of grace embraced all men, it was when God called Abraham and specifically promised him "I will be a God to you and to your seed after you," that the Church began to be separated out from the nations and brought into a definite form as the appointed sphere in history of God's revealing and redeeming activity through which all nations and all creation would be blessed.³

Thus, this Abrahamic covenant is the original creational covenant narrowed and given new redemptive content.⁴ This covenant is then re-enacted with Israel after its redemption from Egypt.⁵ Thus, the election of Israel makes it the focal point, the unique sphere within creation, where the purposes of God are worked out. She is "the critical center in the human race, and in human history."⁶ Here we have an intensification of the covenant as "the sphere within creation and history in which God's promises are given and fulfilled, and it is within the course of promise and fulfillment that conversation with God takes place, and therefore that dialogical theology arises as historical conversation with God."⁷

This historical dialogue with Israel manifests what Torrance calls a "triple activity of grace."

> Throughout the pre-history of the Incarnation, which was itself in a profound sense part of the movement of the Incarnation, God prepared a way, manifested his truth, and assumed man into a life-relation with himself. This triple activity of grace God carried through in Israel. In Israel he prepared a way of covenant love in which he established a union between himself and Israel; within that covenant relation of love God manifested himself as the Truth, bringing Israel into communion with himself; through union and communion God bound Israel to himself as the Lord, the Giver of life, and so set up his Kingdom in the midst of estranged humanity. He began to open up through

---

3. T. F. Torrance, *Theology in Reconstruction*, 194. See T. F. Torrance, *Christian Theology and Scientific Culture*, 84–85.

4. "When God made His Covenant of grace with Abraham it was none other than the Covenant of grace which He established with creation of the world, and which took on a redemptive purpose with the rebellion and fall of man. But with Abraham that Covenant assumed a particular form within history and with one race elected from among all the races of mankind in order that God might prepare a way within humanity for the fulfillment of His Covenant Will for all men." T. F. Torrance, *Conflict and Agreement in the Church: The Ministry and the Sacraments of the Gospel*, 120–21.

5. Ibid., 121.

6. T. F. Torrance, "The Divine Vocation and Destiny of Israel," 86.

7. T. F. Torrance, *The School of Faith: The Catechisms of the Reformed Church*, li.

Israel a new and living way for the redemption of mankind, that was to find its fulfillment in Jesus Christ, the Way, the Truth, and the Life.[8]

With this background, let us sketch the crucial features of Israel's election for our thesis. *First*, the organic relationship between the activity of God's grace in Israel and its fulfillment in Jesus Christ is such that Israel's history is the "pre-history of the Incarnation."[9] By this "pre-history," Torrance does not mean simply the history prior to the incarnation. He states that this pre-history "was itself in a profound sense part of the movement of the Incarnation."

Thus, *second*, there is essentially one movement throughout redemptive history:

> The whole historico-redemptive movement revealed in the Old and New Testaments is to be regarded as essentially one. The Old Testament speaks of the Coming One, and the Coming Kingdom; the New Testament speaks of the One who has come, and of the Kingdom as having arrived in Jesus Christ himself. The Old Testament is the revelation of the *verbum incarnandum*; the New Testament is the revelation of the *verbum incarnatum*: the center of gravity in both is the Incarnation itself, to which the Old Testament is stretched out in expectation, and the New Testament looks back in fulfillment.[10]

We have here something more than an assertion of covenant continuity or of unity in the plan of God. The history of Israel has been assumed into the movement of the incarnation itself. Thus, it is deeply and proleptically conditioned by that controlling "center of gravity."

Third, this means that while Israel and the incarnation mutually condition one another, the relationship is asymmetrical. "The prehistory is critically and creatively reinterpreted by the incarnate Word, and it is only in that light that we must look at the prehistory of the incarnation in Israel."[11]

---

8. T. F. Torrance, "Israel and the Incarnation," 307.

9. "[W]e can say that the history of Israel is the 'pre-history' of Jesus Christ and its word his 'fore-word.' That is to say, it is the pre-history in which He Himself acts and the fore-word in which He Himself speaks." Barth, *CD*, IV.3.1, 66. "It is in the history of Israel, in the Old Testament revelation with its covenant and liturgy and law that the lineaments of the face of God begin to be seen, until the face of God is fully seen in the face of Jesus Christ himself in whom we meet God face to face." T. F. Torrance, *Incarnation*, 44.

10. T. F. Torrance, "Israel and the Incarnation," 306.

11. T. F. Torrance, *Incarnation*, 38.

> Incarnate as the Jew from Bethlehem and Nazareth Jesus Christ stood forth, not only as the controlling center of the mediation of divine revelation in and through Israel, but as himself the personal self-revelation of God to man, the eternal Word of God made flesh once for all within the objective and subjective structures of human existence. Thus Jesus Christ, not Israel, constitutes the reality and substance of God's self-revelation, but Jesus Christ in Israel and not apart from Israel, so that Israel the servant of the Lord is nevertheless included by God for ever within his elected way of mediating knowledge of himself to the world.[12]

Jesus Christ is the center and substance of this movement, yet he is known only in and through Israel.

Fourth, as seen in this Christologically critical and re-interpretive light, Israel becomes the "womb" for the incarnation.

> The story of Israel is the pre-history of the incarnation of the Son of God. Jesus is born through the womb of Israel and within Israel through the womb of the virgin Mary, of the seed of Israel, of the seed of man.[13] And then at long last in the fullness of time when God had prepared in the heart and soul and religion of Israel a womb for the birth of Jesus, a cradle for the babe of Bethlehem, the Saviour of the world was born, the very Son of God—born right in the midst of Israel and all its suffering contradiction of God, and yet right in the midst of the Old Testament faith.[14]

It is clear that Torrance takes this metaphor of the womb in more than a purely metaphorical sense. He can say that, in Israel's history, "the Word of God is on the road to becoming flesh."[15] Israel, then, is ontologically related to Christ who gathers up and fulfills the whole three-fold (preparation of a way, manifestation of God's truth, and assumption of Israel into life relation with God) movement:

---

12. T. F. Torrance, *The Mediation of Christ*, 22–23.

13. T. F. Torrance, *Incarnation*, 41. This notion of Israel as the womb of the incarnation is a favorite root metaphor for Torrance. See T. F. Torrance, *Incarnation*, 43; T. F. Torrance, *Reality and Evangelical Theology*, 87; T. F. Torrance, *God and Rationality*, 149; T. F. Torrance, *The Mediation of Christ*, 18–19; T. F. Torrance, *Theology in Reconstruction*, 145.

14. T. F. Torrance, "Salvation is of the Jews," 166.

15. T. F. Torrance, *Conflict and Agreement in the Church: Order and Disorder*, 266.

> Israel was called to be the bearer of the Messiah, the mother from whom the new race should spring. And so to the end of time it remains true that "salvation is of the Jews." It is not only that Israel was called to be the bearer of the promises of God and therefore to be the messenger of hope, but that throughout her long history in her concrete existence in the flesh, Israel always bore within her the seed of the messianic Saviour and of the messianic race. Throughout all its ordeal of suffering, it was not least that organic union of Israel with Christ that constituted it church and preserved it from extinction, so that when at last it gave birth to the Messiah, its whole historical life was gathered up in him and together with the church of the Gentiles it was constituted one new man, the Israel of God, the universal body of Christ.[16]

Israel is the mother of Christ, she bears the seed of the messianic promise, and her *organic* relationship with Christ constitutes her in her role as church and preserves her. Thus, *fifth*, Israel is the provisional form of the New Covenant[17] and, as such, she has not only historical and epistemic, but ontological priority as the "'mother' of faith in the living God."[18]

Sixth, it is crucial to note in this connection that in the election of Israel God "set up his Kingdom in the midst of estranged humanity."[19] They are the "one people within the *Adamic* race set apart for vicarious mission in the redemption of the many."[20] The election of Israel is not the election of a holy people. Rather, God assumes "Israel in its sinful contradiction into partnership with himself." The election of Israel is the "election of man in corporate enmity to God."[21] Here the Lord enters "into the heart of Israel's

---

16. T. F. Torrance, *Atonement*, 347.

17. T. F. Torrance, "Christian/Jewish Dialogue," 140. Torrance was the chairman of this council and wrote the report which was submitted on behalf of the group to the General Assembly of the Church of Scotland in 1980. "The Church is to be thought of, not as born with Jesus or at Pentecost, but reborn, for it reaches back, through Jesus into the continuities of the people of God in Old Testament times which is no less the people of God. That is to say, the Christian Church has no independent existence apart from Israel, and cannot be understood either in its own origin or in its goal in disjunction from Israel." T. F. Torrance, "Israel: People of God," 3. See also T. F. Torrance, *Theology in Reconstruction*, 204–8.

18. T. F. Torrance, "The Divine Vocation and Destiny of Israel," 87.

19. T. F. Torrance, "Israel and the Incarnation," 307.

20. T. F. Torrance, *Theology in Reconstruction*, 196. Italics mine.

21. T. F. Torrance, *Incarnation*, 52. The election of Israel was "the election of man in his sinful existence and enmity to God." T. F. Torrance, *Theology in Reconstruction*, 197.

estrangement in order to make atonement."[22] Thus, all that is wrought in her organic union with Christ, as the womb of the incarnation, is wrought in the depths of her sinful existence. The coming of the New Covenant in Christ makes it clear that

> Church of God though it was, the holy people bearing the Presence of God in its midst, yet Israel was concluded under sin with the Gentiles, in the solidarity of the whole Adamic race, in the one equal grace of God freely extended to all men.[23]

Seventh, Israel's election means it has a vicarious role in the mediation of both revelation and reconciliation.[24] She is the one elected on behalf of the many. As such, she has a unique service to perform for humanity which both adumbrates, and is illumined by, the election of Jesus Christ:

> The election of one for the salvation of all characterized the whole story of God's dealing with Israel. In Jesus Christ, the incarnate Lord, the election of one for all has become ultimate fact within our human existence. . . . What took place on the cross revealed what was happening to Israel in the election of God.[25]

In the rest of this chapter we shall explore how Torrance unpacks the implications of this election unto vicarious service. We turn first to the mediation of revelation and, later, to the mediation of reconciliation.

THE MEDIATION OF REVELATION

The Intersection of Physical and Spiritual Reality

Torrance speaks of the revelation of God coming to Israel in such a way that it "intersected and integrated its spiritual and physical reality."[26]

> One of the most startling features about the Old Testament Scriptures is the way in which they represent the Word of God as becoming physically implicated with Israel in the very stuff of its

---

22. T. F. Torrance, "Israel and the Incarnation," 310. We shall explore the implications of this when we consider the mediation of reconciliation.

23. T. F. Torrance, *Theology in Reconstruction*, 198.

24. "Israel was thus invested with a vicarious mission and function in mediating the covenant purpose of reconciliation and redemption for all mankind." T. F. Torrance, *The Mediation of Christ*, 32. See also T. F. Torrance, *Theology in Reconstruction*, 194–95.

25. T. F. Torrance, *Incarnation*, 52.

26. T. F. Torrance, *The Mediation of Christ*, 15.

> earthy being and behaviour. Divine revelation did not just bear upon the life and culture of Israel in some tangential fashion, rippling the surface of its moral and religious consciousness, but penetrated into the innermost center of Israel and involved itself in the concrete actuality and locality of its existence in time and space, so that in its articulated form as human word it struck home to Israel with incisive definiteness and specificity.[27]

By the "Word of God" (capital 'W'), Torrance is referring to the Logos, the second Person of the Trinity, the eternal Son of God.[28] He generally refers to the Scriptures as the human response to this Word, as here when he speaks of the Word's "articulated form as human word." We shall explore this relationship shortly, but two themes of importance arise here. First, this non-tangential penetration of the Word gives rise to the unitary, non-dualist[29] cast of the Hebrew mind.

> The Jews in ancient and modern times have always stood for a dynamic outlook upon God and the world which is essentially non-dualist. This is an outlook which contrasts sharply with both deism and pantheism, for it regards God as the mighty living acting God who created the universe out of nothing, continuously sustains it in its being and order and interacts with the life and history of mankind. It is that Hebraic and biblical understanding of the living God which lies behind the New Testament message about the Incarnation, as the Creator Word of God become flesh, and about the death and resurrection of Jesus, as the direct personal intervention of God himself in our human predicament, where we are trapped within our own sin and guilt and violence, in order to save us, and even rescue us, from the clutches of death itself.[30]

---

27. T. F. Torrance, *The Mediation of Christ*, 15.

28. Torrance believes in a *logos asarkos*: "This means that we cannot but think of the incarnation of the Son as *falling within the being and life of God*—although, as we have had occasion to note, the incarnation must be regarded as something 'new' even for God, for the Son was not eternally man any more than the Father was eternally Creator." T. F. Torrance, *The Trinitarian Faith*, 155.

29. Dualisms of various sorts—cosmological (intelligible and sensible realms, time and eternity, physical and spiritual), anthropological (God and man, body and soul), epistemological (form and being, empirical and theoretical), as well as numerous others, are considered by Torrance to be at the root of numerous problems in the history of theology and Western thought in general. The reference here is to the Hebrew outlook which, for Torrance, more seamlessly integrates reality itself and more naturally opens it up for interaction with God. For a comprehensive list of dualisms Torrance rejects see Lee, *Living in Union with Christ*, 14.

30. T. F. Torrance, "The Divine Vocation and Destiny of Israel," 102. See T. F.

Second, and what we wish to highlight, is not simply this "interactionist"[31] model, but the fact that the interaction of the Word of God with Israel invades the fundamental structures of its existence, and those structures belong to the fallen world order. Israel's life and culture, their moral and religious consciousness, their space and time, their concepts and modes of thought, and thus, their very language itself, are all penetrated by the Word in its revealing activity. Revelation is not simply an external word from beyond. It domiciles itself into the full range of Israel's physical and spiritual existence. Our inherited dualisms, Torrance says:

> make us want to detach the religious concept of Israel from the particularity of its physical existence and history in space and time, and to peel away from divine revelation what we tend to regard as its transient physical clothing. That would be a fatal mistake.[32]

In Israel we have a vivid reminder of the fact that "theology cannot be narrowed down to the relations of God and man alone."[33] Rather, it involves what Torrance calls a "triadic"[34] God-man-world relation which takes the created order with utmost seriousness:

> The only knowledge possible for us is that which he mediates to us in and through this world. We do not and cannot know God in disjunction from his relation to this world, as if the world were not his creation or the sphere of his activity toward us. This is not to say that we reach knowledge of God by way of logical inference from the world, but rather that we may know him only within the field of relations actually set up by God in his interaction with the world he has made.[35]

Torrance, "Israel: People of God," 6, where he speaks of the Jewish "massively unitary, non-dualist understanding of the universe."

31. This is Torrance's term for the anti-dualistic model of God's relationship to the world. T. F. Torrance, *Karl Barth: Biblical and Evangelical Theologian*, 136.

32. T. F. Torrance, *The Mediation of Christ*, 16.

33. T. F. Torrance, *Reality and Evangelical Theology*, 25.

34. "So far as theological science is concerned, then, it is evident that we must operate with a *triadic relation*, God/man/world or God/world/man, for it is this world unfolding under man's scientific inquiries which constitutes the medium in which God makes himself known and in which man may express knowledge of him." T. F. Torrance, *Reality and Evangelical Theology*, 27. This "theological science" is theology done in a critically realist framework. See T. F. Torrance, *Karl Barth: Biblical and Evangelical Theologian*, 52–60.

35. T. F. Torrance, *Reality and Evangelical Theology*, 24–25. See T. F. Torrance, *Christian Theology and Scientific Culture*, 113.

Torrance sees the rational order of the world as taking two basic forms, word rationality and number rationality.[36] These correspond, on the one hand, to the world of persons and language, and on the other, to the world of things and scientific description.[37] Speaking of the need for an ontological reference to reality, Torrance says:

> This applies to the whole course and sweep of divine revelation to mankind through Israel, in which word-rationality and number-rationality are inseparably coordinated with one another, that is, in which God's communication to us through word cannot be severed from the determinate structures of the physical creation to which we belong as human beings.[38]

This number-word rationality exists in a universe which is ordered as a series of coordinated levels. The higher, more refined or sophisticated levels interpret and provide control for the levels below, which are open to the higher levels at the boundaries:

> Scientific knowledge embodies layers of coherent comprehension which answer to and are affected by the coordinated layers of orderly relations in reality itself. This integrated complex structure in reality and our corresponding knowledge of it forms an ascending hierarchy of orderly relations which prove to be open upward in ever wider comprehensiveness and profounder ranges of intelligibility but which cannot be flattened downward by being reduced to isomorphic relations on one and the same level. It is characterised throughout by what might be described as the principle of *coherent integration from above*.[39]

The mediation of revelation in this space-time matrix of word and number rationality in the stratified universe is helpfully summarized by Colyer:

---

36. T. F. Torrance, *Reality and Evangelical Theology*, 90; T. F. Torrance, *Christian Theology and Scientific Culture*, 109–44.

37. "No doubt, the created rationalities of word and number are very different, as different as the world of persons and the world of things, but they both go back to the same source in the transcendent Rationality of God and they are both brought together in the incarnation of God's Word in Jesus Christ, for they are upheld and sustained by Him." T. F. Torrance, *God and Rationality*, 164.

38. T. F. Torrance, *Christian Theology and Scientific Culture*, 36.

39. Ibid., 37. Note that the stratification of the universe results in a stratification in our knowledge of it. See T. F. Torrance, "Truth and Authority: Theses on Truth," 216–17, 232–38.

> To grasp what Torrance intends here requires the ability to think of the nation of Israel (and the church) as a spatial-temporal reality spanning the various levels of the created order (from the molecular to the personal and spiritual) and moving through a successive pattern of change and development involving both divine and human agency together.[40]

Torrance summarizes the situation with respect to Israel:

> God's revelation was mediated to Israel in the continuous indivisible field of space-time, in such a way that the physical configurations were inextricably interwoven with its communication and articulation to Israel. That is why . . . revelation and reconciliation had to go together.[41]

Revelation does not consist of free-floating oracles which can prescind from this creational complexity. Nor is the Word inserted into the created order in a hermetically sealed manner. Its mediation is "inextricably interwoven" with the full physical-spiritual range of Israel's life. Thus, creation does not stand simply in an instrumental relation to revelation.

Torrance's last sentence above is of immense importance. It is this feature of revelation, as embedded in this multi-dimensional matrix, which necessitates the fact that revelation entails, and is interlocked with, reconciliation. We shall explore this relation later, but for now we can see that the Word is mediated through fallen men, a fallen nation, fallen conceptualities and thought forms, fallen culture, and a fallen language, all of which depend on fallen lower level (e.g., biological and chemical) structures. In Pauline terms, the Word of God does all that it does in Israel in the sarkic order of this evil age. It is here that the Word begins its long work of shaping and forging Israel in its vicarious service in the mediation of divine revelation.

Permanent Structures of Thought and Speech

Torrance is fond of using the analogy of "conceptual tools" as instruments needed to rightly grasp the revelation of God, particularly as it comes to full expression in Jesus Christ.

> You cannot make anything unless you have the tools with which to form and construct it. You cannot think unless you have tools with which to think and shape the thoughts in your mind and form your judgments. The tools the mind requires are

40. Colyer, *How To Read T. F. Torrance*, 64.
41. T. F. Torrance, *The Mediation of Christ*, 16.

conceptions and categories and formulated ideas. Nor can you make much progress in instruction and learning unless you have appropriate and adequate tools for rational communication. That is surely part of the immense significance of the Old Testament, that is of the whole history of God's dealing with Israel, for it was within Israel that there were shaped and formed the tools which were used in the New Testament to grasp and interpret the bewildering miracle of Jesus.[42] Apart from the Biblical revelation we would not have the tools to grasp the knowledge of God; apart from the long history of the Jews we would not be able to recognize Jesus as the Son of God; apart from the suffering and agony of Israel we could not understand the Cross of Calvary as God's instrument to atone for sin and to enact once and for all His Word of love and pardon and grace. Apart from the context of Israel we could not even begin to understand the bewildering miracle of Jesus. The supreme instrument of God in the salvation of the world is Israel, and out of the womb of Israel, Jesus—the Jew from Nazareth.[43]

Here we have God molding Israel as a potter molds clay in the service of his self-revelation, and providing "a whole set of spiritual tools, appropriate forms of understanding, worship and expression, through which apprehension of God could be made accessible to human beings and knowledge of God could take root in the soil of humanity."[44] The tools Torrance envisions are not discrete, stand-alone instruments, but arise organically in Israel as "a matrix of appropriate thought and language forms for the reception of the incarnational revelation."[45]

In a moving paragraph Torrance describes the tools the Word of God forged for itself in Israel: By elaborate religious ritual and carefully framed laws, by rivers of blood from millions of animal sacrifices, by the broken hearts of Psalmists and the profoundest

---

42. T. F. Torrance, *The School of Faith: The Catechisms of the Reformed Church*, xxx. See T. F. Torrance, "Introduction: Theology and Church"; T. F. Torrance, *The Ground and Grammar of Theology*, 125, 161–62; T. F. Torrance, *God and Rationality*, 95.

43. T. F. Torrance, "Salvation is of the Jews," 167. For this language of grasping the "bewildering miracle of Jesus" in and through Israel see, T. F. Torrance, "Israel and the Incarnation," 319: "Apart from that prepared sphere of revelation and reconciliation no one could have grasped the bewildering miracle of Jesus or begun to understand the Incarnation or the Atonement." Also, T. F. Torrance, *The Mediation of Christ*, 5, 18, 108; T. F. Torrance, "The Divine Vocation and Destiny of Israel," 100.

44. T. F. Torrance, *The Mediation of Christ*, 7.

45. T. F. Torrance, *Theology in Reconstruction*, 145; T. F. Torrance, *God and Rationality*, 147–49; T. F. Torrance, *Reality and Evangelical Theology*, 86–87.

agony of the Prophets, by the tragic story of Israelite politics, and the shattering of their power again and again, God taught the Jews through hundreds and hundreds of years until the truth was imprinted upon their conscience and there was burned into their soul the meaning of holiness and righteousness, of sin and uncleanness, of love and mercy and grace, of faithfulness and forgiveness, justification, reconciliation, atonement, and salvation; the meaning of creation, of the Kingdom of God, of judgment, death, and at last resurrection; the thought of the Messiah, the Suffering Servant, and yet the Prophet, Priest and King. And then at long last in the fullness of time when God had prepared in the heart and soul and religion of Israel a womb for the birth of Jesus, a cradle for the babe of Bethlehem, the Saviour of the world was born, the very Son of God—born right in the midst of Israel and all its suffering contradiction of God, and yet right in the midst of the Old Testament faith.[46]

These interlocked "permanent structures" of thought and speech partake fully in the stratified space-time realities we outlined above. Through Israel, then, knowledge of God is "earthed in human existence,"[47] or "earthed in the clay of humanity."[48] This theology of revelation takes creation, history and culture with utmost seriousness as the complex medium of its communication and mediation. The Word of God "invaded the social matrix of Israel's life, culture, religion and history, and clothed itself with Israel's language."[49] The election of this sinful people to this vicarious service in the mediation of revelation understood in this fashion has foundational significance for Torrance's doctrine of the Christ, the final and definitive revelation of God, assuming to the full our fallen estate. In a statement which summarizes much of what we have said to this point he says:

> Within the universal covenant of God's grace, which takes in the whole creation, Israel was called out from the other nations to

---

46. T. F. Torrance, "Salvation is of the Jews," 166. A virtually identical list is found in T. F. Torrance, *Incarnation*, 42. A slightly different list is found in T. F. Torrance, *The Mediation of Christ*, 18. "Among these permanent structures let me refer to the Word and Name of God, to revelation, mercy, truth, holiness, to messiah, saviour, to prophet, priest and king, father, son, servant, to covenant, sacrifice, forgiveness, reconciliation, redemption, atonement, and those basic patterns of worship which we find set out in the ancient liturgy or in the Psalms. It was indeed in the course of the Old Testament revelation that nearly all the basic concepts we Christians use were hammered out by the Word of God on the anvil of Israel."

47. T. F. Torrance, "Christian/Jewish Dialogue," 140.

48. T. F. Torrance, "The Divine Vocation and Destiny of Israel," 88.

49. T. F. Torrance, *God and Rationality*, 147.

> be the unique historical partner of God's personal and intimate self-revelation, whereby knowledge and worship of the living God might be earthed in human existence, given shape in human understanding and speech, and be mediated to the human race at large. ... By its nature this covenant was not meant to be an end in itself, for through it Israel was steadily and painfully moulded by God into being the instrument of his saving purpose, and made to provide in its very existence among the nations the basis and provisional form of a new covenantal relationship with God which would include all nations.[50]

The church must, as a consequence of her dependence upon this one movement of divine revelation, acknowledge the epistemological priority of the revelation mediated through Israel.

> We need to go to school with the People of Israel, as it were, in order to share with them the training they were given by God through many, many centuries until a matrix of understanding and thought and worship was prepared in Israel appropriate for the reception of God's ultimate self-revelation in Jesus Christ.[51]

This means we cannot abstract "Jesus Christ from the matrix of natural and inherent relations in which he is found."[52] Doing so leads to "plastering upon the face of Jesus a mask of different gentile features which prevents us from seeing him and understanding him as he really is, as a Jew."[53]

Yet, this matrix of relationships does not stand alone. Taking his cue from the scientific achievements of Maxwell and Einstein, Torrance sees a two-fold approach to knowledge. Things must be examined in the matrix of their relationships to other things and also "in the light of their *internal relations* in virtue of which they are what they really are in their inherent constitutive structures whereby they are distinguished from other things."[54] With respect to the knowledge of Christ this entails seeing him in the matrix forged in Israel as well as his internal relations with the Godhead disclosed in the gospel. The two procedures entail one another, yet as we have seen, the center of gravity is Christ's own self-revelation.

---

50. T. F. Torrance, "Christian/Jewish Dialogue," 140.

51. T. F. Torrance, "The Divine Vocation and Destiny of Israel," 97. Also, T. F. Torrance, *The Mediation of Christ*, 12.

52. T. F. Torrance, *The Mediation of Christ*, 2. It is just this kind of abstraction which leads to Torrance's rather dim evaluation of much critical scholarship.

53. Ibid., 19–20.

54. Ibid., 3.

> It is not the substitution of Jewish for Gentile modes of thought that is to be envisaged here, but a "learning obedience" to the Word of God which Gentile modes of thought can only gain in the midst of Israel where the Mind of God and the mind of rebellious man have at last been brought to reconciliation, after long discipline in the history of Israel, in Jesus Christ.[55]

Thus, in interpreting Jesus Christ we do not use only the socio-religious matrix of Israel.[56] All these "conceptual tools" undergo a "recasting and reshaping in their actual use in the New Testament."[57]

> This does not mean that we are simply to interpret Jesus in terms of his background in Israel. The background for Christ the Son of God can only be the background which the fact of the incarnation creates for itself out of our world . . . when the Son of God breaks into that historical development, he throws it all into critical reorientation. The prehistory is critically and creatively reinterpreted by the incarnate Word, and it is only in that light that we must look at the prehistory of the incarnation in Israel.[58]

Nevertheless, as we have seen, the Christ who reorients these structures, is the Jew from Bethlehem, born in Israel, in the womb of the incarnation created by the Word of God. Thus, the tools forged in the depth of Israel in the one Christocentric movement of revelation, maintain an, albeit transformable, epistemic priority.

The Community of Reciprocity

The Community

We have looked at the broad contours of the movement of divine revelation in the election of Israel and, with a view to the mediation of revelation, we

---

55. T. F. Torrance, "Israel and the Incarnation," 320. Here we have an explicit affirmation of the working of the Word of God on the "rebellious mind of man" in Israel and its fulfillment in Jesus Christ. We shall examine this further when we consider the mediation of reconciliation.

56. Kang, "Vicarious Humanity," 143.

57. T. F. Torrance, *The School of Faith: The Catechisms of the Reformed Church*, xxx.

58. T. F. Torrance, *Incarnation*, 38; T. F. Torrance, *Theology in Reconstruction*, 144. Also, T. F. Torrance, *The Mediation of Christ*, 22. In the incarnation "the forms of thought and speech developed in ancient Israel are not only fulfilled but transcended and relativized by the final and permanent forms which the Word has taken in the life and teaching of Jesus Christ." T. F. Torrance, *God and Rationality*, 149.

have seen how it intersects the full range of physical and spiritual reality that Israel inhabits, creating therein a structural matrix of conceptual tools for grasping the mystery of Jesus Christ. Here we turn to another crucial feature created by the Word of God. The election of Israel, Torrance asserts, took the form of a "community of reciprocity."[59] This is a corporate, or communal dialogue between God and Israel which has both vertical (God-Israel) and horizontal (person-person) dimensions.

> The covenant partnership of God with Israel incorporated a brotherly covenant among the members of Israel, and that brotherly covenant was grounded in the covenant relations of God with Israel as a whole. Thus, so to speak, the vertical and the horizontal interrelations of the covenant partnership penetrated each other, constituting a coherent community of reciprocity between God and Israel, and manifesting a community response to the self- revealing and self-giving of God to Israel.[60]

Let us look at this corporate dimension first, before we look at the nature of the reciprocity involved.

Torrance's point here is that Israel as a collective whole is the womb of the incarnation. This is necessary given the fully spatio-temporal invasion of revelation in Israel that we have surveyed. It is in her corporate existence that the permanent structures and tools are formed. Revelation is not a point, a discrete event, or a spasmodic series of episodes limited to a few inspired individuals. It does not intersect Israel tangentially "rippling the surface of its moral and religious consciousness."[61] The unveiling of God to Israel was an "ontological phenomenon" earthing itself in the nation.[62]

> In seeking to understand the role of Israel in the mediation of revelation, therefore, we must consider, not just Jews, not just this or that prophet or this or that author in the Old Testament Scriptures, but Israel as a whole, "all Israel" to use St. Paul's expression, that is, Israel as a coherent entity before God. God mediated his revelation through the totality of Israel's existence and mission, for Israel came into being and has continued in

---

59. T. F. Torrance, *The Mediation of Christ*, 12.

60. T. F. Torrance, *The Mediation of Christ*, 13. See Kruger, "Participation in the Self-Knowledge of God," 52–64. Torrance develops this with an exposition of הסד (hesed) which not only binds Israel to return covenant loyalty to God but requires that same loyalty in brotherly relations. T. F. Torrance, "The Doctrine of Grace in the Old Testament," 57–62.

61. T. F. Torrance, *The Mediation of Christ*, 15.

62. Kruger, "Participation in the Self-Knowledge of God," 69.

existence to remain what it is precisely as the corporate counterpart to the self-revelation and self- communication of God to mankind. This means that we must think of Israel as itself *the Prophet* sent by God, not just Isaiah, or Jeremiah, or Ezekiel, but Israel, while Isaiah, Jeremiah, Ezekiel and all the prophets are to be understood within the one body which had been brought into a special relationship with God within which it was moulded and structured as the earthen vessel to receive and communicate the Word of God to mankind. It was within Israel constituted in that way that God sent the prophets and out of Israel constituted in that way that the Holy Scriptures of the Old Testament were composed and handed down.[63]

This does not, of course, preclude the crucial significance of individual prophets. Notice Torrance's qualification that we must consider not *"just* Isaiah, or Jeremiah, or Ezekiel, but Israel." The prophets arise organically out of, and do not exist in abstraction from, the community.[64] "The kind of reciprocity which the covenant envisaged, however, was of a corporate as well as of a personal nature, for personal relations with God took place within the corporate interaction of Israel with God."[65] The fundamental point Torrance is making is that "revelation and the people called out of the world to receive and embody it, revelation and church, go inseparably together."[66] The divine voice creates the divine community.[67]

---

63. T. F. Torrance, *The Mediation of Christ*, 13–14. Torrance's whole conception of Israel owes much to Barth's discussion: Barth, *CD*, IV.3.1, 38–72. Particularly, here, we note Barth's accent on the whole history of Israel, and not that of any one figure, as being the decisive consideration. "What has spoken for itself to them, and what is meant to speak for itself in their witness—we cannot insist on this too strongly—is the totality and interconnexion of this history . . . the individual accounts of the facts are meant to bring out the structure and contours." Barth, *CD*, IV.3.1, 54. "The history of Israel in its totality and interconnexion is universal prophecy." Barth, *CD*, IV.3.1, 55. "In this unity, more or less clearly disclosed in many other stories of the Old Testament, the history of Israel is an eloquent, prophetic and even mediatorial history." Barth, *CD*, IV.3.1, 63. "Only as a national history, then, did it speak its word, so that this word is not that of the history, action and experience of a single life." Barth, *CD*, IV.3.1, 68.

64. The prophets maintain their decisive significance."The historical dialogue between God and Israel . . . was maintained by a concentration of the speaker-hearer relation in a prophetic nucleus within Israelite society through which the Word of God assumed decisive form in the mouth of men and impinged relentlessly upon Israel's life, interpreting its history, determining its direction, calling it out to be the people or church of God, and opening its future toward the incarnation." T. F. Torrance, *God and Rationality*, 148.

65. T. F. Torrance, *The Mediation of Christ*, 13.

66. Ibid., 14.

67. "The fact that qahal comes from the same root as qol, the word for 'voice,'

There are two interrelated reasons that the mediation of revelation must take this corporate form. First, even in God, the Word does not exist in isolation but within the Trinitarian communion of love. Thus, it necessarily creates such a communion in its self-communication. Second, language is a public, corporate medium. Both ideas are combined when Torrance says:

> Neither in God nor in man is word found in isolation but only in community. In God the Word subsists in the inner consubstantial relations of the Holy Trinity, and in man words have their existence in the public language of expression and communication developed by a community of persons bound together not only by a common world but by a common way of life and culture.[68]

The nature of language itself is important for our purposes. It is "rooted in a society and is kept alive by the exchange and development of thought that takes place through it. It is the currency of social being."[69] Language is an intrinsically corporate medium. Thus, "In order to be heard and understood, and to be communicable as Word, divine revelation penetrates into the speaker-hearer relationship within the interpersonal structure of humanity and becomes speech to man by becoming speech of man to man, spoken and heard through the intelligible medium of a people's language."[70]

This means that in taking up human language for its self-communication the Word of God is not using some neutral or purified instrument, for "every verbal medium is bound up with a long cultural tradition and is inevitably affected by the conceptual habits which may often be inappropriate or misleading."[71]

---

suggests that the Old Testament qahal was the community summoned by the divine voice." T. F. Torrance, "Israel and the Incarnation," 305. "It was the ecclesia or qahal that arose and existed through election, that was actively engaged in God's purpose of revelation." T. F. Torrance, *Theology in Reconstruction*, 195.

68. T. F. Torrance, *God and Rationality*, 146. Also, T. F. Torrance, *Reality and Scientific Theology*, 182, "the Communion of Love in God has interpenetrated our human existence in such a way as to generate within it a community of love which participates in and is sustained by God's own Communion of Love in the consubstantial and interpenetrating relations of Father, Son and Holy Spirit." And, T. F. Torrance, *Reality and Evangelical Theology*, 46, "since it is God as a Communion of personal Being who communicates himself to us through Christ and in his Spirit, it is a community of persons in reciprocity both with God and with one another that is set up."

69. T. F. Torrance, *God and Rationality*, 146.

70. T. F. Torrance, *Reality and Evangelical Theology*, 86. See also, T. F. Torrance, *God and Rationality*, 146.

71. T. F. Torrance, *Christian Theology and Scientific Culture*, 33.

> As the Word of God invaded the social matrix of Israel's life, culture, religion and history, and clothed itself with Israel's language, it had to struggle with the communal meaning already embedded in it in order to assimilate it to God's revelation of Himself. For new understanding to take root within Israel, it had to take shape within Israel's language, and therefore it had to remould the inner structure of the society within which that language had its home and had to determine the whole history of Israel in its physical existence.[72]

The corporate nature of revelation implicates the Word of God in the full range of fallen Israel's communal participation in the fallen structures of space-time, including her language. It is in this sense that Israel as a whole is constituted God's Prophet.

> In this way Israel came to be constituted God's Prophet among the peoples of the earth, that is, his Servant entrusted with the oracles of God and the promises of the Messiah, and to be equipped with ordinances to train it in the ways of righteousness and truth and faith.[73]

She is "in a unique way the bearer of the oracles of God,"[74] his "corporate prophet among the nations."[75] The depth of this corporate union is such that "in a profound sense the Word of God within history took the existence-form of Israel, constituting Israel the great prophetic Word of God addressed to mankind."[76]

Israel, in addition to its prophetic role, is also the corporate people "imprinted with a priestly character and invested with a vicarious mission."[77] Torrance sees the priestly liturgical life of Israel as response to the Word of God. This relation is schematized variously as Moses-Aaron, law-cult, word-mediation, truth-reconciliation, Sinaitic-Levitical,[78] but in such a way that the Word always maintains priority.

---

72. T. F. Torrance, *God and Rationality*, 147. We shall explore this struggle to "remould" Israel further when we consider the mediation of reconciliation. At this point we simply note the struggle of the Word with Israel's language requires its total social transformation.

73. T. F. Torrance, *Theology in Reconstruction*, 195.

74. T. F. Torrance, *Reality and Evangelical Theology*, 87.

75. Klinefelter, "God and Rationality," 148. See Kruger, "Participation in the Self-Knowledge of God," 68–69.

76. T. F. Torrance, "Christian/Jewish Dialogue," 146.

77. T. F. Torrance, *The Mediation of Christ*, 75.

78. T. F. Torrance, *Incarnation*, 46–47, 60; T. F. Torrance, "Israel and the Incarnation," 307–9; T. F. Torrance, *Royal Priesthood: A Theology of Ordained Ministry*, 5–7,

> Over against Moses, and in secondary status, Aaron is regarded as the liturgical priest who carries out in continual cultic witness the actual mediation that came through Moses. In this way, the cult was a liturgical extension into the history of Israel and her worship of the once-and-for-all events of Exodus and Sinai.[79]

This "liturgical extension" means the liturgy, like the Word, had to be "enacted in life and obedience."[80] Thus, Israel as a whole was to be the consecrated and priestly people.[81] Just as the corporate "prophethood" of Israel does not preclude the prophetic tradition, so this need for corporate enactment of the liturgy does not preclude the cult. "Within that actualisation, described as circumcision of the heart or penitence, the cult has its proper place, as Psalm 51 makes so clear."[82]

As the corporate prophet and priestly nation of God, Israel is both the place of his kingly rule and the bearer of messianic promise.

> And so the covenant came to rest upon the twin foundation of the Sinaitic law and the Levitical liturgy, as represented supremely in Moses and Aaron, prophet and priest in essential complementarity and unity. Once this covenantal basis was consolidated in Jerusalem, God manifested his coming Kingdom through the Davidic line of kings, and the Messianic Kingdom came to overarch the covenantal relation of Word and pardon, prophet and priest.[83]

It is Israel's destiny to "open up the way for the one undivided Kingdom of God among men."[84] As the bearer of the oracles of God, she is "a church as much as a people charged with priestly and prophetic significance for all mankind and divinely destined for the universalization of its revelatory mission in the advent of the Son of God himself in space and time."[85]

22; T. F. Torrance, *Conflict and Agreement in the Church: Order and Disorder*, 290; T. F. Torrance, *Theology in Reconstruction*, 194; T. F. Torrance, *Space, Time and Resurrection*, 112–13. We shall look at the historical contours of this relationship when we consider the mediation of reconciliation.

79. T. F. Torrance, *Royal Priesthood: A Theology of Ordained Ministry*, 4. See T. F. Torrance, *Atonement*, 9.

80. T. F. Torrance, *Royal Priesthood: A Theology of Ordained Ministry*, 22.

81. Exod 19:6.

82. T. F. Torrance, *Royal Priesthood: A Theology of Ordained Ministry*, 22.

83. T. F. Torrance, "Israel and the Incarnation," 307–8. See T. F. Torrance, *Incarnation*, 46–47.

84. T. F. Torrance, "The Divine Vocation and Destiny of Israel," 86.

85. T. F. Torrance, *Reality and Evangelical Theology*, 87.

Thus, the whole movement, or "triple activity" of God's grace, by which he assumes Israel into oneness with himself, takes place in terms of prophet, priest and king.[86] As such, it points forward to Christ, "the archetypal Prophet, Priest, and King. He was the King of the Kingdom who provided the way of restoration to the Father."[87] We have considered the "community" dimension of the "community of reciprocity." Now we turn to the nature of the reciprocity involved.

The Reciprocity

The Word of God (understood, again, as the Logos, the eternal Son) reveals himself in such a way as to include within the movement of that revelation the answering word of man. Thus, as we have seen, revelation is not a tangential phenomenon "rippling the surface of Israel's life," but it is a dynamic historical dialogue with the corporate people of God. The reciprocity involved is taken up into the dynamic of revelation itself. Revelation is "actualized" in Israel's response to the Word. Torrance roots this idea in the very nature of the terms used for revelation in Scripture. "In the Hebrew idiom, revelation is not only the uncovering of God but the uncovering of the ear and eye of man for God. It is revelation which achieves its end in man and does not return void to God."[88]

More fundamentally, however, Torrance's thought here is grounded in the very nature of revelation itself and the structure of its movement in Israel. Revelation is such that it must be "actualized within the conditions of our creaturely existence and therefore within the medium of our human

---

86. T. F. Torrance, *Incarnation*, 46; T. F. Torrance, *The Doctrine of Jesus Christ*, 6; T. F. Torrance, "Israel and the Incarnation," 307. This does not entail a one to one correspondence between the "triple activity" (way, truth, life-relation) and prophet, priest and king. The point is simply that the "triple activity" can be seen to take place through the prophet, priest and king triad, both in its corporate form (Israel as a whole) and in the individual prophets, priests and kings.

87. T. F. Torrance, "Israel and the Incarnation," 308.

88. T. F. Torrance, *Theology in Reconstruction*, 129–30. See T. F. Torrance, *The Mediation of Christ*, 11. He speaks of the "doubleness" of "the word to *reveal* in both Hebrew and Greek usage in the Bible, where *reveal* means not only an unveiling or uncovering of God but an uncovering of the ear, or an unveiling of the heart, of man." T. F. Torrance, *Conflict and Agreement in the Church: The Ministry and the Sacraments of the Gospel*, 84. "By revelation is meant . . . not some vague, inarticulate awareness of God projected out of the human consciousness, but an intelligible, articulate revealing of God by God whom we are enabled to apprehend through the creative power of his Word addressed to us, yet a revealing of God by God which is actualized within the conditions of our creaturely existence and therefore within the medium of our human thought and speech." T. F. Torrance, *Reality and Evangelical Theology*, 85.

thought and speech. This is a self-revelation which posits and sustains man as the partner of its full movement from God to man and from man back to God."[89] Here we see that revelation involves the Word of God to man as well as the word of man to God, in what is a circular (from God to man, and back from man to God) or spiraling (this is an extension of the "circular" metaphor which helps bring out the temporal duration) movement.[90]

Yet, these are not two separate movements, "but one two-fold movement, for even the movement from the side of man toward God, free and spontaneous as it is, is coordinated with the movement of God toward man."[91] God posits man in this relationship maintaining his sovereign majesty.[92] Strikingly, Torrance says "the whole fact of Israel entrusted with the oracles of God was itself a mighty response evoked by the Word of God out of the midst of history."[93]

It is within this asymmetrical reciprocity within the space-time existence of corporate Israel that the "permanent structures" are fashioned.

> In the covenanted relationship thus set up between Israel and God, Israel found itself a people invaded by divine revelation and progressively subjected to its molding and informing power in such a way that the responses that divine revelation provoked from it, whether of obedience or disobedience, enlightenment or blindness, were made instruments for its deepening penetration into its existence and understanding until there were forged structures of thought and speech in terms of which it became understandable and communicable.[94]

---

89. T. F. Torrance, *Reality and Evangelical Theology*, 85.

90. T. F. Torrance, *The Mediation of Christ*, 22. "And we have found that in grace and wisdom God adopted a way of making himself known to his people in which the movement of his revelation fulfilled itself not only from the side of God toward man but from the side of man toward God, and so he brought into being ways of human understanding and human obedience to his revelation which were assumed into union with it and constituted the human expression in concept and word of that revelation in its communication to man. That is to say, divine revelation was progressively mediated to mankind in and through Israel in such a way that it provided a true and faithful human response as part of its achievement for us, to us and in us."

91. T. F. Torrance, *Theological Science*, 45.

92. "It is a knowledge made possible under the commanding majesty of the Object which not only establishes itself in our knowledge but does not allow itself to be halted by our creaturely limitations and disabilities, for it creates, bestows, and controls a real knowledge on our part appropriate to it." T. F. Torrance, *Theological Science*, 47.

93. T. F. Torrance, *God and Rationality*, 149. This is also a vivid way of stating the corporate nature of Israel's mediatorial role.

94. T. F. Torrance, *Reality and Evangelical Theology*, 87.

In conjunction with this progressive invasion of Israel by the Word comes a gathering up of the full range of Israel's responses which are then used by that Word for "further penetration" into Israel's existence. The human response is thus assimilated to the divine Word and used as the basis for further communication. It is this spiral molding process in the depth of fallen Israel which gives revelation its bipolar character and makes Israel the means of its mediation to mankind.

The Spiral in Action: The Production of the Old Testament Scriptures

Torrance's thought here is deceptively complex, and thus somewhat opaque. Due to the architectonic nature of his thought, specific narrow examples of this "spiral" in action are hard to come by. Let us try and illustrate the general idea. The Word of God lays hold of Abraham and the patriarchs. They wrestle and struggle with it, sometimes obeying and sometimes disobeying. The various responses lead to new words, or dreams, or visions from God, and the drama deepens. There are various refinements, judgments, recapitulations, and summary movements as the whole layered tapestry thickens. This grand wrestling match with its divine-human cast is chronicled by the author of Genesis in Holy Scripture. In this way the spiraling of the Word, in and through the human response it evokes, is "clothed with Israel's language," forges "permanent structures," and becomes a medium of further communication. The results of this process, in this instance the newly formed nation of Israel at the end of the book of Genesis and the text of Scripture which chronicles the process, are both taken up into the spiral, and the process continues. It is important to see that Israel, and not simply Scripture, continues as the corporate ground of the mediation of revelation. It is Israel *as the bearers of the oracles of God*[95] which is the divine instrument of revelation. Put conversely, it is Scripture in and with and under Israel which mediates the Word.

> ... the Old Testament Scriptures which have been handed down to us are not to be treated as free-floating divine oracles with an independent existence of their own, in spite of their written form, for they cannot properly be detached from their embodiment in the whole historical fact of Israel and its vicarious role

---

95. T. F. Torrance, *Theology in Reconstruction*, 195; T. F. Torrance, *Reality and Evangelical Theology*, 87; T. F. Torrance, *The Mediation of Christ*, 8; T. F. Torrance, *God and Rationality*, 147–48.

in the reception and communication of the Word of God to the human race.[96]

We may extend our examples. The Law and the priestly cult are given in Exodus and Leviticus. The rest of the Pentateuch narrates the spiral of the Word and the various responses of Israel. Much the same can be said for the historical books. In the Psalms the process Torrance has in mind is quite vividly illustrated. Here the psalmists wrestle with the Word of God (that is, with God himself) and the various "structures" it has fashioned (law, cult, community, and the growing canonical writings). They do this in the face of their own personal and communal struggles. This leaves an indelible imprint on the community, not least in the book of Psalms itself. Thus, the spiral deepens, pressing its way down into Israel's national life and out into its messianic future. The important point to grasp is that the human response to the Word is assimilated to the Word, and this response, in and through the community, becomes part of divine revelation. The same process, only in its later spiraling stages, is seen in the prophets as they call Israel back to the law and protest the corruption of the cult.[97]

Thus, not only is the whole fact of Israel a response evoked by, and assimilated to, the Word, but also the Old Testament Scriptures are themselves products of "the ever-deepening, spiral movement of God's self-revelation."[98]

> The Word of God kept pressing for articulation within the corporate medium of covenant reciprocity creating formal and empirical coordinates of its own self-utterance through which it extended its activity in space and time, progressively taking verbal and even written form through the shared understanding and shared response that developed in this people.[99]

---

96. T. F. Torrance, *The Mediation of Christ*, 14–15.

97. T. F. Torrance, *Royal Priesthood: A Theology of Ordained Ministry*, 5–6; T. F. Torrance, *Incarnation*, 47; T. F. Torrance, "Israel and the Incarnation," 309; T. F. Torrance, *Atonement*, 64.

98. T. F. Torrance, *The Mediation of Christ*, 8; T. F. Torrance, "The Divine Vocation and Destiny of Israel," 146.

99. T. F. Torrance, *Reality and Evangelical Theology*, 87. Also, T. F. Torrance, *The Mediation of Christ*, 14–15. The seriousness with which this scriptural intersection with space-time coordinates is taken by Torrance is seen when he says "if we are to understand and interpret divine revelation in the specific spatio-temporal forms which it assumed in and through Israel, we cannot detach the Old Testament Scriptures from the land any more than from the people of Israel. The people of the book and the people of the land belong inseparably together, for they have been forged together by the way that God himself has taken in the actualization and the dynamic course of his covenant partnership with Israel." T. F. Torrance, *The Mediation of Christ*, 16.

Israel 47

It is only across this dynamic historical drama that we see the full significance of this corporate reciprocity in Torrance's statement that it was "within Israel constituted in that way that God sent the prophets and out of Israel constituted in that way that the Holy Scriptures of the Old Testament were composed and handed down."[100]

Revelation and revelation

We must now consider a crucial aspect in Torrance's doctrine of revelation that has not been apparent to this point. It is clear that Israel is the mediator of this spiral-induced revelation; she is distinct, though inseparable, from the revelation itself. But what is the status of the verbal, and ultimately written forms the Word creates as its "empirical correlates"? More precisely, is Holy Scripture revelation? A casual reading of Torrance's description of the process—revelation as "actualized" and "achieving its end in man"—could lead one to an affirmative answer. Yet, one often notices qualifiers such as the human response being "assimilated to" the Word, and becoming the "means" of its further communication.[101] In this case the qualifiers are decisive. Strictly speaking, Scripture is not revelation.[102]

The reason this for this is that, in the full sense of the word, for Torrance only Jesus Christ is revelation.[103] He alone is the perfect Word of God to man *and* the perfect answering word of man to God.

> ... in Jesus Christ the Word of God has become man, has assumed a human form, in order as such to be God's language to man, ... in Jesus Christ there is gathered up and embodied, in obedient response to God, man's true word to God and his

---

100. T. F. Torrance, *The Mediation of Christ*, 14.

101. T. F. Torrance, *Reality and Evangelical Theology*, 85. The subtlety of the qualifiers is fully captured here: "In assuming the form of human speech and writing the revelation of God addressed to man becomes at the same time the obedient response of man to God whereby revelation is anchored and realized in the conditions of human reality."

102. On this whole topic, see Gill, "The Doctrine of Revelation." Expounding the early Barth, Torrance writes: "The Church finds in the Bible a primary datum, which is not to be separated from it nor to be confused with it, which is veiled in the Bible as much as it is unveiled through it, which is both hidden and revealed, namely the Word of God in its primary form, Revelation." The capital R indicates that Jesus Christ, the Word of God, is Revelation. T. F. Torrance, *Karl Barth: An Introduction*, 119.

103. T. F. Torrance, *Theology in Reconstruction*, 130. "The incarnation means that now revelation is determined and shaped by the Humanity of Christ, that we know of no revelation of the Word of God except that which is given through Christ and in the form of Christ."

> true speech about God. Jesus Christ is at once the complete revelation of God to man and the correspondence on man's part to that revelation required by it for the fulfillment of its own revealing movement.[104] . . . He is real word of God to us in such a way that he still remains eternal word of God, word of God addressed to man, but word received, obeyed and lived out as word answering to God in perfect truth, in the concrete faithfulness to God of a life lived from beginning to end in holiness and love and obedience.[105]

As the Word of God to man, and the perfect answering response of man to God, he creatively fulfills and transforms the whole process we have been considering. Jesus Christ is

> . . . himself God and man, in whom the covenanted relationship between God and Israel . . . was gathered up, transformed and fulfilled once for all. In him the revealing of God and the understanding of man fully coincided, the whole Word of God and the perfect response of man were indivisibly united in one Person, the Mediator . . . Jesus Christ in his own personal Being is identical with the Revelation he mediates.[106]

In Jesus Christ alone the revelation of God "completes the circle of its own movement."[107]

Israel's sinfulness prevents the full realization of the spiraling motion. "The Old Testament Scriptures do not hesitate to record that in the long history of its partnership with God, in the mediation of divine revelation and reconciliation, Israel proved to be disobedient and rebellious again and again."[108] Therefore, it is only in Christ where Israel's, and thus our,

---

104. T. F. Torrance, *Theology in Reconstruction*, 129. Also, "In Jesus Christ, as we have seen, we are presented with God's Word to man, and man's obedient response to God incorporated into God's Word as an essential part of it." T. F. Torrance, *God and Rationality*, 151. The whole chapter here, "The Word of God and the Response of Man," 137–164, is relevant.

105. T. F. Torrance, *Incarnation*, 64. See T. F. Torrance, *Reality and Evangelical Theology*, 85–87; T. F. Torrance, *Incarnation*, 126.

106. T. F. Torrance, *The Mediation of Christ*, 9. "And so in the fullness of time Jesus was born of Mary, out of the organic correlation of revelation and response in the life and language of man to be the Word of God heard and expressed in the truth and grace of perfect human response to God the Father." T. F. Torrance, *Reality and Evangelical Theology*, 87–88.

107. T. F. Torrance, *Reality and Evangelical Theology*, 86.

108. T. F. Torrance, "The Divine Vocation and Destiny of Israel," 89.

estrangement and alienation are overcome. Only in him does revelation fully "actualize"[109] itself.

In Christ the Word heals what is assumed. He is the mediator

> who as true God and true Man had chosen Israel as the people in whose midst he penetrated into the innermost existence of man in his estrangement from God, and in the heart of that estrangement he consummated an eternal union between God and man in himself.[110]

The reference to "an eternal union between God and man in himself" refers to the hypostatic union which Torrance conceives of as dynamically carried out in our fallen humanity. It is "the immediate ground for all Christ's mediatorial and reconciling activity in our human existence."[111] The ontological uniqueness of the hypostatic union is the fundamental reason Torrance subordinates Scripture to the revelation of God in Christ:

> Whereas in Jesus Christ the divine Word and the human word are united within one Person, that is hypostatically, in the Bible the divine Word and the human word are only united through dependence upon and participation in Christ, that is, sacramentally.[112] . . . The relation between God's self-revelation and the

---

109. T. F. Torrance, *Theology in Reconstruction*, 196. Torrance can use the language of actualization with respect to Israel, but it is clear that this is a partial, and not a full completion of the circle such as occurs in Christ: "It is of course in the revelation of God actualized in our historical human existence through the instrumentality of Israel and in Jesus Christ the Word made flesh, in whom that actualization of divine revelation was brought to its fulfillment in acutely personal form, that we learn this about the Word of God and the response of man." T. F. Torrance, *God and Rationality*, 138. Of course, this actualization in Christ also happens within Israel, inasmuch as she is the womb of the incarnation: "the movement of God's self-revelation which was brought to its culmination *in Jesus Christ* through the Incarnation when the Word of God actualized itself *within Israel* and within mankind in the visible, tangible form of a particular human being who embodied in himself the personal address of God's Word to man and the personal response of man to God's Word." T. F. Torrance, *The Mediation of Christ*, 78. Italics mine.

110. T. F. Torrance, "Israel and the Incarnation," 311.

111. T. F. Torrance, *The Mediation of Christ*, 65.

112. T. F. Torrance, *Divine Meaning: Studies in Patristic Hermeneutics*, 7. We should note that while the Old Testament Scriptures are our focus here, the same distinction applies to the New Testament Scriptures. While the dynamic of their production is different, they also must be differentiated from, and subordinated to, the revelation that is Jesus Christ. "There are differences between the Old Testament and the New Testament . . . and there are significant differences in the witness between the prophets and apostles, . . . but all these differences are relative compared to their unity in the object, and it is that unity in their object which makes them what they are, *Holy* Scripture in

> Holy Scriptures in which it is mediated is essentially asymmetric. In a profound sense, this is even true of the Word of God and the word of man in Jesus Christ himself, for he is the word of man in answer to God only in that he is first and foremost the Word of God become man. In Jesus Christ himself . . . there is a hypostatic union of divine and human word in his one Person. Therefore in him we have to reckon with a first order relation ontologically inseparable from the fact that the Word *became* man, a relation such that the human word *is* the word of God. But in the . . . Scriptures we have a second order relation in which the human word of Scripture is not ontologically *identical* with the incarnate Word.[113]

The result of this is that Jesus Christ is the Revelation (capital "R") of God, and the Scriptures, assimilated to, and mediatorial instruments of the Divine Word, are revelation (small "r") in a subordinate sense.[114] They are the "written form of the Word of God,"[115] the "divinely inspired"[116] place "where divine revelation might be translated appropriately into human speech and where it might be assimilated and understood in a communicable form."[117] They are a witness to revelation that point beyond themselves to Christ.[118]

---

which God speaks his Word and in which we hear his Word." T. F. Torrance, *Karl Barth: An Introduction*, 120.

113. T. F. Torrance, *Reality and Evangelical Theology*, 94. The same point is made in T. F. Torrance, *Divine Meaning: Studies in Patristic Hermeneutics*, 7. Torrance's major point is simply that "the Holy Scripture *is* not Jesus Christ, the Word of God incarnate." T. F. Torrance, *Reality and Evangelical Theology*, 95. It is important to note that the unity, albeit asymmetric, of the divine and human word in Christ, grounded in the unity of his person, is what saves the spiraling process which comes to fulfillment in him from degenerating into second-order or "sacramental" Nestorianism.

114. McCall, "Theimann, Torrance and Revelation," 138. Gill, "The Doctrine of Revelation," 102. Torrance's whole approach to Scripture and its relation to revelation owes much to Barth, as Gill points out, Gill, "The Doctrine of Revelation," 69–106. For Torrance's dependence upon Barth here, see T. F. Torrance, *Karl Barth: An Introduction*, 109–24. T. F. Torrance, *Karl Barth: Biblical and Evangelical Theologian*, 83–120.

115. T. F. Torrance, *Divine Meaning: Studies in Patristic Hermeneutics*, 5.

116. T. F. Torrance, *The Mediation of Christ*, 120; T. F. Torrance, *The Trinitarian Faith*, 248; T. F. Torrance, *Reality and Evangelical Theology*, 93; T. F. Torrance, *Divine Meaning: Studies in Patristic Hermeneutics*, 5; T. F. Torrance, *Karl Barth: Biblical and Evangelical Theologian*, 101.

117. T. F. Torrance, *Divine Meaning: Studies in Patristic Hermeneutics*, 5.

118. T. F. Torrance, *Reality and Evangelical Theology*, 96, "[T]he Holy Scriptures are not themselves the real Light that Christ is, but are what they are only as enlightened by him and as they therefore bear witness to him beyond themselves." T. F. Torrance, *Reality and Evangelical Theology*, 95. In the case of the Old Testament Scriptures, their

There are two implications of this conception of Old Testament revelation which we must consider. First, for Torrance, the Scriptures partake of human imperfection and inadequacy.

> Although we cannot speak of a direct identity between the human word of Scripture and the Word that was made flesh in Jesus Christ resting in the essence either of the divine Word or the human word, we must speak of an identity between the word of man and the Word of God in the Bible which rests upon the gracious decision of God to unite it with his own Word, and so to give it a divine perfection in spite of its human imperfection.[119]

Human sinfulness, with its concomitant effect on speech, language, and conceptualities, entails for Torrance that "holy Scripture belongs to the sphere where redemption is necessary," and that it "stands with sinners and among sinners, and belongs to the sphere where salvation is bestowed."[120]

This, of course, does not mean that Torrance does not revere Scripture. He says of the New Testament Scriptures, and would surely say of the Old Testament as well, that "they constitute therefore the divinely provided and inspired linguistic medium which remains of authoritative and critical significance for the whole history of the church of Jesus Christ."[121] For Torrance, "The Bible is to be uniquely revered and interpreted as Holy Scripture inspired by the Holy Spirit."[122]

McCall makes an important observation germane to our concerns:

> Surely he is correct in distinguishing between the Bible and the revelation of God in Jesus Christ. But it is not at all apparent that fallibility and error in the former are necessary for this important distinction to be maintained, and Torrance never argues for his position. He simply asserts this without offering reasons to think that this is so.[123]

---

differentiation from the Word of God also points *ahead* to Christ. "In this dynamic mode the Word of God pressed on through the life and experience of Israel toward final and definitive form, but for that reason the scriptural forms inspired by the Spirit proclaimed far more than they could specify at the time and so by their very nature they pointed ahead to the full disclosure of the divine reality they served." T. F. Torrance, *God and Rationality*, 148–49.

119. T. F. Torrance, *Theology in Reconstruction*, 139–40.
120. Ibid., 138.
121. T. F. Torrance, *Reality and Evangelical Theology*, 92–93.
122. Sarisky, "Biblical Interpretation," 335.
123. McCall, "Theimann, Torrance and Revelation," 166.

It is not correct, however, to say Torrance provides no arguments for his position. They consist in the Christological analogy we have considered and the coordinate fact that the Bible "belongs to the sphere where redemption is necessary." He expressly links a "fundamentalist conception of 'verbal inspiration'" with a denial of Christ's assuming our fallen humanity.[124] The shadow of Barth lies in the background here as well. In discussing Barth's conception of revelation, Torrance notes his doctrine of the fallibility of Scripture under the heading of "the unassumed is the unhealed."[125] Barth writes:

> Verbal inspiration does not mean the infallibility of the biblical word in its linguistic, historical and theological character as human word. It means that the fallible and faulty human word is as such used by God and has to be received and heard in spite of its human fallibility.[126]

The affirmation of an infallible Bible, then, entails resisting "the sovereignty of the grace in which God himself became man in Christ to glorify himself in his humanity."[127]

Thus, the offense of the fallible Bible is essentially the offense of the Word made fallen flesh, namely, that "God makes such miraculous use of what he has assumed."[128] Thus, the "innerantist" position is, for Torrance, a Christological error.[129] It fails to reckon with the assumption of our fallen flesh, proleptically in Israel and, finally, in Christ. For Torrance, the "fundamentalist" view would "hypostatize" the relationship between the Word of God and the word of man in Scripture in such a way as to obscure the analogical, and thus eschatological, relation it has with Christ.

Nevertheless, McCall is right to ask if this necessarily entails error in Scripture. If Scripture can be without error, as surely Torrance affirms, most

---

124. T. F. Torrance, *The Mediation of Christ*, 40.

125. T. F. Torrance, *Karl Barth: Biblical and Evangelical Theologian*, 103–5.

126. Barth, *CD*, I.2, 533. See the virtually identical wording in T. F. Torrance, *Theology in Reconstruction*, 139.

127. Barth, *CD*, I.2, 529.

128. T. F. Torrance, *Karl Barth: Biblical and Evangelical Theologian*, 104–5.

129. As such it is also an (over-realized) eschatological error for "we must think of that hypostatic union, however, not in the static categories of patristic thought, but in terms of biblical eschatology, that is, in dynamic categories." T. F. Torrance, *Conflict and Agreement in the Church: The Ministry and the Sacraments of the Gospel*, 171. "If the substance or content of the analogical relation between Christ and His Church [and also between Christ and the Scripture] is the doctrine of Christ Himself, the relationship involved is to be formulated in terms of the doctrine of the Spirit and Eschatology." T. F. Torrance, *Conflict and Agreement in the Church: Order and Disorder*, 233.

of the time, it is not clear why one could not affirm his central concerns, and even the structure of his argument, and still affirm inerrancy. Surely the structure of his theology mitigates against any *a priori* necessity for an infallible Scripture, and perhaps even its actuality, but it does not foreclose the possibility.[130]

Torrance's position is ably summarized as follows: The Word of God comes to us in the human word of Holy Scripture, "pressing its way through the speech of our fallen flesh, graciously assuming it in spite of all its inadequacy and faultiness and imperfection and giving it a holy perfection in the Word of God."[131] The Christological analogy which lies behind this doctrine of Scripture allows Torrance to make the startling assertion that "*the real text* of the New Testament revelation [and surely, in proleptic fashion, the Old Testament revelation as well] is *the humanity of Jesus*.[132]

Torrance makes the connection with our thesis explicit in a telling footnote:

> A full account of the actualization of God's self-revelation in Jesus Christ must reckon with the fact that this is achieved *within our estranged and impaired existence*, and therefore, only through atoning reconciliation and sanctifying re-creation. This is why it would not be theologically proper to offer an account of the inspiration of the Holy Scriptures apart from a doctrine of atoning mediation between the Word of God and the word of man. Thus, the doctrine of Scripture falls apart if Christ does not effect reconciliation *in the depths of our fallen humanity*.[133]

---

130. We note that one would expect some account of how the New Testament Scriptures manifest a realized, analogical-eschatological advance with respect to "imperfection" over the Old Testament Scriptures. This is, however, not forthcoming.

131. T. F. Torrance, *Theology in Reconstruction*, 139. See Kang, "Vicarious Humanity," 272.

132. T. F. Torrance, *The Mediation of Christ*, 78 "As we read the Old Testament and read the New Testament and listen to the Word of God, the real text is not documents of the Pentateuch, the Psalms or the Prophets or the documents of the Gospels and the Epistles, but in and through them all the Word of God struggling with rebellious human existence in Israel on the way to becoming incarnate, and then that Word translated into the flesh and blood and mind and life of a human being in Jesus, in whom we have both the Word of God become man and the perfect response of man to God offered on our behalf."

133. T. F. Torrance, *Reality and Evangelical Theology*, 162–63. Italics mine. Note the similar remark in T. F. Torrance, review of *The Inspiration and Authority of the Bible*, by B.B. Warfield, 106. "There is no question about the fact that a proper doctrine of Scripture must be grounded analogically upon the birth, life, death, and resurrection of Jesus Christ, but in the Incarnation with the hypostatic union of God and Man which it involves, and in Holy Scripture with its derived relation between the Word of God and

The pervasive nature and architectonic importance of Christ's assumption of fallen flesh is vividly illustrated here. Without *this* Christology one does not properly grasp even the emergence of Scripture in the history of Israel.

A second implication of Torrance's doctrine of revelation is that, in the Old Testament, there is no knowledge of God in his internal relations.

> In these Scriptures it is very clear that through his presence and power God was accessible to his people through the covenant relations he had graciously established with them. . . . Nevertheless it is also clear that he did not make *himself* personally accessible to them but remained hidden behind his mighty acts of revelation and salvation.[134] While mediators of divine revelation like Moses were able to speak with God "face to face," and prophets and psalmists clearly had moving intimate experiences with God, nevertheless, before God's Word became flesh in the fullness of time the faithful were not brought into such a close personal relation with God that they came to know him directly in himself as he became known in Jesus Christ.[135]

---

the word of man, we must take seriously the fact that the Word has assumed our fallen humanity, and was made in the likeness of sinful flesh." This failure to grasp the scandal of Christ's assuming of our lost and alienated flesh, which he likens to the scandal of the cross, prompts Torrance to ask: "Is this not the reason why traditional doctrines of the inspiration of the Holy Scripture are strangely not brought into conjunction with the doctrine of atoning redemption?" T. F. Torrance, *Karl Barth: Biblical and Evangelical Theologian*, 105. See T. F. Torrance, review of *The Inspiration and Authority of the Bible*, by B. B. Warfield, 107.

134. T. F. Torrance, *The Christian Doctrine of God*, 68. Likewise, Ebionite Christology leaves one with the "unknowable God of Judaism who does not give human beings access to any knowledge of himself as he is in his own eternal being." T. F. Torrance, *The Trinitarian Faith*, 112. The actuality of revelation, which has come in Christ, is not present in the Old Testament. "There we have the proleptic shadows of the coming reality; they were real as such, but by their very nature pointed beyond themselves toward saving acts of God that were yet to take place. Thus in the Old Testament we have really the Word of God, but it is a Word in promissary form. . . . It is a Word which has not become fully personal and actual. In Jesus Christ, however, we . . . have . . . the Word made flesh, not only revelation of God but such a complete and final revelation that it is itself actually God himself." T. F. Torrance, *The Doctrine of Jesus Christ*, 133–34.

135. T. F. Torrance, *The Trinitarian Faith*, 66. Here, again, Torrance is drawing on Barth's assertion that Israel knew the name of God which was "intended to recall the hiddenness even of the revealed God." This revelation of the Name is fulfilled in the covenant. In Christ the "self-disclosure" and "self-distinction" of God come in a way qualitatively, and not just quantitatively, different from the Old Testament revelation. Barth, *CD*, I.1, 317–18.

The coming of Christ in the flesh entails an "intensifying and interiorizing" of, and not a detachment from, the revelation of God in the Old Testament.[136] The situation is aptly summarized:

> The Christian understanding of God is grounded in and inseparable from the revelation of the one Lord God Almighty given to Israel and mediated to us in the Old Testament Scriptures; and ... there is no access to knowledge of God as he is in himself apart from the reconciliation with God brought about by the cross of Christ.[137]

The Mediation of Revelation: Conclusion

We are now in a position to draw together the key facets of Torrance's doctrine of the mediation of revelation in Israel. The crucial idea for our purposes is that revelation is neither tangential to, nor a sporadic interruption of, the life of the nation of Israel. The Word of God penetrates into the depths of elect Israel, intersecting her variegated physical and spiritual existence across all the levels of her space-time reality. This means the Word implicates itself in the "stuff of its earthly being and behaviour."[138] Nothing, not Israel's language, her culture, her relationships, and especially her recalcitrant humanity, is left untouched by the Word's descent.

Out of this engagement a community of reciprocity is formed. It is in and through this community in all its depth that the individual instruments of revelation (i.e., the prophets) and the empirical correlates to the Word (i.e., the Scriptures of the Old Testament) arise. This dynamic relationship, the womb and pre-history of the incarnation, forges the permanent structures of thought and speech that are needed to rightly grasp the mystery of Christ. The whole process is construed as a spiraling movement from God to Israel and back to God.

What is of particular relevance for our thesis is that this circle is both proleptically conditioned by, and only fully realized in, Christ himself. He is "Revelation" in its ontological depth as the full Word of God to man and the perfect response of man to God. This means that in Israel the spiraling motion is broken, and the circle fails to complete itself properly. All

---

136. T. F. Torrance, *The Christian Doctrine of God*, 55.

137. T. F. Torrance, *The Mediation of Christ*, 105. On the whole matter of the difference in Torrance between Old Testament revelation and its culmination in Christ, see Ho, *A Critical Study on T. F. Torrance's Theology of Incarnation*, 216–27; Morrison, *Knowledge of the Self-Revealing God*, 255, 269–79.

138. T. F. Torrance, *The Mediation of Christ*, 15.

of her responses, whether of obedience or disobedience, are suborned by the spiraling process for the further mediation of revelation. Yet, they possess a historically provisional, and ontologically second-order, relation to the Word which appears in Christ. Thus, for Torrance, one cannot rightly consider the mediation of revelation in Israel without a full affirmation of the Word habituating itself in Israel's, and thus, our fallen humanity. This means that Christ's coming into our fallen existence is utterly necessary to accomplish what the Word was pressing to achieve in Israel's flesh.

Before we consider the actualization of revelation that was achieved in Christ, we must look more closely at the actualization of revelation, however partial, that was achieved in Israel. That is, we must look at both the reasons for, and the telos of, Israel's "broken" response to the Word of God. We shall discuss this under the rubric of the mediation of reconciliation.

THE MEDIATION OF RECONCILIATION

Revelation and Reconciliation

In a fundamental sense, the need for reconciliation exists in any field of knowledge.

> All genuine knowledge involves a cognitive union of the mind with its object, and calls for the removal of any estrangement or alienation that may obstruct or distort it. This is a principle that applies to all spheres of knowledge, and not simply to our knowledge of God.[139]

The need for the removal of estrangement becomes heightened when we are dealing with persons, and thus is particularly acute in our knowledge of God.

---

139. T. F. Torrance, *The Mediation of Christ*, 24–25. This is a bedrock tenet of Torrance's critical realism. The object of inquiry must be allowed to disclose itself to us in accordance with its nature. This is not a philosophical *a priori* for Torrance. It arises out of the actual encounter with God as he has revealed himself: "In the nature of the case a true and adequate account of theological epistemology cannot be gained apart from substantial exposition of the content of the knowledge of God. . . . It is scientifically false to begin with epistemology." T. F. Torrance, *Theological Science*, 10. See T. F. Torrance, *Karl Barth: Biblical and Evangelical Theologian*, 72; T. F. Torrance, "Introduction: Theology and Church," 40–47; T. F. Torrance, *Karl Barth: An Introduction*, 107–8, 141–43. In the foreword to *Reality and Evangelical Theology*, Kurt Richardson writes "It is a posteriori knowing of God which is given in the revelation of the gospel. It is evangelical and theological realism because, while it is human knowledge, it is continually shaped and corrected in us by the Word of God in Scripture. It is critical in terms of criteria outside of ourselves . . . " *Reality and Evangelical Theology*, xv. For a longer discussion see D. F. Kelly, "The Realist Epistemology of Thomas F. Torrance."

> If we are really to know God in accordance with his nature as he discloses himself to us, we require to be adapted in our knowing and personal relations toward him—that is why we cannot know God without love, and if we are estranged without being reconciled to him.[140]

In addition, we must not forget what we looked at under the mediation of revelation. Since revelation entails, as part of its movement, actualization in the life of sinful Israel, by its very nature it is deeply interlocked with reconciliation.[141]

> Revelation involves a communion through the reconciliation of the estranged parties, a reconciliation of the will and mind of man with the will and mind of God. Revelation entails the entry of the Mind of God into our darkness and estrangement in order to redeem our understanding and to achieve its reconciliation to the Mind of God.[142]

In God's election of Israel we have "a divine intention persistently at work which has to do both with revelation and reconciliation."[143] These are not two discrete aspects of God's way with Israel, but rather "reconciliation constitutes the inner dynamic of revelation, and revelation becomes effective precisely as reconciliation for thereby it achieves its end."[144]

It would be overly simplistic to think of the spiraling motion in terms of the Word of God to man being revelation, and the faithful response of man to God as being reconciliation. As shorthand for what Torrance is after, this is an adequate first-order approximation; the process, however, is more complex. The Word of God is always expressed in the word of man, and, however

---

140. T. F. Torrance, *The Mediation of Christ*, 25–26. "The self-revelation of God to be known out of himself as he is according to his own mode of rationality cannot achieve its telos in Torrance's theology unless it is a revelation which effects human reconciliation in the faith-knowing relation within the community of the Church." Morrison, *Knowledge of the Self-Revealing God*, 182.

141. T. F. Torrance, *The Mediation of Christ*, 24. See the discussion in Lee, *Living in Union with Christ*, 103–9.

142. T. F. Torrance, *Theology in Reconstruction*, 133.

143. T. F. Torrance, *The Mediation of Christ*, 5. Israel is the "earthly medium and human counterpart not only of divine revelation but of divine reconciliation." T. F. Torrance, *The Mediation of Christ*, 32. See T. F. Torrance, "The Divine Vocation and Destiny of Israel," 88; T. F. Torrance, "Israel and the Incarnation," 319.

144. T. F. Torrance, *The Mediation of Christ*, 103. Here, as well, Torrance is indebted to Barth. "Revelation takes place in and with reconciliation. Indeed, the latter is also revelation. . . . Revelation takes place as the revelation of reconciliation." Barth, *CD*, IV.3.1, 8. See T. F. Torrance, *Karl Barth: Biblical and Evangelical Theologian*, 114–15.

inadequate, entails some measure of "cognitive union" with the Object. Thus, reconciliation is involved at some level in all revelation. And, of course, the reconciling action of God in drawing Israel to himself, cleansing and restoring them, creates institutions and "empirical correlates" which are themselves revelatory.[145] "Thus the whole course of God's historical interaction with Israel as presented to us in the Old Testament Scriptures made clear that revelation and reconciliation must be locked into each other, for neither can reach its destined end without the other."[146] Therefore, at any point along the spiral we have revelation and reconciliation in dynamic interrelation.[147]

This whole movement is proleptically conditioned by, and comes to fulfillment in, Jesus Christ.[148] In his assumption and healing of our fallen flesh the bi-polarity of revelation and reconciliation becomes a coherent unity. "In the Incarnation revelation and reconciliation are one in the unity of Word and Deed in Christ."[149] Here "the act of his revelation is inseparable from the act of his reconciliation, and the act of his self-impartation is inseparable from the act of his atoning propitiation."[150] It is the hypostatic union, dynamically conceived, which grounds, and in fact, *is* this unity of revelation and reconciliation:

> Thus we must think of the person and work of Christ as completely one, so that he is in himself what he reveals of the Father, and he is in himself all that he does in his life and on the cross in reconciliation. It is only because Jesus is that in himself, and

---

145. "The Bible has to be heard, therefore, as the Word of God within the bi-polarity of revelation and reconciliation." T. F. Torrance, *Theology in Reconstruction*, 139.

146. T. F. Torrance, *The Mediation of Christ*, 102. An example of this inseparability in the one movement of the Word of God in Israel is seen when Torrance says: "Thus the biblical modes of thought have a sacrosanctity, not because they are Hebraic, but because they represent both the way in which God's revelation and reconciliation have taken within the mind of man, and the covenanted patterns of response and obedience to that revelation and reconciliation. Apart from that prepared sphere of revelation and reconciliation no one could have grasp the bewildering miracle of Jesus." Note that the biblical modes of thought are the result of revelation *and* reconciliation, Israel responds to revelation *and* reconciliation, and thus she is the "prepared sphere of revelation *and* reconciliation." T. F. Torrance, "Israel and the Incarnation," 319.

147. Torrance also speaks of "the mutual involution of revelation and reconciliation." T. F. Torrance, *Theology in Reconstruction*, 133.

148. "Christian theology takes its stand in the fullness of time in Christ and looks back from there to interpret the previous history of the covenant." T. F. Torrance, *The School of Faith: The Catechisms of the Reformed Church*, lxi.

149. T. F. Torrance, *Royal Priesthood: A Theology of Ordained Ministry*, 69. See T. F. Torrance, *Theology in Reconstruction*, 132.

150. T. F. Torrance, *Divine Meaning: Studies in Patristic Hermeneutics*, 9. See T. F. Torrance, *The Doctrine of Jesus Christ*, 91–92; Kang, "Vicarious Humanity," 204.

lives it out in himself, that he reveals the Father and reconciles the world.[151]

Here there is no break in the circular or spiral movement.

Yet, in recalcitrant Israel, this is not the case. There the dynamic and interlocked relationship of revelation and reconciliation is expressed in the covenantal tension of law and cult, truth and reconciliation.[152] Within this polarity the Word of God presses for a faithful response, and this requires sinful Israel's reconciliation with God.

The Covenanted Way of Response

The sign of the covenant, in which the various polarities of revelation and reconciliation are held together, is circumcision. This is of immense importance for Torrance. It means that the Word of God has to be "cut into the flesh" of Israel.

> The great sign of the covenant made with Abraham and Isaac was circumcision, for in it the covenant was cut into the flesh of this people, and remained throughout the generations as the sign that the promises of God would be fulfilled in the life of this people only as the word of God was translated into its flesh, into its very existence. It was the sign that at last the covenant has to be written into the heart, in the "crucifixion" of self-will, in the putting off of "the enmity of the flesh."[153]

The Word seeks full-orbed, obedient embodiment, and circumcision covenants Israel to a life of obedience and faith.[154] The Word of God must be "enacted in its flesh,"[155] "done into its existence before God,"[156] and "kneaded into its very existence."[157]

---

151. T. F. Torrance, *Incarnation*, 108. We shall explore this more fully in chapters four through six.

152. Both polarities are held together in the unity of the covenant. T. F. Torrance, *Atonement*, 37.

153. T. F. Torrance, *Incarnation*, 47–48; Kang, "Vicarious Humanity," 152–53; T. F. Torrance, *Atonement*, 43. This entails "the primacy of the covenant, both in law and in cult." T. F. Torrance, *Atonement*, 8. The covenant is not only the will of God for his people, but "the very form of their actual existence" before him. T. F. Torrance, *Atonement*, 38, 43.

154. T. F. Torrance, *Theology in Reconstruction*, 194.

155. T. F. Torrance, *Conflict and Agreement in the Church: The Ministry and the Sacraments of the Gospel*, 98.

156. T. F. Torrance, *Conflict and Agreement in the Church: The Ministry and the Sacraments of the Gospel*, 98, 121; T. F. Torrance, *Royal Priesthood: A Theology of Ordained Ministry*, 6.

157. T. F. Torrance, *Incarnation*, 47; T. F. Torrance, *Conflict and Agreement in the*

> From the Deuteronomic literature on this was given a deeper interpretation in terms of the circumcision of ears, lips, and heart—the whole "inner man," so to speak, had to be circumcised. That is to say, the Covenant will of God had to be inscribed by His finger or by His Spirit upon the tablets of the heart. That idea came to prominence especially in Ezekiel and Jeremiah.[158]

Yet, in addition to circumcision, the covenant has a second sacrament that answers to Israel's weakness and need for atonement as the people in whom the covenant was to be embodied.

> This covenant was sealed with two major "sacraments": circumcision, which inscribed the promise of God's blessing in the flesh and seed of his people and covenanted them to a life of obedience and faith; and the Passover, in which God renewed his covenant promising redemption from the bondage of sin and the tyranny of the powers of evil into fellowship with himself through a sacrifice which God himself would provide.[159]

The sacramental structure of the covenant entails the demand for obedience and the graciously provided remedy for disobedience.[160] God knew that Israel would not be able to faithfully fulfill or embody his will, for "the covenant was not made with a holy people," but with Israel "in its sinful, rebellious and estranged existence."[161] This provides the logic for the cultic dimension of the covenant.

> But God knows that His children are unable to be holy or obedient or perfect before Him; they are unable to fulfill the requirements of His Covenant Will, so that within the Covenant and

Church: Order and Disorder, 290; T. F. Torrance, "Israel and the Incarnation," 309; T. F. Torrance, Atonement, 43.

158. T. F. Torrance, Conflict and Agreement in the Church: The Ministry and the Sacraments of the Gospel, 98.

159. T. F. Torrance, Theology in Reconstruction, 194.

160. Ibid., 195. "Not only, therefore, did he give his people his 'Word and Sacraments' through which he revealed himself familiarly to them and adopted them as his children, but he provided for them a Law which clearly set forth his will, and an order of worship and sacrifice in the cult which supplied his people in their weakness with a covenanted way of response to his will."

161. T. F. Torrance, The Mediation of Christ, 27. "No, the covenant was not made with a holy people . . . for it was a unilateral covenant which depended for its fulfillment upon the unconditional grace of God and the unrelenting purpose of reconciliation which he had pledged to work out through Israel for all peoples. And therefore . . . it depended upon a vicarious way of response to the love of God which God himself provided within the covenant—a way of response which he set out in the liturgy of atoning sacrifice." T. F. Torrance, The Mediation of Christ, 28.

as part of its Covenant mercies He graciously provides a way of response to His Will, a way of obedient conformity to His Covenant which He is pleased to accept as from His people in the Covenant. That was provided in Israel's Cult or *leitourgia*.[162]

This divinely provided "covenant way of response" is what Torrance calls a "third," or "middle," term in the relationship between God and Israel. "We are not concerned here simply with the Will of God and the obedience of man, with the Law of God, and the conformity of man to that divine law, but with a third dimension, with a divinely provided fulfillment of the divine Law."[163] This third term is within the reciprocal polarities of the covenant and not extraneous to them. While it is perfectly legitimate to think of the covenant as having two parties, God and Israel, this middle term, or covenanted way of response provided in the cult, underscores the essentially gracious, non-dualist nature of the relationship.[164] Due to Israel's weakness and frailty, God gratuitously provides a way for the fulfillment of his divine Word.[165]

> Hence within the covenant which, as we have seen, God established and maintained with his people in a unilateral way, and as part of its sheer grace, he freely provided them with a covenanted way of responding to him, a vicarious way in which the covenant might be fulfilled in their midst and on their behalf, so that Israel could come before God forgiven and sanctified in their covenant partnership with him and be consecrated for their priestly mission in the world.[166]

---

162. T. F. Torrance, *Conflict and Agreement in the Church: The Ministry and the Sacraments of the Gospel*, 15–16. This divinely provided way of response is "a witness to his readiness to cleanse and forgive his people within the covenant." T. F. Torrance, *Conflict and Agreement in the Church: The Ministry and the Sacraments of the Gospel*, 121. See T. F. Torrance, *Incarnation*, 56; T. F. Torrance, *Atonement*, 8; T. F. Torrance, *Theology in Reconstruction*, 194–95.

163. T. F. Torrance, *Conflict and Agreement in the Church: The Ministry and the Sacraments of the Gospel*, 15.

164. "We normally think of the covenant as having two parties, God and Abraham, or God and Israel. And that is certainly in accordance with the Word of God in the institution of the covenant partnership. 'I am the Almighty God; walk before me and be perfect.' . . . There is another factor to be taken into account however, a middle term between the polarities of the covenant, God and Abraham, or God and Israel, namely a *covenanted way of response* such as a divinely provided sacrifice replacing the best that the human partner may think he can offer, as in the paradigm case of the offering God provided instead of Isaac, Abraham's beloved son." T. F. Torrance, *The Mediation of Christ*, 73–74.

165. T. F. Torrance, *Conflict and Agreement in the Church: The Ministry and the Sacraments of the Gospel*, 121; T. F. Torrance, *God and Rationality*, 158.

166. T. F. Torrance, *The Mediation of Christ*, 74.

Thus, Israel is taught in the cult that she is unable to obey, much less placate or manipulate God. An obedient response must be provided by sheer grace within the corporate reciprocity of the covenant. "Thus no unprescribed oblation, no uncovenanted offering, no strange fire, no incense of their own recipe, and no ritual of their own inventing, were to be intruded into their worship of God."[167]

Yet Israel cannot rely on the cult as a talisman, for it too, grounded in the covenant, is to be kneaded into her recalcitrant flesh. After all, as we have seen, the whole cult was a liturgical extension into the life of Israel of the once for all events which established the covenant at Sinai.[168] "Law and cult have no place in God's will merely as such; they have their place only as they are kneaded into the very existence and understanding and life of Israel."[169] They are not "mere letter and liturgy."[170] As the law is to be inscribed on the heart of Israel, so the cultic pattern needs to be acted out in obedience.[171]

Thus, the cult points to a fundamental enigma in the divinely provided covenant way of response. It points to Israel's waywardness, its inability to fulfill the terms of the covenant, yet the cult must be joined to, and fleshed out as, obedience. The insistence on obedience precisely at the place of a

---

167. Ibid. "Everything about the sanctuary and everything that was prescribed to be done within it as the place where God had recorded his name, the holy place of meeting and witness between God and his covenanted people, was designed to testify to the fact that God alone can expiate guilt, forgive sin and bring about propitiation between himself and his people Israel. Hence the very priesthood itself, the sacrifices, offerings and oblations which the priests alone were consecrated to take in their hands, together with all the liturgical ordinances, were regarded as constituting the vicarious way of covenant response in faith, obedience and worship which God had freely provided for Israel out of his steadfast love." T. F. Torrance, *The Mediation of Christ*, 74–75. "It is the very grace of God in providing the covenanted way of response that placed the whole of Israel's existence and even her most holy offerings under judgment." Kruger, "Participation in the Self-Knowledge of God," 7.

168. T. F. Torrance, *Atonement*, 9, 15–16; T. F. Torrance, *Royal Priesthood: A Theology of Ordained Ministry*, 4.

169. T. F. Torrance, *Incarnation*, 47; T. F. Torrance, *Atonement*, 57. It should be noted that this way of putting the matter requires a minor clarification in the notion of the "covenanted way of response." We might say that the cult is the focused arena of the covenanted way of response in which Israel's inability, and the need for atoning sacrifice, is highlighted. Thus, while Torrance often speaks of the cult as the divinely provided way of response, it is also clear that the whole of the covenant (law and cult) is to meet with an obedient response from Israel. Therefore, Torrance can speak of them jointly as Israel's "covenanted way of response" that must be "impregnated in its understanding and sculptured into its very being." T. F. Torrance, *The Mediation of Christ*, 74–75.

170. T. F. Torrance, "Israel and the Incarnation," 308–9; T. F. Torrance, *Incarnation*, 47.

171. T. F. Torrance, *Conflict and Agreement in the Church: The Ministry and the Sacraments of the Gospel*, 16.

graciously provided way of response points us to the reality that this middle, or third, term in the covenant is realized only in the life, death and resurrection of Jesus Christ in our humanity.[172] The covenanted way of response points ahead to the vicarious humanity of Christ where enacted obedience and atoning sacrifice are one.[173]

The cult, or the covenanted way of response, then, bears witness to two realities. The response must be made by Israel, and yet Israel's response must be displaced. This is what Torrance sees in the fulfillment of the covenanted way of response. Jesus Christ is man, and responds as man, yet due to the hypostatic union, he is at the same time God, and thus his human response is "divinely provided." In other language, Jesus Christ both represents us, acting on our behalf, and in one indivisible movement, substitutes for us, displacing our response.[174] He does "in our stead, and in our place and on our behalf what we are unable to do."[175] In this sense the shape of the cult is a second-order, sacramental reflection of Christology.[176]

---

172. There is also an important anticipatory fulfillment of the covenant way of response and, indeed, the whole priestly-cultic aspect of the covenant, in the servant of the Lord which we shall consider below.

173. Kang, "Vicarious Humanity," 339–48. We shall look further at this in chapter 4.

174. T. F. Torrance, *Theology in Reconstruction*, 156–57.

175. T. F. Torrance, *Conflict and Agreement in the Church: The Ministry and the Sacraments of the Gospel*, 124. By this combination of terms Torrance means representation and substitution. "The radical nature of Jesus' mediation of our human response to God can be made apparent by bringing together and thinking into each other the concepts of representation and substitution. It will not do to think of what Christ has done for us only in terms of representation, for that would imply that Jesus represents, or stands for, our response, that he is the leader of humanity in humanity's act of response to God. On the other hand, if Jesus is a substitute in detachment from us, who simply acts in our stead in an external, formal or forensic way, then his response has no ontological bearing upon us but is an empty transaction over our heads. A merely representative or a merely substitutionary concept of vicarious mediation is bereft of any actual saving significance. But if representation and substitution are combined and allowed to interpenetrate each other within the incarnational union of the Son of God with us in which he has actually taken our sin and guilt upon his own being, then we may have a profounder and truer grasp of the vicarious humanity in the mediatorship of Christ, as one in which he acts in our place, in our stead, on our behalf but out of the ontological depths of our actual human being." T. F. Torrance, *The Mediation of Christ*, 80–81. See T. F. Torrance, *Royal Priesthood: A Theology of Ordained Ministry*, 14. T. F. Torrance, *Karl Barth: Biblical and Evangelical Theologian*, 234–35.

176. T. F. Torrance, *God and Rationality*, 158. What was gratuitously provided in the cult was "what took place in Jesus Christ in the whole course of His obedience from His birth to His death on the Cross, for He fulfilled in Himself the Word of God tabernacling among men, the covenanted way of response to God set forth in the ancient cult, and constituted Himself our Temple, our Priest, our Offering and our Worship." See T. F. Torrance, *Royal Priesthood: A Theology of Ordained Ministry*, 5–7.

For our purposes, it is important that this fulfillment of the covenanted way of response takes place in the "ontological depths" of our humanity. Just as the covenant was to be wrought out in the depths of Israel's fallen humanity, so in Christ the covenanted way of response adumbrated by the cult is fulfilled inside of our alienation and guilt. "As God and yet as Man, Jesus Christ penetrated into the midst of our humanity in order to overcome our estrangement and to reconcile us to the Father."[177] This entails both the priestly obedience which Israel as our representative has failed to offer, and bearing the judgment against disobedience to which we were liable.[178]

The Conflict with the Carnal Mind

As the chosen mediators of reconciliation, called to embody the covenant both as law and as cult, Israel finds itself invaded by the Word of God. This produces an intense, "running conflict between divine revelation and what St. Paul called 'the carnal mind.'"[179] It is Israel "with all its recalcitrance and intractability, with all its resentment against his love," that God chooses.[180] It is not that Israel is any better or worse than any other people, but rather, the covenant relation is like a furnace in which "the innate resistance of the human soul and mind resulting from the alienation of man from God inevitably became intensified."[181] The removal of estrangement, which all knowledge entails and which makes reconciliation the "inner dynamic" of revelation, is pursued most ruthlessly in this divinely established reciprocity. The fire of God's love and holiness and truth "cuts against the grain of its natural existence," and "its religious desires and forms of worship."[182] In

---

177. T. F. Torrance, *Theology in Reconstruction*, 133. "He is the mediator between God and man and between man and God who constitutes in himself the divine-human bridge across the chasm of alienation, disruption and death." T. F. Torrance, *Divine and Contingent Order*, 137. Importantly, this includes the creational and social coefficient we looked at earlier: "In order to achieve its end, the self-address of God to man in Jesus Christ had to penetrate, domicile itself, and take form within the interpersonal reciprocities of human society and thereby within the address of man to man." T. F. Torrance, *Reality and Evangelical Theology*, 91; T. F. Torrance, *God and Rationality*, 151. We shall explore this penetration into our darkness more fully later, especially in chapter 5.

178. T. F. Torrance, *The Mediation of Christ*, 41. We shall look at the relationship of this obedience and judgment when we consider "condemning sin in the flesh" in chapter 5, and the cross of Christ in chapter 6.

179. T. F. Torrance, *The Mediation of Christ*, 10.

180. T. F. Torrance, *Incarnation*, 42.

181. T. F. Torrance, *The Mediation of Christ*, 10.

182. Ibid. Here Torrance refers to Israel's propensity to engage in the idolatrous practices of its neighbors.

order for revelation to complete itself as reconciliation it had to wage war against "all in-built bias against it," "break through the barriers of naturalistic and pagan convention,"[183] and turn "the soul and mind of this people inside out."[184] The result is what Torrance calls "a kind of 'love-hate' relation between Israel and God."[185]

This reality means the spiraling movement of the Word of God in Israel "was far from being an easy or painless process."[186] It was rather an agonizing drama which Torrance graphically describes as "an ordeal by history and judgment,"[187] or a "harrowing experience."[188] Herein lies the source of Israel's long historical ordeal of "the most appalling suffering."[189] While Israel suffered from other nations, it suffered above all from God, "for divine revelation was a fire in the mind and soul and memory of Israel burning away all that was in conflict with God's holiness, mercy and truth."[190] The very intimacy of the covenant "had the effect of intensifying the stubbornness of its self-will."[191]

Though we considered them earlier under the mediation of revelation, here we learn that Israel's ordeal as the mediator of *reconciliation* is also a crucial part of the restructuring movement that produces the matrix of concepts, or permanent structures of thought and speech about God. This includes the Old Testament Scriptures, which themselves document the escalating fiery ordeal of which they are a by-product.[192]

---

183. T. F. Torrance, "The Divine Vocation and Destiny of Israel," 88.

184. T. F. Torrance, *The Mediation of Christ*, 10.

185. Ibid. Or, Israel "shattered itself on the unswerving persistence of the divine purpose of love." T. F. Torrance, *Incarnation*, 47.

186. T. F. Torrance, *The Mediation of Christ*, 8.

187. T. F. Torrance, *Incarnation*, 42.

188. T. F. Torrance, *The Mediation of Christ*, 8. God's self-revelation is "carried through the most harrowing and profound historical experience the world has ever known, in the whole life and agony of Israel." T. F. Torrance, *Incarnation*, 46.

189. T. F. Torrance, *The Mediation of Christ*, 8. "The role for which Israel was elected was agonizingly difficult: to be the human bearer of divine revelation and thus to suffer from its flame as no other people has ever had to suffer." T. F. Torrance, "The Divine Vocation and Destiny of Israel," 88.

190. T. F. Torrance, *The Mediation of Christ*, 8. Provocatively, Torrance sees the suffering caused by the enmity of the human heart against the Word of God, and the oddity or strangeness this gives Israel, as the source of anti-semitism. Their struggle mirrors our own enmity against God and we vent our resentment against God on Israel. T. F. Torrance, *The Mediation of Christ*, 11.

191. T. F. Torrance, "The Divine Vocation and Destiny of Israel," 89.

192. Ibid., 88.

> The Word of God ... used the reactions of the succeeding generations, whether of assent or dissent, obedience or disobedience, apostasy or reform, as the instruments for ever-deepening penetration into Israel's existence and as the means through which it became understandable and communicable as God's Word to man.[193]

It is important to note that *all* of Israel's responses, whether of obedience or disobedience, were made instruments for the Word's "deepening penetration into its existence."[194] It is not that Israel does not sometimes respond in obedience; nevertheless, her history as the vicarious representative of the human heart in its enmity toward God is a tragic one marred by disobedience and idolatry. Thus she suffers from the "flame" of divine revelation.

This suffering is inevitable for it is part of Israel's vicarious calling and destiny as the prepared sphere of reconciliation, the one place where the Word of God fully engages and summons the fallen nature of humanity. "God insisted on assuming Israel in its sinful contradiction into partnership with Himself—hence the profoundest agony of psalmist and prophet alike."[195]

> But it is important to see that this obstinate behaviour on Israel's part was an inescapable and essential ingredient in its vicarious mission, for it was with Israel in its capacity as a representative of human nature in its stubborn estrangement from God, and with Israel precisely in its sinful existence, that God bound himself for ever in a covenant or partnership of steadfast love.[196]

The vicarious election of Israel, thus, implies the vicarious rejection of Israel.[197]

This suffering also intensifies as the covenant history unfolds. The more the Word of God penetrates and embodies itself in Israel, the more the enmity of man is revealed and the more she suffers.

---

193. Ibid., 88–89. See T. F. Torrance, *The Mediation of Christ*, 12, 77–78; T. F. Torrance, *God and Rationality*, 147–48; T. F. Torrance, *Reality and Scientific Theology*, 87.

194. T. F. Torrance, *Reality and Evangelical Theology*, 87.

195. T. F. Torrance, *Incarnation*, 48.

196. T. F. Torrance, "The Divine Vocation and Destiny of Israel," 89. "If the Jew, caught up in man's conflict with God through the vicarious role God has put upon him could not but react as he did, he was acting in our place and representing our rejection of God's self-giving, so that divine reconciliation might come to us as well and be grounded in the depths of our being." T. F. Torrance, *The Mediation of Christ*, 35.

197. Kang, "Vicarious Humanity," 145–67; T. F. Torrance, *Theology in Reconstruction*, 197; T. F. Torrance, *Conflict and Agreement in the Church: Order and Disorder*, 294.

God used the historical experience of Israel to reveal Himself more and more profoundly and to give Himself more completely to Israel. He used the suffering and judgment of Israel to reveal the terrible nature of sin as contradiction to God's love and grace, to uncover the deep enmity of humanity in its persistent self-will before God in his divine self-giving. But transcending all, God used this nation in the ordeal of history and suffering to reveal his own infinite love and the undeflected persistence of his holy will to bring forgiveness and reconciliation.[198]

The Historical Contours of the Conflict

Let us look more closely at the historical contours of this running conflict. We recall that Torrance sees the covenant playing out in the complementary duality of law and cult, word and mediation, Moses and Aaron, prophet and priest. In this framework the Word, which always retains its primacy, presses relentlessly for an obedient response, thus inducing Israel's long trauma.

This conflict is manifested first in the polarity of Moses and Aaron, Sinaitic law and Levitical liturgy.[199] This provides the backdrop for Israel's repeated rebellions against Moses. He is the mediator of the Word insisting it be done into sinful Israel's flesh. In this role he anticipates the later prophets in their confrontation with the nation.[200] As the servant of the Lord, "Moses stood in the gap . . . he interceded for Israel in its great sin, acting as the representative and mediator of the people before the wrath of God."[201] In his vicarious suffering and intercession, Moses, in conjunction with Aaron's priestly sacrificial witness, anticipates the Isaianic Servant.[202]

---

198. T. F. Torrance, *Incarnation*, 47.

199. "The priesthood of the Old Testament in its double character, as mediation of God's Word and priestly witness to God's revealed Will, is given very clear interpretation in the account of the relations of Moses and Aaron, brother priests of the tribe of Levi." T. F. Torrance, *Royal Priesthood: A Theology of Ordained Ministry*, 3.

200. T. F. Torrance, *The Mediation of Christ*, 77. "Throughout all the vicissitudes of Israel's national, social and religious existence the Word of God came to Israel mediated through servants of the Lord like Moses, Elijah, Jeremiah, sometimes like a refining fire, sometimes like a hammer breaking the rocks in pieces, sometimes as a still small voice, but always in such a way that the holy presence of God himself in his Word imprinted his truth upon the innermost being of this people with the result that all its relations with God were intensified in obedience and disobedience, in faithfulness and unfaithfulness alike."

201. T. F. Torrance, *Atonement*, 43.

202. Ibid., 21, 43; T. F. Torrance, *Royal Priesthood: A Theology of Ordained Ministry*, 6; T. F. Torrance, *The Mediation of Christ*, 75–76.

The next phase of this historical ordeal is seen in the long conflict between prophet and priest. While the law and the cult in themselves, especially in light of the covenant sign of circumcision, call for embodiment, Israel's disobedience precipitates the ministry of the prophets.

> All through the history of Israel that Word was behind the law and the cult, the prophets came forward under the constraint of the Word to insist that the Word must become flesh, that is, must be allowed to enter into the very existence of Israel, in judgment and mercy.[203]

This, Torrance says, "was surely the great prophetic burden of Deutero-Isaiah and Jeremiah."[204] The cult must not become an idolatrous substitute for obedience.

> The worst thing that could be done with such a Covenant would be to turn the symbolic ritual into an end in itself, as a means of acting upon God and bending His will to serve the ends of men. That is precisely what Israel tried to do again and again, so that God sent the prophets to protest against their use of the Cult and to demand obedience rather than sacrifice.[205] The prophets, some of whom came from the priesthood, insisted that this vicarious response had to be enacted by way of obedience into the life and existence of Israel in order to be efficacious reality, and pointed ahead to the Servant of the Lord as the chosen instrument for its actualization.[206]

The prophetic witness testifies to the supremacy of the Word and the need for a repentant restructuring within the fallen mind and life of Israel without which the cult is a mockery.[207] Yet the prophets are repeatedly re-

---

203. T. F. Torrance, *Incarnation*, 60. "Through the cult Israel had been taught that the covenant could be fulfilled only through an obedient response or sacrifice provided by God himself from within the covenant, but through the prophets Israel learned that such an obedient response had to be translated into its very existence and life and made to issue out of it." T. F. Torrance, *Theology in Reconstruction*, 196.

204. T. F. Torrance, *Incarnation*, 47; T. F. Torrance, "Israel and the Incarnation," 309; T. F. Torrance, *Conflict and Agreement in the Church: Order and Disorder*, 290.

205. T. F. Torrance, *Conflict and Agreement in the Church: The Ministry and the Sacraments of the Gospel*, 121–22; T. F. Torrance, *Atonement*, 64; T. F. Torrance, *Atonement*, 271–72; T. F. Torrance, *Royal Priesthood: A Theology of Ordained Ministry*, 22.

206. T. F. Torrance, *God and Rationality*, 158. We shall consider this more fully under "The Servant of the Lord."

207. "Against that independence and perversion of priesthood and priestly liturgy God sent the prophets, most of them out of the priesthood itself, to protest against the transmutation of liturgy into idolatry, against the transmutation of liturgical forms of

jected, and Israel's hardening and the concomitant "appalling suffering" intensifies.[208] In the end, the temple itself is destroyed.

Throughout the historical unfolding of this conflict a number of other features emerge. Israel's vicarious rejection, to which we have already alluded, becomes more pronounced and vivid as the spiraling process intensifies. Torrance takes the representative role of Israel's reprobation with full seriousness. It is for our sakes that they are cast off. This is representative and substitutionary rejection.

> If Israel again and again was disobedient and rejected the claims of God's love, in a profound sense it had to do so in our place and for our sakes. And if in the process of mediating divine revelation Israel became blind to the way of God's grace (Isaiah 42:19)—it had to become blind that we might see. And whenever Israel found itself overwhelmed in the horror of divine rejection (Psalm 22:1) that too had to take place that the world might be reconciled to God.[209]

Torrance sees this rejection, which becomes clear in the latter portions of Israel's history, as already implied in the cult itself. He interprets the two sacrifices of the Day of Atonement, the bloody sacrifice and the scapegoat (the "living sacrifice"), as signifying not only the provision of a covenanted way of response but also the calling of Israel to be cast off as a mute, sin-bearing witness to the world.[210]

As the "covenant bonds between Israel and God" are drawn closer, Israel "draws back from its calling and reacts against God, because our estranged human nature, our self-centeredness and our self-will in Israel are brought into conflict with God's will."[211] However, this does not thwart the gracious self-giving of God. He "uses this very state of affairs to ground his

---

witness into hardened and self-sufficient forms that only ministered to Israel's false security" T. F. Torrance, *Royal Priesthood: A Theology of Ordained Ministry*, 5.

208. "However when the priesthood became so very corrupt, God raised up prophets like Amos who had no relation to the priesthood and who came voicing the word of God in criticism of cultic performances. In this prophetic ministry, there was evident an attack upon the independence of the cult, a prophetic and eschatological suspension of liturgy in the demand for obedience to the will of God rather than ceremonial ritual. Hence at last when the prophets were spurned, God promised he would destroy the temple and its liturgy and so overthrow the false security of Israel which rested upon a sinful perversion of the holy liturgy." T. F. Torrance, *Atonement*, 64.

209. T. F. Torrance, "The Divine Vocation and Destiny of Israel," 89.

210. Ibid., 99–101; T. F. Torrance, "Israel and the Incarnation," 169–70.

211. T. F. Torrance, "The Divine Vocation and Destiny of Israel," 93.

self-giving to mankind more deeply than ever in human existence."[212] This is the triumph of the grace of God precisely in and through Israel's darkness. "Even if Israel persists in adulterating its relationship with God, he will not divorce Israel," for the covenant bond "will finally triumph over all estrangement and bring about reconciliation and peace."[213]

> That intensification, however, is not to be regarded simply as an accidental result of the covenant but rather as something which God deliberately took into the full design of his reconciling activity, for it was the will and way of God's grace to effect reconciliation with man at his very worst, precisely in his state of rebellion against God.[214]

This overcoming and use of Israel's rejection, which is at the same time a confirmation of her role in the mediation of reconciliation, is seen most graphically in "Israel's strange rejection of its own Messiah in the crucifixion of Christ." It is

> something which, in its service of God's covenant-will, to bring about the reconciliation of all mankind and in the fulfillment of its God-given vicarious mission, Israel *had* to do. Thus Israel's rejection of Christ implicated it in the depths of Christ's own vicarious passion and atoning reconciliation.[215]

Intertwined with this mission of vicarious suffering and rejection is another important dynamic. The covenant always had a dual character in that it was particular and universal. This is particularly clear in the case of Abraham who is elected so that through him the nations would be blessed.[216] In Israel this duality takes on a paradoxical nature as her history advances.

> The movement was paradoxical in character—the more particular it became, the more universal it also became; the deeper the bond between God and man was driven in the human existence of Israel, the closer redemption made contact with creation; the more intimately Israel was tied to the one and only God, the God of all, the more the activity of grace broke through the limitations of national Israel and reached out into all the world.[217]

212. Ibid., 93.
213. T. F. Torrance, *The Mediation of Christ*, 27.
214. Ibid., 28.
215. T. F. Torrance, "The Divine Vocation and Destiny of Israel," 93–94.
216. Gen 12:1–3.
217. T. F. Torrance, *Atonement*, 50–51. It is important to note that driving revelation and reconciliation into Israel's existence drives it deeply into creation. This is another

Torrance seems to be thinking of the gradual unveiling of the international purposes of God, present from the beginning to be sure, but stated with greater frequency and intensity as revelation unfolds, for example in the Psalms and the Prophets. Thus, the election of one for all is not a static affair. Acute personalization or particularization leads to universalization.

This paradox is rooted in the very nature of Israel's calling to be God's people (λαος). Torrance will often view the whole dynamic of Israel's suffering under the rubric of her aspiring to be a nation (ἔθνος) like the surrounding nations, as opposed to being God's λαος.[218] This is a fundamental way the enmity of the human heart surfaces in Israel.[219]

> That was particularly apparent in the election of Israel to be God's *laos*, people, upon which Israel's aspirations to be *ethnos*, nation, were shattered again and again. . . . It was characteristic of the whole activity of God's grace that it should suborn the very refusal of Israel to be *laos* to minister to its purpose of universal blessing and redemption. And so the more like a single *ethnos* Israel become the more it had to be scattered in diaspora over the face of the whole earth.[220]

Thus, the acute particularization of the covenant leads to exile and diaspora (acute universalization in judgment). We shall see how this dynamic continues when we look at the Servant of the Lord, and finally, how "at last in the acute particularization of the covenantal bond between Israel and God in Jesus, it became absolutely universal for all men."[221]

To complete our survey of this historical conflict we turn to the period of the exile. Torrance sees this era in terms of the conflict between prophet and priest, where the prophet, and thus the Word of God, becomes wholly

---

reason the cultural-linguistic, layered space-time reality discussed earlier is important.

218. Ibid., 346. "Thus there arose and persisted through the history of Israel a struggle between Israel and its Lord, between its 'ethnic' aspirations to be a nation like the other nations of the earth and its 'laic' calling to be a people in covenant-communion with God. It was this conflict that plunged Israel into its long ordeal of suffering."

219. This dynamic, like the dynamic of Israel's vicarious rejection generally, highlights the essentially corporate nature of the mediation of reconciliation for the sake of the world. As such, Israel "cannot completely nationalize its own existence without detaching itself from the very covenant with God which constitutes it the people that it always has been and is." T. F. Torrance, *The Mediation of Christ*, 14.

220. T. F. Torrance, *Incarnation*, 51. The will to be ἔθνος "entailed political and national disaster for Israel. . . . That was part of the deepest agony of Jeremiah." T. F. Torrance, "Israel and the Incarnation," 309.

221. T. F. Torrance, "Israel and the Incarnation," 312.

marginalized. Though the law is present, and the cult revived, the situation results in what Torrance calls "liturgized law" and "legalized liturgy."[222]

> We find a rehabilitation of the ancient cult in final liturgical form[223] but we find also a rehabilitation of the Word of God, mainly in the form of "Instruction." Now there begins the era of liturgised law and legalized liturgy. Already the scribe emerges into prominence along with the priest. Law and liturgy go hand in hand, but in such a way that they are made self-sufficient and independent, liturgised Scripture and legalized priestcraft. Here there is no room for the prophet, the direct intervention of the charismatic Word, for the Word of God is made of none effect by the traditions of men.[224]

It is into this situation that Jesus Christ penetrated as the Word of God, the fulfillment of the law and cult. This penetration necessarily involved a judgment on the whole cultic-legal system, which Torrance sees announced in the ministry of the "cult-prophet" John the Baptist.[225]

The Servant of the Lord

We turn now to consider the figure who, in the midst of the historical conflict, emerges in the Servant Songs of Isaiah. The Servant of the Lord has a crucial role in integrating many of the strands of Torrance's thought on the spiraling movement of the Word of God, particularly with respect to the mediation of reconciliation in Israel. Here we should note that the whole spiraling movement we have been examining narrows as Israel's history

---

222. T. F. Torrance, *Atonement*, 64–65.

223. Ibid., 42.

224. T. F. Torrance, *Royal Priesthood: A Theology of Ordained Ministry*, 7. "In this developing situation Ezekiel had already seen the Shekinah leaving the Temple as it had left Aaron's Tabernacle in his revolt from Moses, and the seventy-fourth Psalm says: 'We see not our signs. There is no more any prophet.' Without the priestly mediation of the Word of God and its dynamic intervention in the life of Israel, Israel is delivered over to God-forsakenness, hardened by sin in the very use of the ordinances of grace. And Daniel speaks of the sealing up of sins and the sealing up of vision and prophecy until the coming of the Anointed (ch. 9.24f)."

225. T. F. Torrance, *Atonement*, 65–66. The movement proceeds, says Torrance, relying on John's Gospel, from Jesus' baptism to his cleansing of the temple and his decisive proclamation, "Destroy this temple, and in three days I will raise it up." As we shall see, Torrance's exposition of Jesus' baptism is of critical importance in his understanding that Christ assumed our fallen humanity.

proceeds, and in the Servant we have an anticipation of the "acute personalization" which will culminate in Jesus Christ.[226]

> The whole conception of the suffering servant represents the activity of God whereby he begins to draw together the cords of the covenant in which he had bound Israel to Himself as his chosen partner in covenant history; it represents the saving activity of God in which he began to narrow down his assumption of Israel into union with himself toward the point of the incarnation where, in the midst of Israel, he was to assume man into oneness with himself in the ultimate act of incarnation and reconciliation.[227]

Behind this narrowing is the election of corporate Israel to be God's Servant. "Israel was called to be the Servant of the Lord, the one people within the Adamic race set apart for vicarious mission in the redemption of the many."[228] What is being narrowed down, then, is God's "assumption of Israel into union with himself." She is the corporate prophet and priest, and she is elected to be the Servant of the Lord. Torrance explicitly links up these corporate functions: "In this way Israel came to be constituted God's Prophet among the peoples of the earth, that is, his Servant entrusted with the oracles of God and the promises of the Messiah."[229] Thus, Israel is the "servant of God's reconciling love for all men."[230] It is the narrowing down of Israel as God's elected Servant which lies behind Torrance's reading of the texts in Isaiah.

This gives us a new angle into Torrance's understanding of the need for the law and the cult to be cut into Israel's very existence, which he calls "the

---

226. Scandrett, "Suffering Servant," 44: "If an 'ever-deepening, spiral movement' is one that both deepens and narrows to a point, and the Incarnation is the culmination of God's self-revelation to Israel it follows that Torrance sees the Incarnation as the point toward which that spiral is both moving and narrowing. Assuming this to be the case, it would also follow that Torrance understands the later period of Israel's history—and thus, the later Old Testament texts such as the Prophets—to contain more densely focused thematic material relevant to a proper understanding of the Incarnation." Herein lies the significance of the Servant Songs. "God had, as it were, lassoed Israel by the cords of his covenant love and drew them increasingly tighter as his partnership with Israel held on its reconciling course through history." T. F. Torrance, *The Mediation of Christ*, 28. See T. F. Torrance, *Theology in Reconstruction*, 197.

227. T. F. Torrance, *Incarnation*, 47; T. F. Torrance, "Israel and the Incarnation," 309.

228. T. F. Torrance, *Theology in Reconstruction*, 196.

229. Ibid., 195. It should be noted that Torrance often capitalizes "Servant" in this context to indicate the inner connection between Israel and the Isaianic Servant. See T. F. Torrance, "The Divine Vocation and Destiny of Israel," 88.

230. T. F. Torrance, *The Mediation of Christ*, 32.

great prophetic burden of Deutero-Isaiah and Jeremiah," and the suffering which ensues.

> So long as the cords of the covenant were not drawn tight, and God remained, so to speak, at a distance, the conflict was not very sharp, but the closer God drew near the more the human self-will of Israel asserted itself in resistance to its divine vocation. Thus the more fully God gave himself to this people, the more he forced it to be what it actually was, what we all are, in the self-willed isolation of fallen humanity from God.[231]

This intensification of suffering is the result of an intensification of Israel's sinfulness. This ordeal, which follows from Israel's vicarious and representative enmity against God, is part of "the breaking and making of Israel as the Servant of the Lord."[232] The whole historical conflict between prophet and priest can be tersely summarized as leading to the Servant of the Lord.

> The prophets, some of whom came from the priesthood, insisted that this vicarious response had to be enacted by way of obedience into the life and existence of Israel in order to be efficacious reality, and pointed ahead to the Servant of the Lord as the chosen instrument for its actualization.[233] The very self-giving of God in holy love not only revealed Israel's sin, but intensified it; it intensified the enmity between Israel and Yahweh and intensified the contradiction between Yahweh and Israel—hence "the Suffering Servant."[234]

Therefore, we must also understand Israel's rejection, not simply as that of the elected representative of Adamic humanity, but as part of its vicarious passion as God's Servant.

---

231. Ibid., 28, 102.

232. T. F. Torrance, "Israel and the Incarnation," 309; T. F. Torrance, *Incarnation*, 47; T. F. Torrance, *Conflict and Agreement in the Church: Order and Disorder*, 290; T. F. Torrance, *Theology in Reconstruction*, 197.

233. T. F. Torrance, *God and Rationality*, 158. "The cult-prophets, in language drawn from the priestly sacrifices, and the great salvation-events of the Exodus, liturgically extended in them, place before Israel the doctrine of the Suffering Servant." T. F. Torrance, *Atonement*, 21. The whole cult is "bent forward" to the Servant and, ultimately, to the New Covenant. T. F. Torrance, *Atonement*, 9; T. F. Torrance, *Royal Priesthood: A Theology of Ordained Ministry*, 6.

234. This assumption of sinful Israel leads to the "identity by assumption" of the suffering of Israel with the suffering of the Messiah "so poignantly described in Isaiah 53." T. F. Torrance, *Incarnation*, 48; T. F. Torrance, "Israel and the Incarnation," 309–10; T. F. Torrance, *Conflict and Agreement in the Church: Order and Disorder*, 291.

How could it be otherwise when God entered into the heart of Israel's estrangement in order to make atonement, when the assumption of refractory Israel into oneness with God intensified judgment upon Israel's self-will as well as fulfilled the self-giving of God to Israel in love? Israel becomes blinder and blinder— who is blind but my servant? (Is. 42:19)[235]

All of these themes—election, the corporate nature of Israel's mediation, the law and the cult (as a covenanted way of response) and their need for embodiment, the consequent suffering and rejection of sinful Israel— converge as the cords of the covenant are tightened and the mysterious Servant of the Lord emerges. With this background, let us turn to Torrance's understanding of the Servant himself.

The Servant is Israel, the one elected on behalf of the many, assumed into union with the Word of God.[236] We have seen the pervasive way in which Torrance describes the Word's engagement with our sinful humanity in Israel, but here the language becomes intensely personal. We have noted that Torrance takes the corporate nature of the servant quite seriously. The Servant is, first of all, Israel. Nevertheless,

> even there it is evident that as the Word became one with Israel, it became more and more one Israelite, for that is the only way in which the Word assumes a human nature and existence into oneness with himself. Thus, while in one sense, the suffering servant was Israel assumed into oneness with the Word, it is primarily to be understood as the Word identifying Himself with Israel, and becoming one particular Israelite, an individual person, the Messiah.[237]

Torrance provocatively asserts that "the servant of the Lord was the hypostatized actualization within the flesh and blood existence of Israel of the divinely provided way of covenant response set forth in the cult."[238]

---

235. T. F. Torrance, *Incarnation*, 49; T. F. Torrance, "The Divine Vocation and Destiny of Israel," 89. See T. F. Torrance, "Israel and the Incarnation," 310. "Thus the election of Israel as the Servant of the Lord meant that it was elected to be used even in its refusal of grace that through it the ultimate self-giving of God to man in spite of his sin and because of his sin might take place—elected, that is, to act in representative capacity for all peoples in their rejection of God's will." T. F. Torrance, *Theology in Reconstruction*, 197.

236. T. F. Torrance, "Israel and the Incarnation," 312; T. F. Torrance, *Incarnation*, 51.

237. T. F. Torrance, *Incarnation*, 51–52. See T. F. Torrance, "Israel and the Incarnation," 312; T. F. Torrance, *Theology in Reconstruction*, 197.

238. T. F. Torrance, *The Mediation of Christ*, 75–76. See Scandrett, "Suffering Servant," 56. The oneness of Israel with the Word belongs "to the very essence of the

What is at play here is the one and many dynamic of Israel's election being narrowed to the one, and thus particularized as part of the particular-universal dynamic we saw earlier. Herein lies the significance of the promises of light to the Gentiles and salvation to the ends of the earth, with their messianic telos, which cluster around the appearance of the Servant.

> Thus the ultimate self-giving of God to Israel in its historical particularity narrowing down to one particular Jew, meant the universalisation and transcendence of the Old Testament form of the covenant, and the setting of the relation of God to man on a wholly new basis in which redemption was more than the restoration of Israel, more than an event that penetrated back into the foundations of creation; it was a new creation in which the fullness of the eternal purpose of God was to be realised in an altogether transcendent way.[239]

Another crucial convergence in the figure of the Servant is that in him we have the divinely provided way of covenant response. This is deeply embedded with the one and many dynamic.

> Not only must the whole of Israel obediently fulfill the covenant as the servant of the Lord, but the enactment of the principle of atoning redemption through vicarious sacrifice in the midst of Israel means that one servant, gathering up all Israel in himself, will bear the sins of many, fulfilling on behalf of all the covenant will of God from the side of God and from the side of man, and so be the redeemer, the holy one of Israel. All these lines converge here, at the servant.[240]

Isaianic notion of the suffering servant." T. F. Torrance, *Incarnation*, 57.

239. T. F. Torrance, *Incarnation*, 52. See T. F. Torrance, "Israel and the Incarnation," 312. T. F. Torrance, *Conflict and Agreement in the Church: Order and Disorder*, 294. "This vicarious mission of Israel was the subject of considerable attention in the Isaianic prophecies, notably in the 'Servant' passages, in which it is shown how deeply Israel suffered and had to suffer in its vicarious mission as bearer of divine revelation, and mediator of the covenant on behalf of the race, bringing light to the Gentiles and salvation to the ends of the earth, but subject at the same time to divine judgements upon its own unfaithfulness and calamities at the hands of other nations. In the heart of this presentation the notions of the suffering Servant, the Holy One of Israel and the Redeemer are drawn closely together in an enigmatically anonymous figure in whom the suffering ordeal and priestly destiny of Israel are gathered up, personified and infiltrated with universal significance, and made to point ahead to the consummation of God's redemptive purpose of peace in a triumphant Messianic era which will transcend the history of Israel itself." T. F. Torrance, "Christian/Jewish Dialogue," 141.

240. T. F. Torrance, *Incarnation*, 44.

Through the Servant, conceived, first as Israel, and then as the Messiah, the covenant is cut into the flesh, and thus, vicariously fulfilled for all.[241]

At this point Torrance sees a telescoping of the basic Moses-Aaron, law-cult, prophet-priest, word-mediation duality of the covenant in the figure of the Servant. In Moses, the servant of the Lord, and in his vicarious intercession before the wrath of God, through which the covenant is renewed, Torrance sees a figure "that ultimately lies behind the conception of the servant in Deutero-Isaiah."[242] In addition to this faithful word-mediation, the servant offers the faithful covenanted way of response in atoning sacrifice.

> Here the two aspects of priesthood are brought into one, for the conceptions of Moses and Aaron are telescoped together in the vicarious life of the Servant of the Lord in order to set forth at once the redeeming action of God for Israel, and the sacrifice of obedience enacted into the life of Israel. That is the wonderful climax of the Old Testament, where it points to the union of God and man in Messianic redemption and breaks into the Gospel.[243]

Here we must recall that the covenanted way of response centered in the cult assumes Israel's disobedience and inability, yet the cult could not be divorced from obedience. This pointed to the need for both representation (Israel must obey out of the depths of her humanity) and substitution (Israel's response must be displaced). Notice in the citation above, that the sacrifice is "enacted into the life of Israel" (representation) and, at the same time, is "the redeeming action of God *for* Israel" (substitution). Torrance designates this combination as "total substitution."[244] This means that the sacrificial obedience which the Servant offers for Israel must spring out of the depths of Israel's alienated humanity.

> This leads us to the heart of Torrance's understanding of the vicarious work of the Suffering Servant, which is accomplished not merely on behalf of Israel in a representative sense, but from within Israel and therefore as Israel in a participatory sense.[245]

---

241. T. F. Torrance, *Conflict and Agreement in the Church: The Ministry and the Sacraments of the Gospel*, 98.

242. T. F. Torrance, *Atonement*, 42–43.

243. T. F. Torrance, *Royal Priesthood: A Theology of Ordained Ministry*, 6; T. F. Torrance, *Atonement*, 21.

244. T. F. Torrance, *Karl Barth: Biblical and Evangelical Theologian*, 234–36; T. F. Torrance, *The Mediation of Christ*, 80–81; T. F. Torrance, *The Trinitarian Faith*, 167–68.

245. Scandrett, "Suffering Servant," 63.

We can illumine this by looking at two aspects of the cult, one of which we have considered briefly. First, in the ritual for the Day of Atonement Torrance speaks of a "blood sacrifice," and in the scapegoat, a "living sacrifice." In the blood sacrifice the accent is on substitution, and in the living sacrifice it is on representation. Both of these were reflected and personalized in Isaiah's account of the vicarious affliction of the Suffering Servant, and finally "blended together" in Jesus' "mission as the Servant of the Lord."[246]

Second, Torrance gathers up all the various cultic themes relating to redemption under three Hebrew terms: כפר, פדה, and גאל.[247] *Padah* (with its cognates) is taken to represent the dramatic aspect of the atonement and is "essentially an act of redemption from unlawful thraldom."[248] *Kipper* (with its cognates) focuses on the priestly-cultic dimension of the atonement. Here Torrance sees a substitutionary act of expiation which is also forensic.[249] *Goel* speaks of what Torrance calls the ontological dimension of redemption. Here the focus is on the person of the mediator rather than the act of mediation. The *goel* brings redemption out of bondage or forfeited rights "through kinship or some other bond of affinity."[250] The term *goel* is, significantly, applied to God himself in the Old Testament, and with particular frequency in the latter parts of Isaiah.[251] All three terms have a Mosaic background and converge on the Servant.

> It is particularly significant that all three concepts are used to speak of the redemption of Israel out of Egypt in the Passover and the Exodus, which constitutes the paradigm instance of divine redemption. They are also used, however, in Deutero-Isaiah in association with the promise given to Israel of a new Exodus when the Holy One of Israel will redeem God's people through his anointed servant who mediates the covenant and is afflicted with the judgments of God.[252]

---

246. T. F. Torrance, *The Mediation of Christ*, 36–37; T. F. Torrance, "The Divine Vocation and Destiny of Israel," 99–100.

247. T. F. Torrance, *Atonement*, 27–56. It is important to recognize that these terms are reinterpreted in the gospel, and that they overlap and defy any easy schematization. T. F. Torrance, *Atonement*, 52. The terms are also discussed in T. F. Torrance, *The Trinitarian Faith*, 170–75; T. F. Torrance, "The Atonement. The Singularity of Christ," 239–40.

248. T. F. Torrance, *The Trinitarian Faith*, 170.

249. Ibid.; T. F. Torrance, *Atonement*, 53.

250. T. F. Torrance, *The Trinitarian Faith*, 171.

251. T. F. Torrance, *Atonement*, 46.

252. T. F. Torrance, *The Trinitarian Faith*, 171. Also, T. F. Torrance, *Atonement*, 51.

These texts in the latter part of Isaiah, as the place where the cords of the covenant are drawn most tightly, come "within a hair's breadth" of identifying the Holy One of Israel, the divine *Goel*, and the servant of the Lord. The two figures converge, virtually "coinciding through the embodiment of reconciliation in the very existence of Israel, which pointed ahead to the Incarnation."[253]

The reference to reconciliation being embodied in the very existence of Israel indicates that the ontological dimension of redemption represented by the *goel* is, for Torrance, the one that provides the coherence and ground of the overall atoning work. The *goel* provides the priestly-cultic and dramatic aspects of redemption, representing and substituting for Israel. This points forward to the incarnation and Torrance's view that atonement takes place within "the incarnate constitution of the mediator."[254] The critical point here is that even as God assumed sinful Israel into union with himself—drew all the cords of the covenant together in the figure of the Servant who is "of" sinful Israel, and yet her substitute—so in Christ, the *goel* and Suffering Servant, incarnate atonement occurs "within the ontological roots and actual condition of the human and creaturely existence he assumed in order to save."[255] In this way the various aspects of atoning mediation adumbrated by the cult, converging on the one and many reality of the Servant, and ultimately Jesus Christ, form a coherent pattern. It is a pattern "which inevitably disappears whenever they are torn away from their biblical roots and their unifying ground in the incarnational assumption of *sinful* humanity."[256]

The Mediation of Reconciliation: Conclusion

Our conclusions here are, in many ways, simply the obverse of our conclusions on Israel's mediation of revelation, for there is a "mutual involution" of revelation and reconciliation in her history. Torrance's conception of the mediation of reconciliation is of one piece with the affirmation of his realist epistemology that all knowledge involves cognitive union with the object, and thus, the removal of estrangement. This becomes particularly intense

---

253. T. F. Torrance, *The Mediation of Christ*, 28, 76. To make the identification at this point in history "would have implied that God had become incarnate within the existence of his people." T. F. Torrance, *The Trinitarian Faith*, 171; T. F. Torrance, *Atonement*, 48.

254. T. F. Torrance, *The Mediation of Christ*, 63, 66–67; T. F. Torrance, *The Trinitarian Faith*, 154–62; T. F. Torrance, *The School of Faith: The Catechisms of the Reformed Church*, lxxxi–xcv.

255. T. F. Torrance, *The Trinitarian Faith*, 158.

256. Ibid., 168. Italics mine.

in the realm of our knowledge of, and thus reconciliation with, the Holy One of Israel. From the sign of the covenant given to Abraham, through Moses and the law, through the cult as the covenanted way of response and the prophetic critique of its abuse, and down to the figure of the Servant, the covenant seeks embodiment, and revelation seeks its actualization as reconciliation. The covenant must be "done into the flesh," yet God knows that Israel will fail to fully embody it, and thus, provides a covenanted way of response in the cult. Yet, the cult itself cannot be divorced from obedience, for atoning mediation must be accomplished in the depths of Israel's "recalcitrant humanity." Thus, it becomes clear that Israel must be both represented and displaced in "total substitution." This dynamic, and Israel's sinful inability to "complete the circle" of the Word's movement, is what drives history agonizingly forward toward the New Covenant in Christ.

In this situation the Word has a running conflict with our "carnal mind" vicariously represented in Israel. We looked at the contours of this conflict and the "appalling suffering" it produced for Israel. It is this process, in conjunction with the mediation of revelation, which produces the various "empirical coordinates" of the Word, such as the Old Testament Scriptures and the institutions of Israel's national life. Here we saw that Israel's vicarious election entails her vicarious rejection as the mediator of reconciliation.

As the "cords of the covenant" are tightened, the dynamic of the one for the many produces a paradoxical particularization and universalization. It is in this situation that the enigmatic and, for Torrance's theology, momentous figure of the Servant of the Lord appears. Here the covenant is enacted into Israel's flesh in One who both participates in her alienation and substitutes for her. The Servant is Israel in her vicarious suffering and rejection, but ultimately, in the complete enactment of the covenant, points beyond her to the Messiah.

The depth of this enactment is so deep, and Israel's alienation so profound, that the very form of the covenant must change. It must be transcended, transformed and universalized in the "acute particularization" of Jesus Christ. Indeed, in Christ, redemption "penetrated back into the foundations of creation; it was a new creation."[257]

---

257. T. F. Torrance, *Incarnation*, 51–52; T. F. Torrance, *Conflict and Agreement in the Church: Order and Disorder*, 293–94. "But once the covenant came to be enacted so deeply into the existence of Israel that it was written into the 'inner man,' its whole form would change. It would be a new covenant. Such a total 'circumcision' was fulfilled at last in the flesh of Jesus Christ, for through his crucifixion, the new covenant was inaugurated, and the new and living way was opened up in the humanity of the Son of Man." T. F. Torrance, *Incarnation*, 48.

Historically, we looked at the contours of the conflict of the Word of God with Israel's carnal mind down to the post-exilic period of legalized liturgy and liturgized law. It is in this situation that Jesus Christ comes. He steps into the "tradition of the cult-prophets" as the Word of God in "the midst of our religious estrangement from God which rests upon a perversion both of Scripture and priesthood, and calls scribe and priest alike to account."[258] Here the prophetic role is restored to its primacy and the covenanted way of response is fully enacted in his obedient vicarious humanity.[259] The integrity of the duality of the covenant in word and mediation is now realized.

As this movement presses toward the cross we find that Israel's "strange rejection of its own Messiah" has "implicated it in the depths of Christ's own vicarious passion and atoning reconciliation."[260] For there "the vicarious passion of Israel, the servant of the Lord, was gathered up fulfilled and transcended in the atoning passion of God incarnate offered on behalf of Israel and all peoples."[261] Thus, Israel's passion and rejection is not mere prelude to a work done on Israel or "over her head."

> The rejection of Israel is only to be understood in the light of the substitutionary nature of the cross, for Israel's rejection is bound up with the atoning rejection of the man on the cross, or rather his acceptance of the sentence of our rejection. Paul did not hesitate to speak of the rejection of Israel as the reconciling of the world in language almost identical with his assertion that by the death of his Son we are reconciled to God. See Rom 5:10 with Rom 11:15.[262]

---

258. T. F. Torrance, *Royal Priesthood: A Theology of Ordained Ministry*, 8.

259. T. F. Torrance, *Conflict and Agreement in the Church: Order and Disorder*, 15–16.

260. T. F. Torrance, "The Divine Vocation and Destiny of Israel," 93–94.

261. Ibid., 89–90.

262. T. F. Torrance, *Incarnation*, 54–55. So strong and organic is the connection of the passion of Israel and Jesus Christ, that even Israel's rejection carries within it the seed of their resurrection (restoration). The two Pauline texts which Torrance alludes to here, startlingly, place reconciliation through the death of Christ and reconciliation through the passion and rejection of Israel in the closest relation: "The inner connection between Israel and Christ is so close and strong that St. Paul insists that it carries with it the restoration and resurrection of Israel. Thus on the one hand he can say: 'If when we were enemies we were reconciled by the death of his Son, how much more shall we be saved by his Life!' (Rom. 5:10). But on the other hand he can also say: 'For if their casting away [i.e., of Jews] meant the reconciling of the world, what will their inclusion mean but life from the dead?' (Rom. 11:15)." T. F. Torrance, "The Divine Vocation and Destiny of Israel," 91.

Indeed, it was only the "organic union of Israel with Christ that ... preserved it from extinction throughout all its ordeal of suffering."[263] Her agony, the contour of her harrowing history, is the womb, or pre-history, not of the Incarnation considered abstractly, but of incarnate atonement enacted in the depths of our fallen humanity.

> To be the bearer of divine revelation is to suffer, and not only to suffer but to be killed and made alive again, and not only to be made alive but to be continually renewed and refashioned under its creative impact. That is the pre-history of the crucifixion and resurrection of Jesus in Israel.[264]

ANALYSIS AND CRITIQUE

T. F. Torrance's reading of Israel's history is a penetrating piece of Christological exegesis with great integrative force. The whole panorama of Israel's election and ordeal as the mediator of divine revelation and reconciliation is both shaped by, and informs, a deep and coherent Christological center. Here we come to see that Jesus, the controlling center of the whole movement, is "embedded in history, embedded therefore in the hard stubborn history of Israel."[265] The result is a powerful example of theological "depth exegesis" where Torrance discerns, in and through the "trees" of the text, the "forest" of the commanding movement of the Word of the living God.[266]

---

263. T. F. Torrance, *Theology in Reconstruction*, 197.

264. T. F. Torrance, *The Mediation of Christ*, 11. "[T]he passion of Jesus is not presented in the pages of the New Testament as symbolic of a spiritual notion of sacrifice, but as the direct outcome of all that went before it in Israel, as the obedient fulfillment of God's saving intervention in all the long story of this stubborn people gathered by God into covenant with himself." T. F. Torrance, *Incarnation*, 17.

265. T. F. Torrance, *Incarnation*, 16.

266. Sarisky, "Biblical Interpretation," 333. "Depth exegesis is a reading strategy that takes its cue from the Bible's status as a signum, a text which certainly has literary and historical features, but which ultimately serves to reveal a transcendent res. One of the hallmarks of depth exegesis is Torrance's attempt to avoid dualism, according to which the literary and historical framework within which God is apprehended is broken off from the divine reality to which the framework refers. Torrance's reading program presupposes a theological construal of the Bible and results in interpretative judgments which are particularly sensitive to the overall scope of the scriptural witness." The exposition we have surveyed is a result of what Torrance calls "indwelling" the Scriptures. Here we "acquire the habit of looking *through* the various books and passages of the Scriptures and allowing their message to be interiorised in the depths of our mind. In this way a structural kinship becomes built up between our knowing and what we seek to know, which enables us intuitively to grasp the conjoint meaning latent in the

The Word-response, revelation-reconciliation dynamic which drives Israel's history, and produces the Old Testament and its institutions, is carefully construed as a second-order, or "sacramental" manifestation and anticipation of the union of the Word of God and the obedient response of man in Jesus Christ. Revelation and reconciliation are inseparable in the unity of his person as the God-Man. Israel is in a Christologically structured and organic relation with the Word, who is on the road to becoming flesh in her existence. It is this fundamental frame which enables Torrance to make the connections he makes.

Torrance's reading strategy has a number of advantages. First, it gives depth to the doctrine of revelation. Revelation is not tangential or episodic. It is rooted in the corporate election and vicarious vocation of Israel. The Word penetrates Israel's existence, and within the community of reciprocity, assumes her humanity into its movement. That movement engages, not simply human instruments of revelation conceived as atomistic individuals, but members of a community whose language, culture, and space-time structures are all intersected by the Word and gathered up in the spiraling dynamic. Surely, discussions about applying Christological analogies to the relationship of the divine and human aspects of Scripture can be enriched by Torrance's account of the production of the Old Testament Scriptures. In particular, the humanity of the Bible is here earthed in a robust way that gives full place to the fallen, and communal or embedded, nature of the inspired writers from which the text springs forth. While Torrance thinks this entails the inadequacy and imperfection of the text through which the Word nonetheless speaks, we have seen that this is not a necessary implication. Traditional accounts of Scripture as the Word of God can strengthen and deepen their conception of its humanity from Torrance's account.

Second, in giving a deeply "creational" and social dimension to the Word's movement in Israel, we can anticipate a reason why Torrance thinks it unavoidable that Christ assume our fallen nature. While he never gives us a definition, it is apparent that, for Torrance, human nature is not simply the instantiation of a set of abstract properties in a concrete particular. Human nature has dynamic, temporal, cultural-relational, and linguistic dimensions. It cannot abstract itself from the fallen sarkic order. Whether one

---

biblical texts which we could not derive simply from the particularities and explicit features of the documents themselves. As our minds dwell in the Scriptures we find diverse passages coming together in our meditation and resonating with one another so that a spontaneous organization of natural coherences running through them arises and a crystallisation of the truths to which they conjointly direct us takes place in our understanding of them." T. F. Torrance, *The Christian Doctrine of God*, 37. For more on this indwelling see T. F. Torrance, *Belief in Science and in Christian Life*, 1–48.

adopts Torrance's conception of Christ's humanity or not, his presentation is a helpful reminder that human nature cannot be isolated from the space-time matrix in which it exists.

Third, Torrance's account of reconciliation as vicariously enacted in the depths of Israel's darkness gives the ordeal of Israel's passion and suffering more depth than if it were simply viewed as a failed prelude to redemption. They are "implicated in the passion of Christ." Israel's rejection means the world's reconciliation. This gives the whole law-cult, prophet-priest conflict, as it presses for the embodiment of the covenant, its telos. Here there emerges the need for an ontologically grounded covenant way of response which is representative and, at the same time, an act of substitution. This act must be rendered from within the corporate reciprocity that fallen Israel has with the living God. This comes forth proleptically in the one and many reality of the Servant, and ultimately, in Christ.[267] Torrance's claim, which we shall examine later, is that this ontological grounding of the atonement, first "sacramentally" in Israel, and finally in the incarnate constitution of the mediator, maintains and integrates the other aspects of redemption, including the forensic. Another advantage of this organic and incarnational conception of the relation between Israel and Christ is that it highlights the organic ontological roots of the *church* in Israel (Eph 2; Rom 11).

While we grant the power of Torrance's overall presentation, there are a number of questions that can be put to it. First, what of the immense suffering of Israel in Egypt? This suffering which, arguably, may be as traumatic as anything later in her history, and undeniably is much more prolonged, happens at the earliest portion of her history when the "cords of the covenant" are drawn most loosely. Virtually all of Torrance's exposition, after Abraham and the establishment of the covenant sign, starts with Sinai.[268] One could also ask how the exile of 722 B.C. fits into the spiral. If the Word keeps pressing Israel harder as the covenant history unfolds, increasing the divine self-giving, how do we explain the long silence in the post-exilic period? We

---

267. Even if one wants to see the Servant as Christ, *rather than* corporate Israel, surely he is Christ as the fulfillment of Israel's ordeal. Torrance's reading, while it may lose some force, would still be valid.

268. In one sense, since the ordeal in Egypt ends with the Passover lamb it could be proleptic of Israel's whole history. This is likely Torrance's conception. "In the Old Testament such a redeemer was known as the *go'el*, who claims the cause of another as his own, and stands in for him when he cannot redeem himself. That was applied in the prophecies of the book of Isaiah to God's advocacy of Israel, not only in its deliverance from Egypt as his first-born son, but to the messianic redemption of Israel in the future into unbroken communion with himself." T. F. Torrance, "The Atonement. The Singularity of Christ," 241. Regardless, this early and intense suffering is not easily integrated with his narration of the subsequent history.

must remember that the spiral is a metaphor for Torrance, but it clearly has some anomalies. This dynamic of increasing resistance, increasing suffering, and increasing divine self-giving, is something we shall examine closely as it works itself out in Christ's humanity.

Second, there is some ambiguity as to what the embodiment of the cult means. This arises from the fact that, while the covenant, especially the law, must be written into the heart, it is difficult to apply this to the whole range of sacrifices and offerings in the priesthood. How is the *cult* kneaded into Israel's flesh? The textual support here is not as great as for the embodiment of the law and seems to require only that the cult not be divorced from obedience. It is relatively easy to see that Israel periodically embodies that law and periodically denies it. What is harder to grasp is how they, even sporadically, embody the cult. All knowledge of, and obedience to God involves the removal of estrangement and, thus, reconciliation. But it is unclear as to how this reconciliation, in any given instance, which is facilitated by the cult, is an *embodiment* of the cult. As this embodiment works itself out historically, especially in the Servant, who is the focus of Torrance's thought in this regard, it becomes Israel's total vicarious rejection. This rejection is, to be sure, "implicated in the passion of Christ," and thus, an embodiment of the cult. But this happens by the grace and holiness of God using Israel's blindness—*its refusal to embody the cult*—as the instrument of its cultic embodiment in judgment. This still leaves somewhat obscure the standing demand, as part of the covenant, that the cult be done into the flesh.

Another way to state the ambiguity is to ask why Israel is successful in mediating the oracles of God, but only negatively, through rejection, in embodying the cult. If, taking into account the caveats about their interlocked nature, we associate the Scriptures with the mediation of revelation, and the cult with the mediation of reconciliation, does this not imply that revelation and reconciliation are interlocked more loosely, even asymmetrically, in Israel's history? The net effect of this, we feel, is to cast a shadow over the *ontological* unity of revelation and reconciliation in Israel's history. This will play itself out when we look at how Christ both embodies the cult from within the depths of our condemned humanity, and is, at the same time, the obedient Amen to God from within that humanity.

What is important for our thesis is that this reading of Israel's covenant relationship with God is unthinkable without Torrance's Christology, and in particular, the assumption of Israel's, and thus our, fallen humanity. This we believe has been indisputably established. All the basic structures of Torrance's Christology emerge here: revelation and reconciliation, incarnate atonement, the conjunction of holiness and judgment working with increasing intensity on Israel's recalcitrant flesh, the conflict with the carnal mind, Israel and the Servant as the one and the many, and the covenant way of response which is not a third term in the relation between God and Israel. At every point the presentation depends on the Word's assuming *fallen* Israel into union with himself. Thus, the assumption of fallen humanity is not simply a feature of Torrance's reading; it *pervades* and, indeed, gives birth to the shape of the overall presentation. Simply put, the bottom falls out of this account of Israel as "the pre-history of the incarnation," if it is not driven by a Christology in which Christ assumes our fallen humanity from the womb of the Virgin Mary, in the womb of Israel, the womb of the incarnation. The purpose of our next chapter is to begin to examine how this comes to pass in the incarnation of the Son of God, the Servant of the Lord.

3

ONCE AND FOR ALL UNION
The Word Made Flesh

IN THIS CHAPTER WE shall begin to examine T. F. Torrance's doctrine of the fallen humanity of Christ as it takes shape in the biblical narrative of his earthly life. In his Edinburgh Christology lectures, Torrance divides this material into what he calls "the once and for all union of God and man," and "the continuous union in the life of Jesus."[1] The first concerns the event of the incarnation narrowly construed and is Torrance's remarkably full exposition of the virgin birth. The second covers the historical life of Christ as it unfolds in the Gospels. This chapter shall expound the "once and for all union." The subsequent chapter will take up the fallen humanity in more explicitly theological perspective in preparation for examining the "continuous union" in chapter 5.

THE WORD MADE FLESH

In Jesus Christ, the demand that the Word behind the law and the cult be cut into Israel's sinful existence comes to fruition. In the fullness of time, as "flesh of our flesh in Israel, the holy Son of God incorporated Himself into the continuity of sinful human existence."[2] It is against this deep background in Israel that Torrance expounds the Johannine phrase "the Word

---

1. T. F. Torrance, *Incarnation*. Chapters 3 and 4, respectively.
2. T. F. Torrance, *Atonement*, 346.

became flesh." This terminology means "John is saying that Jesus Christ is himself the tabernacle of God among men and women, himself the Word of God enshrined in the flesh."[3]

The crucial question is what does John mean by the word "flesh" (σαρχ)? Does this term describe "some neutral human nature," or does it describe "our actual human nature and existence in bondage and estrangement," and thus under the judgment of God? Torrance answers emphatically:

> It was certainly into a state of enmity that the Word penetrated in becoming flesh, into darkness and blindness, that is, into the situation where light and darkness are in conflict and where his own receive him not. There can be no doubt that the New Testament speaks of the flesh of Jesus as the concrete form of our human nature marked by Adam's fall, the human nature which seen from the cross is at enmity with God and needs to be reconciled to God. In becoming flesh the Word penetrated into hostile territory, into our human alienation and estrangement from God. When the Word became flesh, he became all that we are in our opposition to God.[4]

In the same context Torrance cites Romans 8:3, which affirms that Christ was made "in the likeness of sinful flesh." He consistently takes this to mean our actual twisted and disordered human nature.

Much of what Torrance says regarding the humanity assumed by Christ can be accounted for in traditional categories, such as assuming a mortal, corruptible body, facing temptation, bearing our curse, stepping into our situation under the wrath of God, etc. Yet, as the citation above indicates, it is clear that, in his mature thought, he has more than this in view. Early in his career, as shown in the 1938–39 Auburn Seminary lectures, there is some hesitancy about ascribing corruption, and thereby concupiscence, to the humanity of Christ.[5] Nevertheless, the flesh which Jesus assumes is still called "the actual form of our humanity under the fall," and "is not to be thought of in some neutral sense, but as really *our* flesh."[6] In a 1941 essay, Torrance relates the immanence of God to the fact that "Christ was made sin for us." In him God comes "near to sinful man, inasmuch as he was 'made in the likeness of sinful flesh.'" Liberal theology "refuses to take the

---

3. T. F. Torrance, *Incarnation*, 60.

4. Ibid., 61. The phrase, "the concrete form of our human nature marked by Adam's fall," comes from Barth. Barth, *CD*, I.2 151.

5. See the respective discussions on the question of concupiscence in the early Torrance in Rankin, "Carnal Union," 101–10; Guthridge, "Christology," 158.

6. T. F. Torrance, *The Doctrine of Jesus Christ*, 121.

thought of this identification of God in Christ with human sin seriously," and thus must be charged with a false transcendence.[7]

The question at this early date is how and when the flesh Christ assumed is sanctified. In contrast to Edward Irving, who taught that, having assumed our fallen humanity, Christ remained sinless in it through the indwelling Holy Spirit, Torrance ascribes Christ's purity to his divine person.[8] This purity is whole and intact from the onset of the union in the womb of the virgin Mary. "In this union the flesh of Christ becomes holy. . . . Thus we are to think of Christ's flesh as perfectly and completely sinless in his own nature, and not simply in virtue of the Spirit as Irving puts it."[9] The result is that, after the virgin birth, the early Torrance speaks of Christ entering "the sphere of our corrupted humanity," or "our sphere of sin and temptation."[10]

Nevertheless, as early as 1954 Torrance affirms that Christ enters "our estrangement in the contradiction of sin," "penetrates into our sinful humanity," and works out reconciliation "in the midst of our humanity and alienation."[11] By 1956 he declares, "though conceived by the Holy Spirit and born of the Virgin Mary, Jesus was yet born in the womb of a sinner, within the compass of our sinful flesh."[12] We read of Christ being "born into our alienation, our God-forsakenness and darkness," and growing up "within our bondage and ignorance."[13] In this context he begins to speak of Christ "bending back" the wayward will of man into submission to the will of God.[14] Expressions of this sort occur with great frequency throughout Torrance's work and continue to the end of his career.

Thus, despite the early ambiguity, it is clear that when the Word became σαρχ, he took "our human nature as we have it in the fallen world."[15] This entry into our estate is total. It includes, importantly, the assumption of our fallen and "diseased mind," for Christ enters "the root of our estranged

---

7. T. F. Torrance, "Predestination in Christ," 133.

8. T. F. Torrance, *The Doctrine of Jesus Christ*, 122–24. "We cannot think of Jesus as having original sin, for his Person was Divine."

9. Ibid., 122.

10. Ibid., 122–23.

11. T. F. Torrance, "Atonement and Oneness," 247.

12. T. F. Torrance, "The Place of Christology," 18.

13. Ibid. In 1958, we have the unambiguous statement that Christ "was made in the likeness of the flesh of sin in order that he might condemn sin in our flesh, submit our fallen humanity to the divine judgment on the Cross, and so make expiation for our sin." T. F. Torrance, "What is the Church?," 13.

14. T. F. Torrance, "The Place of Christology," 18.

15. T. F. Torrance, *Incarnation*, 62.

mental existence,"[16] and there works out "reconciliation deep within the rational center of human being."[17]

The importance of this doctrine for Torrance cannot be overstated:

> One thing should be abundantly clear, that if Jesus Christ did not assume our fallen flesh, our fallen humanity, then our fallen humanity is untouched by his work—for "the unassumed is the unredeemed,"[18] as Gregory Nazianzen put it.[19]

This fundamental truth, which the church must relearn, having suppressed it,[20] was the "great soteriological principle of the early church,"[21] without which the Fathers "reckoned the church would be soteriologically and evangelically deficient."[22] To deny it "is to deny the very foundation of our redemption in Christ."[23] Rejection of the non-assumptus leads to "the Latin heresy," which consists of construing salvation in wholly forensic and external categories, and results in an instrumental conception of the humanity of Christ.[24] Torrance states the implication of the denial starkly: "How could it be said that Christ really took our place, took our cause upon himself in order to redeem us? What could we then have to do with him?"[25]

16. T. F. Torrance, "The Reconciliation of Mind," 5.

17. T. F. Torrance, *The Mediation of Christ*, 39.

18. This phrase is also known by its Latin shorthand as the "non-assumptus." From this point on, I shall use "the non-assumptus" as equivalent to "Christ's assumption of our fallen humanity."

19. T. F. Torrance, *Incarnation*, 62. See T. F. Torrance, "The Atonement. The Singularity of Christ," 237–38; T. F. Torrance, *Incarnation*, 201; T. F. Torrance, *Conflict and Agreement in the Church: Order and Disorder*, 175–78; T. F. Torrance, *Karl Barth: Biblical and Evangelical Theologian*, 104.

20. T. F. Torrance, *The Mediation of Christ*, 39.

21. T. F. Torrance, "The Legacy of Karl Barth (1886–1968)," 306; T. F. Torrance, *Karl Barth: Biblical and Evangelical Theologian*, 179.

22. T. F. Torrance, "The Reconciliation of Mind," 5. Here Torrance notes that this "is a truth which I first learned from my beloved Edinburgh teacher, H. R. Mackintosh, who had himself been profoundly influenced by the Christology of these Greek fathers. But it was only when I studied Karl Barth's account of this doctrine that its truth broke in upon my mind in a quite unforgettable way." For more on the patristic background of the non-assumptus see T. F. Torrance, *The Trinitarian Faith*, 149–67; T. F. Torrance, *The Christian Frame of Mind*, 6–11.

23. T. F. Torrance, *Conflict and Agreement in the Church: Order and Disorder*, 175.

24. This is one of Torrance's favorite ways of describing Western legal conceptions of the atonement. T. F. Torrance, "Karl Barth and the Latin Heresy," 476–79; T. F. Torrance, "The Atonement. The Singularity of Christ," 238; T. F. Torrance, *The Mediation of Christ*, 40.

25. T. F. Torrance, *Incarnation*, 62. "Otherwise our actual human nature, mental and physical, would not have been brought within the sanctifying and renewing activity

It would mean that the love of God had stopped short of union with us in our actual condition.[26]

However, Torrance also asserts "that in the very act of assuming our flesh the Word sanctified and hallowed it."[27] Since Torrance conceives of the hypostatic union dynamically, this sanctifying and atoning action refers primarily to the whole of Christ's incarnate life.

> The atonement began with the virgin birth of Christ, entered upon active operation at His baptism and reached its culmination in the crucifixion—the whole of Christ's life and ministry were involved in the work of reconciliation as well as His death.[28]

It is the reality of this healing union, the subject of which is the holy Son of God, which enables Torrance to repeatedly affirm that Christ wears our sinful humanity sinlessly.[29] In the act of taking our flesh, and throughout his life in it, he does not do in the flesh what we do, namely, sin.[30] In fact, both early and later in his career, Torrance affirms the impossibility of sin based on the divine subject of the incarnation. "If God the Word became flesh, and God the Word is the subject of the incarnation, how could God sin?"[31]

Our concern at this point is not with how this is worked out in the continuous union of Christ's life of obedience, but rather with the once for all event of the virgin birth. While Torrance views these as inseparable aspects

---

of the Saviour." T. F. Torrance, *Karl Barth: Biblical and Evangelical Theologian*, 104. If salvation "does not take place in the ontological depths of human being," then "there is no profound cleansing of the roots of the human conscience through the blood of Christ, no radical transformation or rebirth of human being in him." T. F. Torrance, *The Mediation of Christ*, 62.

26. T. F. Torrance, *Theology in Reconciliation*, 201. "Although it was not often perceived, the really fatal elements derived from an Apollinarian orientation in Christology and soteriology, namely, failure to appreciate the principle that what Christ has not taken into himself from us has not been saved, together with failure to appreciate the fact that if Christ did not have a human mind or a rational soul, the Son of God did not really become incarnate in human being, and his love stopped short of union with us in our actual condition."

27. T. F. Torrance, *Incarnation*, 63.

28. T. F. Torrance, "Atonement and Oneness," 252.

29. T. F. Torrance, *Atonement*, 371.

30. T. F. Torrance, *Incarnation*, 63. "In the concrete likeness of the flesh of sin, he is unlike the sinner."

31. Ibid. For the earlier view, see the Augustinian discussion of peccability in T. F. Torrance, *The Doctrine of Jesus Christ*, 125–30.

of one complex event, there are distinct moments in the overall movement,³² and thus the virgin birth can be distinguished from the whole.

> The *egeneto*³³ refers to a *completed event*, one that has taken place once and for all in the union of God and man in Jesus Christ; but it is also a historical event, a dynamic event, a real happening in the time of this world which is coincident with the whole historical life of Jesus. While therefore the incarnation refers in one sense to that unique event when the Word entered time and joined human existence, it also refers to the whole life and work of Jesus, from his birth at Bethlehem to his resurrection from the dead.³⁴

The result is that "the incarnation is itself the *sanctification* of our human life in Jesus Christ."³⁵ He sanctifies our fallen human nature *both* "in the very act of assumption and all through his holy life lived in it from beginning to end."³⁶ Thus, the virgin birth, what Torrance calls the "incarnation in its narrower sense," is a redeeming event.³⁷ With this background, we turn to Torrance's exposition of the virgin birth in the New Testament.

---

32. T. F. Torrance, "Atonement and Oneness," 248.

33. The reference is to the word translated "made" or "became" in John 1:14.

34. T. F. Torrance, *Incarnation*, 67. We feel there is a lack of conceptual clarity here. If the *egeneto* is itself a completed event, and if it *also* refers to, and *is coincident with*, the whole historical life, it is difficult to see how any differentiation can be maintained. Yet, Torrance does make distinctions within the one movement.

35. In assuming our fallen nature he "began its redemption and healing." T. F. Torrance, *Incarnation*, 204. "[T]hat identification of himself with us in our sin is already our assumption and exaltation," but this saving union "reaches its supreme point in the cross." T. F. Torrance, *Atonement*, 150. The passion "began with his very birth . . . but it was in the Cross itself that it had its telos or consummation." T. F. Torrance, *Theology in Reconstruction*, 154. Alternatively, the resurrection is seen as the telos: "atoning reconciliation began to be actualized with the conception and birth of Jesus of the Virgin Mary," and "was brought to its triumphant fulfillment . . . in the resurrection." T. F. Torrance, *The Mediation of Christ*, 41; T. F. Torrance, *Conflict and Agreement in the Church: Order and Disorder*, 242.

36. T. F. Torrance, *Theology in Reconstruction*, 155.

37. Ibid., 156; T. F. Torrance, *The School of Faith: The Catechisms of the Reformed Church*, lxxxv. In this context of the virgin birth as a redeeming event, Torrance adds: "In his holy assumption of our unholy humanity, his purity wipes away our impurity, his holiness covers our corruption." T. F. Torrance, *Incarnation*, 82. The incarnation in the broader sense, which we shall look at later, is not just a once for all event but includes the whole incarnate life of Christ "from his birth of the virgin Mary to his resurrection." T. F. Torrance, *Christian Theology and Scientific Culture*, 96.

THE VIRGIN BIRTH[38]

John

Surprisingly, Torrance spends very little time on the virgin birth in the Synoptic Gospels.[39] The theologically substantive points he makes come from texts in John and Paul, which are not always seen as references to the virgin birth. Regarding John 1:13, "who were born, not of blood, nor of the will of the flesh, nor of the will of man, but of God," Torrance asks if "who were born" should be singular, in which case the reference would be to Jesus, or plural, where the reference would be to believers. Even granting the plural reading, he sees an "extended reference to the virgin birth," in that the word for man is ἀνδρὸς and not ἀνθρώπου, that is, a male or a husband, and not man generically.[40]

What this does is establish a correspondence between Christ's sanctifying birth "from above"[41] and our own rebirth out of sin. Thus, in light of 1 John 5:18,[42] Torrance concludes, "it is upon Christ's unique birth once and for all that our birth depends and in his birth that we are given to share."[43]

> What happened once and for all, in utter uniqueness in Jesus Christ, happens in every instance of rebirth into Christ, when Christ enters into our hearts and recreates us. Just as he was born from above of the Holy Spirit, so we are born from above of the Holy Spirit through sharing in his birth.[44]

---

38. Throughout this discussion Torrance is indebted to Barth, *CD*, I.2 172–202. See also T. F. Torrance, "Karl Barth and Patristic Theology," 233. The material in this section from the *Incarnation* volume of the Christology lectures appears, with very little change, in T. F. Torrance, "The Doctrine of the Virgin Birth," 8–25.

39. There is, however, this forceful assertion: "The genealogy of Jesus recorded in the gospel according to St. Matthew showed that Jesus was incorporated into a long line of sinners . . . he made the generations of humanity his very own, summing up in himself our sinful stock, precisely in order to forgive, heal and sanctify it in himself. . . . Thus atoning reconciliation began to be actualized with the conception and birth of Jesus of the Virgin Mary." T. F. Torrance, *The Mediation of Christ*, 41.

40. T. F. Torrance, *Incarnation*, 90. The editor notes here that the NIV has "a husband's will." In addition, Torrance adduces manuscript and, in his view more weighty, patristic evidence for the singular reading.

41. Torrance takes being "born from above" in John 3 as having "primary objective reference to Christ himself," and cites Irenaeus as a witness.

42. "We know that any one born of God does not sin, but he who was born of God keeps him."

43. T. F. Torrance, *Incarnation*, 91. T. F. Torrance, "The Mission of the Church," 133.

44. T. F. Torrance, *Incarnation*, 101.

Here we note Torrance's persistent conviction that there are not two unions (the incarnational union of Christ with us, and our spiritual union with him), but one union of Christ with us in which we are given to share.[45]

> There are not two unions, the one which Christ has with us which he established in his incarnation, and another which we have with him through the Spirit or through faith. There is only one union which Christ has created between himself and us and us and himself, and in which we participate through the Spirit which he has given us.[46]

What is often underemphasized in this connection is the fact that it is Christ's assumption of our actual twisted humanity, conceived in an ontologically realist manner, which drives this notion of a singular union. This shall become clear as our exposition proceeds. The implication, at this point, is that in baptism we are born from above because we are incorporated into Christ's birth of the Spirit from above. Thus baptism "reposes upon the virgin birth of Christ as well as upon his death and resurrection."[47]

Paul

Torrance sees a similar pattern in the way Paul contrasts Christ and Adam. "Christ as the new man comes likewise from God. His likeness to Adam was not in sin, but in coming into existence and in representative capacity." The normal New Testament word for human birth, γενναν, is "not used of Adam and Paul never uses it of Christ."[48] First Corinthians 15:47[49] means Christ, like Adam, came into being by divine initiative, and is a virtual affirmation of the virgin birth.

Galatians 4 is viewed in much the same way. Throughout the chapter Paul uses γενναν to speak of human birth,[50] but in Galatians 4:4 he uses

---

45. Rankin, "Carnal Union," 119–45; Lee, *Living in Union with Christ*, 201–2; Kang, "Vicarious Humanity," 307–8; T. F. Torrance, *The Mediation of Christ*, 66–67; T. F. Torrance, *The School of Faith: The Catechisms of the Reformed Church*, cvi–cxi.

46. T. F. Torrance, "The Mission of the Church," 133.

47. T. F. Torrance, *Incarnation*, 91. A virtually identical discussion is found in T. F. Torrance, *Conflict and Agreement in the Church: The Ministry and the Sacraments of the Gospel*, 118–19.

48. T. F. Torrance, *Incarnation*, 92.

49. "The first man was from the earth, a man of dust; the second man is from heaven."

50. Galatians 4:23, 24, 29.

γινεσθαι (γενόμενον) to speak of the earthly origins of Jesus.[51] "That is the strongest disavowal of birth by ordinary human generation in regard to the birth of Jesus."[52]

Since Christ was "made[53] of a woman, made under the law . . . that we might receive the adoption of sons,"[54] and Galatians 3 links our sonship with being baptized into Christ, Torrance concludes:

> To be incorporated by baptism into Christ is to partake of his Spirit of sonship which he is able to bestow on us men and women because of his own coming into existence of a woman, as a real man. So Paul can also say, like John, when Christ was born I was born a son of God, for in baptism I partake of Christ and his Spirit of sonship.[55]

Thus, for Paul and John the virgin birth shows its deep significance by being implicitly woven into the texture of their theology.

THE VIRGIN BIRTH IN DOCTRINAL PERSPECTIVE

The virgin birth is not a theory explaining how the Son became man, but rather "an indication of what happened within humanity when the Son of God became man."[56] Thus, it cannot be "understood apart from the whole mystery of Christ," for it is a sign pointing to the mystery of the hypostatic union. Nevertheless, it does have much to tell us about the way this mystery

---

51. See also Rom 1:3 and Phil 2:7.

52. T. F. Torrance, *Incarnation*, 93.

53. In accord with the linguistic argument, "made," following the KJV, not "born," is Torrance's preferred translation.

54. Gal 4:4.

55. T. F. Torrance, *Incarnation*, 93. "St. Paul could say, 'It pleased God to reveal His Son in me.' In a profound sense the Word becomes flesh in the Christian by his incorporation into Christ . . . and that is why real faith is always a virgin birth in the soul, for Christ, as St. Paul says, becomes formed within the believer." T. F. Torrance, *Conflict and Agreement in the Church: The Ministry and the Sacraments of the Gospel*, 70. "When were you born again? In your conversion? In your baptism? The profoundest answer you can give to that question is, when Jesus Christ was born from above by the Holy Spirit. The birth of Jesus was the birth of the new man, and it is in Him and through sharing in His birth that we are born again." T. F. Torrance, *Conflict and Agreement in the Church: The Ministry and the Sacraments of the Gospel*, 128.

56. T. F. Torrance, *Incarnation*, 94–95. Here we see again that the virgin birth into our humanity is conceived as a compressed version of the dynamic hypostatic union wrought out in Christ's historical life.

has taken "in its insertion into our fallen human existence at the very beginning of the earthly life of Jesus."[57]

Since the virgin birth points to the mystery of Christ's person, and the resurrection reveals that mystery, the two are inseparable. The virgin birth "and the resurrection of Jesus from the virgin tomb are twin signs which mark out the mystery of Christ."[58] Like the denial of the non-assumptus, "to bracket off the Virgin Birth from the death and resurrection of Christ, inevitably leads to a deficient understanding of the atonement as only an external transaction expressible in legal terms."[59] This is the case precisely because the virgin birth and the resurrection delimit the assumption and healing of our fallen flesh. The incarnation is a once for all act of assumption of our sinful flesh, *and* a continuous union "carried all the way through our estranged state under bondage into the freedom and triumph of the resurrection."[60] At the virgin birth the mystery is veiled because it "is inserted into the flesh of sin, the *sarx hamartias*, as St. Paul called it."[61] The resurrection, thus, authenticates the virgin birth. "It is the unveiling of what was veiled, the resurrection out of our mortality of what was inserted into it and recreated within it."[62] The humiliation of Jesus, as well as the new life of our humanity, begins at Bethlehem, and both are carried through into the unveiling of the resurrection. Thus, "the virgin birth is the basis of the mystery of the resurrection."[63]

Torrance summarizes his teaching on the virgin birth under a series of headings. *First*, it establishes the reality of Jesus' humanity. There is both

---

57. Ibid., 95–96.

58. Ibid., 96; T. F. Torrance, *Conflict and Agreement in the Church: The Ministry and the Sacraments of the Gospel*, 160; T. F. Torrance, "The First-Born of All Creation," 12, 14. The ontologically realist manner in which Torrance sees our rebirth as reposing on, or participating in, *both* of these "twin signs" is seen in the answer he gave to a highlander's question during his time as moderator of the General Assembly of the Church of Scotland. Asked if he were born again, Torrance replied in the affirmative. Asked when he had been born again, Torrance replied "when Jesus Christ was born of the Virgin Mary and rose from the virgin tomb." T. F. Torrance, *The Mediation of Christ*, 85–86.

59. T. F. Torrance, "The Truth of the Virgin Birth."

60. T. F. Torrance, *Incarnation*, 96. "Both these acts were sovereign creative acts of God's grace in and upon and out of our fallen humanity." Torrance finds the assumption of our fallen humanity, and thus the bracketing of the virgin birth and the resurrection, as well as our own participation in his birth from above in our baptism in Irenaeus. See T. F. Torrance, "The Kerygmatic Proclamation of the Gospel," 116–17.

61. T. F. Torrance, *Incarnation*, 97.

62. Ibid.

63. Ibid.

continuity and discontinuity here.⁶⁴ He was born in "the same flesh as our flesh," yet "he was not born as other men are of the will of the flesh."⁶⁵ This also entails the denial of any synergism. Man is involved, "but he is the predicate, not the subject, not the lord of the event."⁶⁶ *Second*, the virgin birth entails the disqualification of human capability in approaching God. *Third*, the virgin birth is not an entirely new act of creation, "not a *creatio ex nihilo*, but a *creatio ex virgine*."⁶⁷ It presupposes the first creation and its fall, and is the beginning of the new creation.⁶⁸ *Fourth*, the virgin birth represents a break in the sinful autonomy of man. Our very existence is "involved in original sin."⁶⁹ His birth into our condition, "far from acquiescing in its sin, resists it, sanctifying what sin had corrupted, and unites it again to the purity of God."⁷⁰ Thus, in contrast to the doctrine of the immaculate conception of Mary, we have an event which means "that out of Mary a sinner, by pure act of God, Jesus is born . . . and that his very birth sanctified Mary, for it is through her Son that she is redeemed and given to share in the purity and holiness of God."⁷¹ The setting aside of human autonomy is seen

---

64. "It was a real birth. . . . Jesus was not a product of a casual historical continuity, nevertheless the Incarnation was a coming of God right into the midst of human conditions. Jesus was not created *ex nihilo*, but *ex virgine*, therefore right in the midst of human choices and decisions." T. F. Torrance, "Predestination in Christ," 130. See T. F. Torrance, *Scottish Theology: From John Knox to John McLeod Campbell*, 14.

65. T. F. Torrance, *Incarnation*, 98.

66. Ibid., 99. "The word became flesh, not through any synergistic activity, but a gracious decision on the part of God. . . . Jesus was not born because of the sovereignty of man, not through the will of the flesh." T. F. Torrance, "Predestination in Christ," 130.

67. T. F. Torrance, *Incarnation*, 100.

68. Ibid., 99–100.

69. Ibid., 100. It is important to note that in calling the virgin birth a sanctifying act Torrance habitually, as here, brings it into close connection with the removal of original sin. Yet it is clear that it is only so inasmuch as it is the origin of the continuous union carried out in Christ's whole life. See T. F. Torrance, *Incarnation*, 82.

70. T. F. Torrance, *Incarnation*, 100.

71. Ibid. Torrance sees the emergence of the doctrine of the immaculate conception as the long term result of denying that in the virgin birth Christ assumes our sinful flesh. "Thus there developed especially in Latin theology from the fifth century a steadily growing rejection of the fact that it was our alienated, fallen, and sinful humanity that the Holy Son of God assumed . . . which forced Roman Catholic theology into the strange notion of the immaculate conception." T. F. Torrance, *The Mediation of Christ*, 40. Also, T. F. Torrance, "Karl Barth and the Latin Heresy," 476–77; T. F. Torrance, *Conflict and Agreement in the Church: Order and Disorder*, 149. Of course, classical Protestantism denies the assumption of sinful flesh by Christ and also rejects the immaculate conception. While Torrance acknowledges this state of affairs in the West, he sees an equally strange notion in the "fundamentalist conception of 'verbal inspiration' of the Bible." T. F. Torrance, *The Mediation of Christ*, 40. As we saw adumbrated in

in the fact that "man in the person of Joseph is set aside."[72] *Fifth*, the virgin birth is the archetype for all of God's gracious actions. Mary, seen as passive and receptive, is "the normative pattern of the believer in his or her attitude toward the Word announced in the gospel, which tells men and women of the divine act of grace and decision taken already on their behalf in Christ."[73] This point is thus a fuller statement of the fact that our rebirth reposes on Christ's birth of the virgin. All of this means that in the virgin birth "we have a powerful force keeping the church faithful to the basic doctrine of salvation and justification by the grace of God alone."[74]

ANALYSIS AND CRITIQUE

While Torrance provides a robust and illuminating theological discussion of the virgin birth, his presentation raises a number of questions from the vantage point of our thesis. Torrance is emphatic that Jesus "incorporated himself into the continuity of sinful human existence." The whole exposition of Israel's ordeal, which we looked at in the last chapter, prepares the way for this conclusion. The virgin birth, as we have repeatedly seen, despite the absence of a human father, "was truly of the flesh just like that of all other human beings."[75] Jesus, within the matrix of Israel, assumes our fallen, alienated humanity. Yet we are also told that the virgin birth represents a break in the sinful autonomy of man. It is a sovereign act where man and his sinful will, "man in the person of Joseph, is set aside." Christ "breaks through the continuity of adamic existence and opens up a new continuity in a new Adam, a new humanity." Thus, Jesus "was therefore *both* in continuity and discontinuity with our fallen humanity."[76]

The basic framework on which this analysis rests is beyond dispute. The virgin birth as an event, through the flesh of Mary in the womb of Israel,

---

the production of the Old Testament Scriptures in Israel, the assumption of our fallen humanity entails the assumption of the fallen human word of the Bible.

72. T. F. Torrance, *Incarnation*, 100.

73. Ibid., 101; T. F. Torrance, *The Mediation of Christ*, 95. In the context of a discussion of predestination, Torrance sees in the relation between the human and divine in the virgin birth the rejection of three common soteriological options. "We have here therefore a repudiation of adoptionism, that is, correspondingly, Pelagianism . . . the repudiation of docetism, that is, correspondingly, determinism . . . the repudiation of Arianism, that is synergism." T. F. Torrance, "Predestination in Christ," 131. We shall examine this further in chapter 6.

74. T. F. Torrance, *Incarnation*, 104.

75. T. F. Torrance, *The Trinitarian Faith*, 151.

76. T. F. Torrance, *Incarnation*, 94.

has horizontal continuity with our humanity. In addition, through the sovereign work of the Spirit in the descent of the Son, it vertically intersects that history, so there is also discontinuity. On the traditional view, the continuity lies in the fact that Christ is fully human, mortal, and subject to temptation. The discontinuity lies in his human nature being preserved from intrinsic corruption. This, with all due respect for the mysterious ground on which we tread, gives Jesus continuity with our humanity and discontinuity with respect to its "fallenness." Torrance, however, affirms continuity and discontinuity with our *fallen* humanity. This conception is less clear.

Of course, the reason for this break in sinful continuity is that the virgin birth is a redeeming, sanctifying event. When the holy Son of God unites himself to our corruption, the incarnation in the "narrower sense" cannot but be a healing event. Torrance can speak, as we have seen above, of this sanctification as if it were fully accomplished. The rationale for this lies in the holistic way he views the hypostatic union as a single, complex, dynamic whole. Incarnation and atonement entail one another. The person and work of Christ are inseparable. The work of Christ is not "added to" the hypostatic union but simply is the hypostatic union in action.[77] Thus, the "parts" in the historical existence of the Son interpenetrate one another and cannot be artificially separated. As a result, since the hypostatic union commences in the virgin birth, Torrance sometimes speaks of it in terms of what is accomplished by the union as a whole.

Two things are certain. Torrance grants that the union has certain "moments," and his whole treatment of the life of Christ takes seriously the linear sequence and distinguishable quality of the events in view. Thus, organic inseparability notwithstanding, we cannot simply opt out of chronological questions. Second, he is emphatic that the post virgin birth humanity of Christ is our flesh of sin, for he wrestles with it, "bends it back," throughout the whole course of his life. Large swaths of Torrance's analysis assume not only the full presence of our corruption throughout Christ's life, but the ever-increasing intensity of the conflict between our sin and the faithfulness of God within the incarnate constitution of the mediator.[78] Strikingly, he can even say "that the union of God and man in Jesus Christ is not thought of as somehow ontologically complete at Bethlehem."[79] The hypostatic union does not reach its telos until the cross and resurrection.

77. We shall examine some of these "Torrancian" commonplaces in the next chapter.

78. For one example, see T. F. Torrance, "The Atoning Obedience of Christ," 70–71. We shall discuss this further when we look at the "continuous union" in chapters four and five.

79. T. F. Torrance, *Scottish Theology: From John Knox to John McLeod Campbell*, 14: "It begins there by entry into the enmity between the justice of God and our sin, but it

This leaves us with a few critical questions. In what sense does the virgin birth sanctify the humanity Christ assumed?[80] What is the relationship between the sanctification in the virgin birth and the sanctification throughout the whole life of Christ? Is there something analogous to the definitive, progressive, and final sanctification of the believer at work here? In what state does this healing assumption leave the post virgin birth humanity of Christ? Put in Torrance's own terms, just how is Christ's humanity our actual, concrete humanity marked by the fall, *and* in discontinuity with our fallen humanity? Any discontinuity at all, it would seem, leaves Christ with something other than our fallen humanity at the very outset of his life. Of course, the *ground* of the discontinuity lies in the fact that our diseased humanity is now united to the Word of God; but if this were the *sum* of the discontinuity, as much of Torrance's post virgin birth analysis seems to assume, why is "man, in the person of Joseph," set aside?[81]

Clearly, *something* redemptive happens to our humanity in the very act of its assumption.[82] Torrance himself attributes it to the joint action of the second and third persons of the Trinity. It is the Son and Word of God who takes on our flesh, and the conception itself is a *creatio ex virgine*, a transcendent "act of the Spirit . . . which breaks into our humanity."[83] Yet, we are not told precisely what this narrow atoning event consists of, or how it relates to the whole, and that lack of clarity hangs over the subsequent discussion of Christ's life.

We can focus our concern here, and anticipate our future discussion of the continuous union, in the following manner. It is clear that in assuming our flesh, Christ assumes a will which is enslaved, alienated, and in bondage to sin. Torrance regularly uses the harshest "Reformed" language about the bondage of the will Christ assumes. What precisely happens to this will and, by implication, to the nature of which it is a part, in the virgin birth?

If it is *healed* in the act of being assumed, then Christ's human nature, post virgin birth, is not in fact fallen, and this is clearly not Torrance's doctrine.[84] If the human will is *regenerated* in the act of assumption, then

---

is completed in the death, resurrection and ascension of Christ."

80. Macleod, "T. F. Torrance and Scottish Theology," 67. After citing a couple of Torrance's assertions on the virgin birth as a sanctifying event, Macleod says "such statements desperately need clarification."

81. Would not a birth, albeit from above, in which, from the moment of conception, the Word assumed the humanity of Mary *and* Joseph be more in accord with assuming our fallen humanity?

82. Even Mary's humanity, as we saw, is said to be sanctified by the virgin birth.

83. T. F. Torrance, *Incarnation*, 95.

84. This is so, in spite of the fact that Torrance insists that the act of assumption

Christ's post virgin birth humanity would be equivalent to our redeemed, but sub-eschatological humanity, and this is clearly not Torrance's doctrine. If the human will is *enabled*[85] in the act of assumption, giving it a measure of freedom whereby it can deliberate, wrestle against itself, and choose obedience, then Christ's post virgin birth humanity would be *almost* our fallen humanity, but not identical with it, and this is clearly not Torrance's doctrine. Yet, it seems that this third option, or something like it, is what Torrance assumes, since it alone allows the humanity of Jesus to be a genuine actor in synergistically (along with the divine nature and the presence of the Spirit) "bending back" the fallen will in conformity to the divine will. This would create a two-stage process. First, in the virgin birth, the will is sanctified, thereby gaining a measure of deliberative capacity. Then, throughout the dynamic, historical union, into the telos of the resurrection, the will is fully healed. This appears to simply convert a Reformed conception of the fallen human will into a more "semi-Pelagian" one by means of the virgin birth.

We are fully aware that this "ordo salutis" characterization is not something Torrance ever attempts. He insists on the holistic nature of what happens to our humanity in Christ. The union *as a whole* is what he calls the "great *paliggenesia*" of our humanity.[86] Yet, as we indicated above, the

---

entails the healing of our flesh.

85. Here we have in mind something weaker than the previous option which left Christ with a humanity identical to that of Christians.

86. T. F. Torrance, "The Atoning Obedience of Christ," 71; T. F. Torrance, *Incarnation*, 119; T. F. Torrance, *The School of Faith: The Catechisms of the Reformed Church*, xx–viii. The reference is to the Greek word translated "regeneration." See Matthew 19:28, Titus 3:5. "It is significant that the New Testament does not use the term regeneration (*paliggenesia*), as so often modern evangelical theology does, for what goes on in the human heart. It is used only of the great regeneration that took place in and through the Incarnation and of the final transformation of the world when Jesus Christ shall come again to judge the quick and the dead and make all things new." Torrance is surely correct about the Matthew 19:28 text and its relation to the end of all things. But the Titus 3:5 text is almost surely about "what happens in the human heart," since it is a *washing* of regeneration coordinate with the renewal of the Holy Spirit who was poured out *on us*. Torrance himself, in another context, sees the text as referring to Christian baptism. However, he sees Christian baptism as reposing on the baptism of Christ and, more decisively, upon the whole descent and ascent of the Son. "The baptismal language of descent and ascent applies fundamentally to the descent of the Son of God into our mortal humanity and to His ascension to the right hand of the Father." T. F. Torrance, *Conflict and Agreement in the Church: The Ministry and the Sacraments of the Gospel*, 109. See T. F. Torrance, *Incarnation*, 76–77. It is in this sense that Torrance affirms "the Gospel speaks of regeneration as wholly bound up with Jesus Christ." T. F. Torrance, *The Mediation of Christ*, 85. We shall refer to this further when we look at the baptism of Jesus in chapter 5.

question cannot be avoided, precisely because he insists that the virgin birth is itself a sanctification of our nature. The presence of one complex, interlocked event, does not, even in his own exposition, eliminate sequence and decisive moments.[87] His silence on the nature of "initial" sanctification in the decisive moment the virgin birth results in a lack of clarity about the fallen nature of the assumed humanity. More narrowly, this raises the question of the clarity of the state of Christ's will. That is, precisely how does the fallen human will of Christ get "bent back" into conformity with the divine will by the vicarious *humanity* of Christ? We shall have occasion to return to this question later.

---

87. The baptism of Jesus, the cross, and the resurrection are all viewed, as we shall see, as decisive "moments" within the great *paliggenesia*.

4

THE CONTINUOUS UNION
Theological Foundations

IN THIS CHAPTER WE shall consider a number of tightly coupled concepts that apply to the whole historical obedience of Christ. It is our intention to deal with the basic constituents of Torrance's Christology and to illumine the crucial role played by the assumption of our fallen humanity. In the following chapter we shall examine the "continuous union of God and man" in the historical life of Christ. However, a pervasive set of theological foundations are necessary to focus properly on any given aspect of Christ's historical life. It is to that basic theological substructure of Christ's historical life that we now turn.

THE HOMOOUSION

The consubstantial relation between the Father and the Son as expressed at the Council of Nicea by the term *homoousios* is, for Torrance, "of staggering significance." It "is the ontological and epistemological linchpin of Christian theology. With it, everything hangs together; without it, everything ultimately falls apart."[1] Though they are impossible to separate, we shall consider the homoousion's ontological significance first and then look at its

---

1. T. F. Torrance, *The Ground and Grammar of Theology*, 160–61. See T. F. Torrance, *The Christian Doctrine of God*, 95. The homoousion expresses "the heart and substance of our Christian Faith." T. F. Torrance, "The Evangelical Significance," 165.

epistemological ramifications.² These two dimensions of the homoousion correspond to the person and work of Christ conceived as reconciliation and revelation, respectively.³ Finally, as a prelude to the next section, we shall examine the link between the homoousion and the hypostatic union.

The Ontological Significance of the Homoousion

The homoousion brings "to decisive expression the ontological substructure upon which the evangelical message of the New Testament about Jesus Christ" rests.⁴ It teaches us that what God is towards us in Jesus Christ, he is eternally and antecedently in himself.⁵ "The *homoousion* asserts that God *is* eternally in himself what he *is* in Jesus Christ, and, therefore, there is no dark unknown God behind the back of Jesus Christ."⁶

---

2. "In the *homoousion* the understanding of the Church is firmly set on a unitary basis which is both epistemological and ontological, for it entails a unity in being and a unity in intelligibility in God's *self*-giving and *self*-revelation in Jesus Christ, and correspondingly in our knowing of him in so far as it is allowed to fall under the compelling power of that *self*-giving and *self*-revealing in Jesus Christ." T. F. Torrance, "Theological Realism," 185–86.

3. T. F. Torrance, "The Evangelical Significance," 165–66.

4. T. F. Torrance, *The Trinitarian Faith*, 127. Thus, we shall consider what Torrance sometimes calls "the evangelical significance of the homoousion" in this section on its ontological significance. The two conceptions are virtually identical. See T. F. Torrance, "The Evangelical Significance."

5. T. F. Torrance, *The Christian Doctrine of God*, 21, 72, 80, 93–95, 98, 115, 130, 143, 158–59, 177; T. F. Torrance, *The Ground and Grammar of Theology*, 39–40, 159–61; T. F. Torrance, *The Trinitarian Faith*, 125–45; T. F. Torrance, *The Incarnation: Ecumenical Studies*, xvii–xx; T. F. Torrance, *Trinitarian Perspectives: Toward Doctrinal Agreement*, 9–10, 24, 81, 104; T. F. Torrance, "Theological Realism," 185; T. F. Torrance, *Christian Theology and Scientific Culture*, 106; T. F. Torrance, "Truth and Authority: Theses on Truth," 215; T. F. Torrance, "The Evangelical Significance."

6. T. F. Torrance, *The Trinitarian Faith*, 135. The expression "there is no God behind the back of Jesus" is common in Torrance. See T. F. Torrance, *The Mediation of Christ*, 59–60, 100; T. F. Torrance, *Karl Barth: Biblical and Evangelical Theologian*, 140; T. F. Torrance, *The Incarnation: Ecumenical Studies*, xvii; T. F. Torrance, *The Christian Doctrine of God*, 199, 243; T. F. Torrance, *The Doctrine of Jesus Christ*, 15, 101; T. F. Torrance, *Christian Theology and Scientific Culture*, 115; T. F. Torrance, *The Centrality of Christ*, 27; T. F. Torrance, "Introduction: Theology and Church," 46. "There is an absolutely faithful relation between what God is toward us in the Gospel and what he is in himself, for God is not one thing in Jesus Christ and another thing behind the back of Jesus Christ." T. F. Torrance, "The Legacy of Karl Barth (1886–1968)," 299. The decree of election, as traditionally understood, is criticized for going "behind the back of Jesus Christ," and dividing Christ from God. T. F. Torrance, "Universalism of Election?," 315; T. F. Torrance, *Scottish Theology: From John Knox to John McLeod Campbell*, 133, 172; T. F. Torrance, *Christian Theology and Scientific Culture*, 134–35; T. F. Torrance, "The

What kind of God would we have, then, if Jesus Christ were not the *self*-revelation or *self*-communication of God, if God were not inherently and eternally in his own being what the Gospel tells us he is in Jesus Christ? Would "God" then not be someone who does not care to reveal himself to us? Would it not mean that God has not condescended to impart himself to us in Jesus Christ, and that his love has stopped short of becoming one with us? It would surely mean that there is no ontological, and therefore no epistemological, connection between the love of Jesus and the love of God.[7]

Thus, there is a oneness in being and agency between Jesus and the Father[8] and, consequently, a oneness between the economic Trinity and the ontological Trinity.[9] These three conceptions—oneness in being and

---

Distinctive Character," 4–5; T. F. Torrance, "Predestination in Christ," 110–11; Habets, "The Doctrine of Election," 335–38; T. F. Torrance, *Christian Theology and Scientific Culture*, 134–35; T. F. Torrance, "The Evangelical Significance," 166. The pastoral significance of the matter seems to have been brought home to Torrance during his time in Italy during the Second World War. A dying soldier asked him if God was really like Jesus: "I assured him ... that God is indeed really like Jesus, and that there is no unknown God behind the back of Jesus for us to fear; to see the Lord Jesus is to see the very face of God." T. F. Torrance, *Preaching Christ Today*, 55. See T. F. Torrance, *The Mediation of Christ*, 59.

7. T. F. Torrance, *The Trinitarian Faith*, 134. See T. F. Torrance, *The Mediation of Christ*, 59. We saw similar language concerning God's love stopping short of becoming one with us used to defend the non-assumptus.

8. T. F. Torrance, *The Mediation of Christ*, 23; T. F. Torrance, *Trinitarian Perspectives: Toward Doctrinal Agreement*, 10; T. F. Torrance, *Preaching Christ Today*, 14.

9. This does not mean that what is revealed in the economy can be read back into the eternal being of God, but that, while distinctions may be made, no separation is possible. "If the economic or evangelical Trinity and the ontological or theological Trinity were disparate, this would bring into question whether *God himself* was the actual content of his revelation, and whether *God himself* was really in Jesus Christ reconciling the world to himself." Thus, "the economic Trinity and the ontological Trinity overlap with one another and belong to one another." T. F. Torrance, *The Christian Doctrine of God*, 7–8. For discussions of what can and cannot be read back into the ontological Trinity from the economic Trinity, see T. F. Torrance, *Trinitarian Perspectives: Toward Doctrinal Agreement*, 77–88; T. F. Torrance, *The Christian Doctrine of God*, 97, 108–9; T. F. Torrance, *Divine Meaning: Studies in Patristic Hermeneutics*, 343–44; T. F. Torrance, "Theological Realism," 190–91. Torrance affirms the *logos asarkos*, and he does not think the temporal and causal relations in our creaturely existence can be read back into the being of God. Thus, while the incarnation is "new," even for God, the crucial point of the bond between the economic and ontological trinities is that "the incarnation and the atoning mediation of the Son of God ... have an essential place in the very Life of God." T. F. Torrance, *The Christian Doctrine of God*, 97; T. F. Torrance, *The Mediation of Christ*, 54, 64, 112, 114; T. F. Torrance, *The Ground and Grammar of Theology*, 160; T. F. Torrance, "The Atonement. The Singularity of Christ," 232.

agency between Jesus and the Father, unity of the economic and the ontological Trinities, and "no God behind the back of Jesus"—entail one another. Torrance brings them together in the following full statement of the matter.

> That is the fiducial significance of the central clause in the Nicene Creed, that there is a oneness in Being and Agency between Jesus Christ the incarnate Son and God the Father. What God is in eternity, Jesus Christ is in space and time, and what Jesus Christ is in space and time, God is in his eternity. . . . There is thus no God behind the back of Jesus Christ, but only this God whose face we see in the face of the Lord Jesus. There is no *deus absconditus*, no dark inscrutable God, no arbitrary Deity of whom we can know nothing but before whom we can only tremble as our guilty conscience paints harsh streaks upon his face. No, there are no dark spots in God of which we need to be afraid; there is nothing in God for which Jesus Christ does not go bail in virtue of the perfect oneness in being and nature between God and himself.[10]

The evangelical implications of this can be summarized by saying that what Jesus is and does, God is and does, and thus all his actions possess divine validity.[11]

> Everything hinges upon the fact that he who became incarnate in Jesus Christ, he who mediates divine revelation and reconciliation . . . is God of God, Light of Light, very God of very God . . . for it is in virtue of his Deity that his saving work as man has its validity.[12] The evangelical significance of the *homoousion* is very apparent in its direct bearing upon the saving acts of Jesus Christ, in healing, forgiving, reconciling and redeeming lost humanity, for it is asserted in the strongest way that they are all done out of a relation of unbroken oneness and communion between Jesus Christ and God the Father . . . thereby identifying the saving acts of Jesus Christ in the gospel as the downright acts of God himself "for us and our salvation."[13]

---

10. T. F. Torrance, *The Christian Doctrine of God*, 243.

11. T. F. Torrance, "The Evangelical Significance," 167.

12. T. F. Torrance, *The Mediation of Christ*, 54–55.

13. T. F. Torrance, *The Trinitarian Faith*, 141. Even what we discern of the inner life of God through the homoousion is, in the words of H. R. Mackintosh, "apprehended by us for the sake of its redemptive expression, not for the internal analysis of its content." Mackintosh, *Person of Christ*, 526. See Colyer, *How To Read T. F. Torrance*, 297; T. F. Torrance, *The Christian Doctrine of God*, 91. "That is the immense significance of the *homoousion, of one substance with the Father*, for the compassion, healing and forgiving of Jesus are rooted and grounded in the eternal being of God, and as such are divinely

To detach Jesus from God would make all he said and did of only "passing and ephemeral significance."[14]

Torrance often expresses the significance of the homoousion by saying that the Fathers emphasized the being of God in his acts, while the Reformers emphasized the acts of God in his being.[15]

> The fathers of the early Church were concerned in the *homoousion* to assert the belief that when God communicates himself to us in Christ it is none other than God himself in his own divine Being that is revealed. The fathers of the Reformation were concerned to apply the *homoousion* to salvation in Christ, insisting that when God gives himself to us in him it is none other than God himself who is at work. God himself is active in his saving gifts and benefits—that is to say, they applied the *homoousion* to the doctrine of grace.[16]

While this distinction can be confusing, we take it to be equivalent to asserting a oneness in being (the patristic emphasis) and a oneness in agency (the Reformation emphasis) between Jesus and the Father. The latter gives the homoousion a more explicitly soteriological dimension. The bottom falls out of the revealing and reconciling *actions* of Jesus if he is not one with the Father.[17] The homoousion, thus, grounds not only the being (ontological significance), but the saving acts (evangelical significance) of Jesus Christ, in God.[18]

---

and eternally valid." T. F. Torrance, "The Evangelical Significance," 166.

14. T. F. Torrance, *Preaching Christ Today*, 16; T. F. Torrance, *The Mediation of Christ*, 57–58.

15. T. F. Torrance, *Incarnation*, 85. "Accepting fully the patristic doctrine of the Being of God in His Acts in Christ, the Reformation insisted on stressing the Acts of God in the Being of Christ, and in so doing carried through a great transition in theological thinking from a more static mode to a more dynamic mode." T. F. Torrance, *Theology in Reconstruction*, 265.

16. T. F. Torrance, *Theology in Reconstruction*, 265, 182–83. See T. F. Torrance, *Karl Barth: Biblical and Evangelical Theologian*, 174–76; T. F. Torrance, "The Distinctive Character," 3.

17. T. F. Torrance, *The Mediation of Christ*, 57–58, 124; T. F. Torrance, *The Incarnation: Ecumenical Studies*, xii–xvii.

18. "[W]hat he *is* and *does* as Son of the Father falls within the eternal Being of the Godhead." T. F. Torrance, *The Mediation of Christ*, 54. Italics mine. See T. F. Torrance, *The Trinitarian Faith*, 155.

No Third Party: The Act of God as Man

This ontological or evangelical aspect of the homoousion is important to keep in mind when Torrance says that, in assuming our flesh of sin, Jesus *steps into* a situation of intense, and progressively intensifying conflict. "He stepped into the conflict between the covenant faithfulness of God and the unfaithfulness of man and took the conflict into His own flesh as the Incarnate Son and bore it to the very end."[19]

> We must think of the work of the cross, therefore, as beginning immediately with his birth, increasing in his growth into manhood, and deepening in intensity as he entered his public ministry. His whole life is his passion, for his very incarnation as union of God and man is an intervention into the enmity between God and mankind.[20]

Yet, in light of the homoousion, Torrance is emphatic that, despite the language of stepping into, or intervening in, a conflict between God and man, it is "not as a third party" that Christ works out his atoning obedience. The homoousion guards against any disjunction between the humanity and deity of Christ, and thus against docetic Christologies from above, and ebionite Christologies from below, both of which damage "the undivided wholeness of his divine-human reality as the Son of God become man."[21] Rather,

> Jesus Christ steps into the situation where God judges mankind and where mankind contradicts God. He steps in not as a third party but as the God who judges man, and steps into the place of man who sins against God and is judged by God.[22]

As the incarnate God-man he shares in the conflict from both sides.

> He shared in it from both sides, from the side of God who is offended by man and from the side of man who is under the divine judgment of death. Within our flesh He was thus act

---

19. T. F. Torrance, "Atonement and Oneness," 251; T. F. Torrance, *Conflict and Agreement in the Church: Order and Disorder*, 244–45; T. F. Torrance, *Incarnation*, 110–12; T. F. Torrance, *The Mediation of Christ*, 82; T. F. Torrance, *When Christ Comes and Comes Again*, 17, 41.

20. T. F. Torrance, *Incarnation*, 110.

21. T. F. Torrance, *The Christian Doctrine of God*, 114–15. See T. F. Torrance, *The Doctrine of Jesus Christ*, 63–66; T. F. Torrance, *Karl Barth: Biblical and Evangelical Theologian*, 103; T. F. Torrance, "The Kerygmatic Proclamation of the Gospel," 115.

22. T. F. Torrance, *Incarnation*, 110–11; T. F. Torrance, *The School of Faith: The Catechisms of the Reformed Church*, lxxxix.

of God the Judge condemning sin in the flesh, and within our flesh where man has no justification before God, He the Just in the place of the unjust stood under judgment and rendered to God the answer of complete obedience, even to the death of the Cross.[23]

It is important to see that it is God himself, God the Son, who steps into our situation. Torrance uses a great deal of language about what Jesus does as God, and what he also does as man. He is the Word of God to man and the answering word of man to God. He is God the judge and man the judged. The sheer volume of this language can mislead one into thinking that there is a species of Nestorianism at work.[24] Yet, it is clear that there is only one actor in the atoning union. The atonement is his person at work, and his person is divine.[25] But, atonement is a divine act that, *within it*, is also a fully human action.

> God is the Subject of the whole atoning action: "God was in Christ reconciling the world unto Himself," and yet on the other hand Jesus Christ is Himself the *hilasmos*, for within the divine act of atonement Jesus as Man has a particular place in obedience. Reconciliation is God's supreme action, but within it, it is the concrete action of Jesus Christ that reconciles us.[26]

Here it is significant that Torrance sees the homoousion as being predicated of the *incarnate* Christ.

> The homoousion applies to the relation between the *incarnate* Son and God the Father. . . . That is to say, it grounds the reality of our Lord's *humanity*, and of all that was revealed and done

---

23. T. F. Torrance, *Conflict and Agreement in the Church: Order and Disorder*, 245.

24. These types of "as God to man, and as man to God" statements, at least when applied to the bulk of Jesus' life, are really Torrance's shorthand for "as 'God as man' to man, and as 'God as man' back to God," through he rarely puts it in that, admittedly more Alexandrian, way. However, note: "The saving reality with which we are concerned here is the twofold but indivisible activity of God, of God as God upon man and of God as man towards himself." T. F. Torrance, *Theology in Reconciliation*, 118. His concern in the standard formulation is simply to stress the full and integral humanity in the one, indivisible action of the God-man.

25. T. F. Torrance, *The Mediation of Christ*, 113.

26. T. F. Torrance, *Conflict and Agreement in the Church: Order and Disorder*, 243. Atonement is thus not done "over the head of man . . . the atonement is act of God, supremely act of God, but that act of God is incarnated in human flesh, giving the human full place within the divine action issuing forth out of man's life." Torrance often brings the anhypostasia-enhypostasia couplet to bear on this analysis, but we shall reserve our interaction with that subject for the last section (III) of this chapter.

for our sakes by Jesus, in an indivisible union with the eternal being of God.[27]

This is seen in the consideration that "the clauses of the Creed that speak of the incarnation . . . are dominated by a *soteriological* concern, 'for us men and for our salvation.'"[28] The church set its confession of the deity of Christ in this soteriological context.[29] Thus, "both ends of the homoousion, the divine and the human, had to be secured."[30]

> Only at that point where in Jesus Christ the Incarnate Word is *homoousios* with us in our human nature and *homoousios* with God in his divine Being, is there a real revelation and therefore a knowing of God which derives from the eternal Being of God as he is in himself.[31]

Therefore, the soteriological import of the homoousion includes a human and a divine pole in the incarnate person of the Son. "If Jesus Christ the incarnate Son is not true God from true God, then we are not saved, for it is only God who can save; but if Jesus Christ is not truly man, the salvation does not touch our human existence and condition."[32]

While the concept of "two ends" of the homoousion might seem peculiar, it rests not only on the soteriological context of the Creed, but also on the subsequent confrontation with Apollinarianism leading up to Constantinople, during which Gregory of Nazianzus articulated the non-assumptus.[33] Thus, the "human end" of the homoousion entails the assump-

---

27. "It is the wholeness of Christ's humanity that we have to keep in mind here—that is, the completely human, spatio-temporal being of Jesus who is our brother, flesh of our flesh and blood of our blood. It is precisely as the incarnate Son shares with the Father his eternal being and nature, that he also shares with us our contingent and mortal being and nature." T. F. Torrance, *The Trinitarian Faith*, 135–36.

28. T. F. Torrance, *The Trinitarian Faith*, 146–47; T. F. Torrance, *Space, Time and Incarnation*, 3; T. F. Torrance, *Divine Meaning: Studies in Patristic Hermeneutics*, 344.

29. T. F. Torrance, *The Christian Doctrine of God*, 94; T. F. Torrance, *The Trinitarian Faith*, 8, 146–49.

30. T. F. Torrance, *The Trinitarian Faith*, 146, 203.

31. T. F. Torrance, *Theology in Reconstruction*, 214.

32. T. F. Torrance, *The Trinitarian Faith*, 149.

33. "The *homoousion* was of course introduced in the first instance to argue for Christ's complete identity with God the Father, and only sixty years later to assert his consubstantiality with human beings. But the principle which Gregory of Nazianzus formulated epigrammatically . . . is already clearly enunciated in Irenaeus and thereafter repeatedly. . . . At Constantinople the *homoousion* is a bi-polar formula—Christ is of one substance with both God and man." Gorringe, "Not Assumed Is Not Healed," 482, 487.

tion of our fallen flesh, for it "applies to the incarnate Savior *and* his saving passion."³⁴ Following Athanasius, Torrance sees an unbreakable bond between the consubstantiality of the incarnate Son with the Father (the divine end of the homoousion) and his condescension into our estate (the human end of the homoousion).³⁵ In the midst of a critique of Arianism, the result of which is that "the relation between Jesus Christ and God can only be construed in *moral* terms,"³⁶ Torrance concludes that in Arianism

> divine salvation does not take place in the ontological depths of human being and reconciliation with God does not penetrate into the underlying structures of human existence.... But if Jesus Christ is God the Creator himself become incarnate among us, he saves and heals by opening up the dark, twisted depths of our human being and cleansing, reconciling and recreating us from within the very foundations of our existence.³⁷

Thus, the homoousion implies and includes as part of its bi-polar incarnational and soteriological context, the non-assumptus.

Nevertheless, the "two ends" of the homoousion do not imply two actions in the life and death of Jesus. There is one complex action which is both manward and Godward.³⁸ This means that incarnate atonement is to be construed not "just in terms of God's mighty act of salvation upon our humanity, but in terms of its actualisation within the depths of our human existence."³⁹ Atonement is "not simply an act of God in man, but an act of God *as* man."⁴⁰ It is "as very God," that "Jesus judges man and [through

---

34. T. F. Torrance, *The Christian Doctrine of God*, 254. Italics mine. "[I]n the Lord Jesus Christ God has wholly and unconditionally committed himself to us in the incarnation of his Son, so that all he eternally is ... is irrevocably pledged in the birth, life, death and resurrection of Jesus Christ for us and for our salvation." T. F. Torrance, *The Mediation of Christ*, 125.

35. T. F. Torrance, *Divine Meaning: Studies in Patristic Hermeneutics*, 250, 254, 262–64, 269.

36. T. F. Torrance, *The Mediation of Christ*, 61.

37. Ibid., 62.

38. T. F. Torrance, *Incarnation*, 195.

39. T. F. Torrance, *The Trinitarian Faith*, 4. In the one indivisible act of the God-man there is no divine atonement "done over the head" of man, nor is there a Pelagian act of man appeasing God. "Even as man in atoning action, Christ is act of God and ... even as God in atoning action, Christ is act of man." T. F. Torrance, *Atonement*, 76–77.

40. T. F. Torrance, *Incarnation*, 195. This is a frequent expression in Torrance. See T. F. Torrance, *The Mediation of Christ*, 56; T. F. Torrance, *The Christian Doctrine of God*, 40–41; T. F. Torrance, *The Trinitarian Faith*, 55, 136; T. F. Torrance, *Theology in Reconciliation*, 157–58, 227–28; T. F. Torrance, "The First-Born of All Creation," 14. "This has been very well put by the late Dr. F. W. Camfield in the *Scottish Journal of*

his human obedience] condemns sin in the flesh."[41] It is upon this concrete human action *within the divine action* that Torrance lays such immense stress. In terms of the homoousion, the divinity of the action highlights its ontological significance; that it is act of God as man highlights its evangelical significance. In the incarnate Son, we have a divine-human word where "we are unable to separate the human word from the divine, for the Word of God to us is precisely this one divine-human Word in the mutual involution of revelation and reconciliation."[42]

It is in this framework that the non-assumptus, as the human pole of the homoousion, is crucial in giving full place to the reality of the human action. This delivers atonement from being sheer act of God "over our heads," and gives genuine integrity to the human action.

> If Christ assumed neutral or perfect human nature, and assumed it into oneness with his own divine person who could not choose to sin any more than he could choose not to be God,[43] then the humanity of Christ is merely instrumental in the hands of God. But if so, then salvation is only an act of God done upon us and for us, and not also a real human act done in our place and issuing out of our humanity.[44]

Thus, the "third term," or the divinely provided "covenanted way of response," which the cult was in the covenant with Israel, finds its fulfillment in the One who is not a "third term" in the relation between God and

---

Theology: It was not Godhead qua Godhead that atoned; it was the God-manhood. And that means not simply God in man but God as man. The manhood was integral and essential and not merely instrumental." T. F. Torrance, *Conflict and Agreement in the Church: Order and Disorder*, 243–44. The statement alluded to is found in Camfield, "Ideal of Substitution," 292.

41. T. F. Torrance, *Incarnation*, 111.

42. T. F. Torrance, *Theology in Reconstruction*, 133. Here we see both the ontological and evangelical significance of the homoousion without the express terminology.

43. This phrase is particularly puzzling, and not simply because of Torrance's Augustinian discussion of peccability in the early Auburn lectures. As we have seen, he says the act of assuming our sinful flesh in the virgin birth was a sanctifying and atoning action. There, he adds, "How could it be otherwise when he, the Holy One took on himself our unholy flesh? . . . If God the Word became flesh, God the Word is the subject of the incarnation, and how could God sin? How could God deny God, be against himself, divest himself of his holiness and purity?" T. F. Torrance, *Incarnation*, 63. Apparently, the inability of the divine Person to sin makes neutral humanity instrumental, and yet has a sanctifying effect on fallen humanity.

44. T. F. Torrance, *Incarnation*, 212.

man, but who is God *as* man—that is, in the vicarious assumption of, and obedience within, our humanity by Jesus Christ, the Son of God.[45]

> We are not concerned simply with a divine revelation which demands from us all a human response, but with a divine revelation which already includes a true and appropriate and fully human response as part of its achievement for us and to us and in us. Thus the Incarnation shows us that the revelation of God fulfilled in Jesus Christ provides us with a truly human but divinely prepared response.[46]

"There are, then, three factors to be taken into account, God and mankind, or God and his people, the two parties of the covenant partnership, but within that polarity, the all-important middle factor, *the vicarious humanity of Jesus*."[47]

The Epistemological Significance of the Homoousion

Against the epistemological dualism[48] of the ancient world, Torrance asserts "the epistemological force of the *homoousion* . . . for the mediation of

---

45. T. F. Torrance, *Conflict and Agreement in the Church: The Ministry and the Sacraments of the Gospel*, 16, 122; T. F. Torrance, *God and Rationality*, 145, 158.

46. T. F. Torrance, *Theology in Reconstruction*, 131–32. See T. F. Torrance, *God and Rationality*, 145. T. F. Torrance, *Theology in Reconciliation*, 103, 209–10. T. F. Torrance, *Theological Science*, 50.

47. T. F. Torrance, *The Mediation of Christ*, 77. We can summarize this as follows: there are three factors (God-mankind-Jesus Christ), two ends of the homoousion (human and divine), and one actor or action (God as man).

48. T. F. Torrance, *The Ground and Grammar of Theology*, 15–43. Torrance has in mind a disjunction between the sensible and intelligible worlds, often referred to as the *cosmos aisthetos* and the *cosmos noetos*, respectively. See T. F. Torrance, *Theology in Reconciliation*, 240; T. F. Torrance, "Theological Realism," 171; T. F. Torrance, *Christian Theology and Scientific Culture*, 88; T. F. Torrance, *Karl Barth: An Introduction*, 77. "The Platonic separation between the sensible world and the intelligible world, hardened by Aristotle, governed the disjunction between action and reflection, event and idea, becoming and being, the material and the spiritual, the visible and the invisible, the temporal and the eternal, and was built by Ptolemy into a scientific cosmology that was to dominate European thought for more than a millennium. The combined effect of this all-pervading dualism was to shut God out of the world of empirical actuality in space and time." T. F. Torrance, *The Trinitarian Faith*, 47. Thus, the epistemological dimension of this dualism is coupled with, and inseparable from, the Greek cosmological dualism "between God and creation, which lay at the heart of Arian theology." T. F. Torrance, *Theology in Reconciliation*, 224; T. F. Torrance, "Truth and Authority: Theses on Truth," 219. In periods when these dualisms have been dominant "the demand for a natural theology has been urgent, in order to find a way of throwing a logical bridge between the world and God if only to give some kind of rational support for faith. But

knowledge of God in his intrinsic reality and intelligibility."[49] Since Jesus is homoousios with the Father, "his incarnate life on earth has a place of unique and controlling finality in our knowledge of God." More bluntly, "Jesus Christ is the one place in space and time where we may really know the Father."[50] As the Logos incarnate he "is the source of all our knowledge of God,"[51] for it is only in Christ "that God has communicated himself to us."[52] Since this is divine *self*-communication, the homoousion "tells us that God himself is the reality and content of his revelation . . . that God's self-revelation is God."[53] For our experience of God in Christ, this "means that our knowing of God is not somehow refracted in its ultimate reference, but actually terminates on the Reality of God."[54]

> It is in him as the *Logos* of God that all true conceptuality in our knowledge of God is to be found, that is, not as something that is detachable from God or accidentally related to him, but as ultimately and objectively grounded in him.[55]

---

as modern analysis has made clear again and again no such bridge is possible." T. F. Torrance, *Reality and Evangelical Theology*, 32. "By giving conceptual expression to the oneness between the Son of God become man in our world of space and time and God the Creator of heaven and earth and of all visible and invisible reality, the early church set aside at a stroke the epistemological dualism of Greek thought." T. F. Torrance, *Preaching Christ Today*, 16. For a brief general discussion see Marley, *Dualism*.

49. T. F. Torrance, *The Ground and Grammar of Theology*, 40.

50. Ibid. This exclusivity of the knowledge of God in the incarnate Christ is likened by Torrance to Fermat's principle that the shortest path between two points taken by light invalidates, *a posteriori*, the consideration of all other options. T. F. Torrance, *Space, Time and Incarnation*, 66–67; T. F. Torrance, *Theological Science*, 103, 341. "The Incarnation as the actual self-revelation of God means the setting aside of all other knowledge of God as invalid." T. F. Torrance, *The Doctrine of Jesus Christ*, 96.

51. T. F. Torrance, *Divine Meaning: Studies in Patristic Hermeneutics*, 230.

52. Ibid., 385 "It is not difficult to notice the point in Torrance's emphasis on the exclusive character of God's self-revelation in his incarnate Son. He is arguing that the Nicene Fathers and Athanasius in particular, with their application of the *homoousion* as an epistemological principle, ruled out all other channels of coming to a knowledge of God." Luoma, *Incarnation and Physics*, 35.

53. T. F. Torrance, "The Legacy of Karl Barth (1886–1968)," 299; T. F. Torrance, *The Trinitarian Faith*, 135; T. F. Torrance, *Reality and Evangelical Theology*, 14, 18; T. F. Torrance, *Karl Barth: An Introduction*, 113, 145–46.

54. T. F. Torrance, *The Ground and Grammar of Theology*, 161.

55. T. F. Torrance, *Divine Meaning: Studies in Patristic Hermeneutics*, 248. Both ends of the homoousion are necessary for this epistemic bridge: "Because Jesus Christ is God of God and man of man in himself, in Christ we who are creatures of this world may know God in such a way that our knowledge of him rests upon the reality of God himself." T. F. Torrance, *The Ground and Grammar of Theology*, 40. See T. F. Torrance, *The Trinitarian Faith*, 32; T. F. Torrance, *Reality and Evangelical Theology*, 21, 23; T. F.

There is an epistemological convergence here between the bi-polar homoousion and the divinely given way of covenant response. In Christ, the human and divine words are not held together "in some kind of 'Nestorian' dualism, but with the indivisible, all-significant middle term, the divinely provided response in the vicarious humanity of Jesus Christ."[56] Neither do we have the human word "displaced in some Apollinarian fashion," but rather "fully and finally established in its genuine humanity through the regenerating and humanizing work of the Word made flesh."[57] The human word of Christ is anchored in the divine Word because of the non-assumptus, or what Torrance here calls "the regenerating and humanizing work" of the incarnate Son.

Our participation in this knowledge, then, is grounded in the economic condescension of the consubstantial Word who "has adapted himself to us in our weakness and lack of ability in order to effect real communication with us."[58] In this descent, Christ's ignorance

> was not just an appearance of ignorance . . . [which] would have emptied the economic condescension of the Son to save and redeem of any reality. Unless the Son of God had assumed the whole nature of man, including his ignorance, man could not have been saved.[59]

Thus, the epistemological significance of the homoousion, and the real knowledge of God it affords, cannot be grasped apart from Christ's obedience in our fallen humanity. In this divine accommodation to our ignorance, God also "lifts us up to communion with Himself through reconciling and

---

Torrance, *Reality and Scientific Theology*, 186.

56. T. F. Torrance, *Reality and Evangelical Theology*, 88.

57. T. F. Torrance, *God and Rationality*, 142.

58. T. F. Torrance, *Theology in Reconstruction*, 38.

59. T. F. Torrance, *The Trinitarian Faith*, 187. This is also expounded in terms of the "uncreated Light of God" which, "adapts itself to the lowly understanding of our finite minds and at the same time through its creative touch elevates them to communion with God." Thus, "through the accomplishment of reconciliation . . . sin is forgiven and all its defilement is removed so that our minds may become clean like transparent windows through which there may stream the illuminating and transforming radiation of divine Light." Thus, actual knowledge of God is mediated "through the incarnation and passion" of him in whom the invisible Light of God is made visible, and in indissoluble oneness with the eternal Word and Love of God, is made accessible to mankind." T. F. Torrance, *Christian Theology and Scientific Culture*, 93–94. Here, the light of God has "penetrated into the great darkness of our rebellious self-alienation from God in which even the light that is in us has become darkness, in order to redeem us from its power and bring us to the Light of divine Life." T. F. Torrance, *Christian Theology and Scientific Culture*, 97.

adapting us in conformity to Himself."⁶⁰ This descent, then, "has its counterpart in a movement of *prokope*,"⁶¹ a term which, for Torrance, refers to Christ's obedience within our estate.

> The Son of God has descended into our human ignorance, in order that as Word of God he might penetrate into our human modes of knowing and speaking, and . . . impart to us knowledge of the true God . . . within our ignorance and darkness the Son of God has lived out a life in which through his obedience to the Father, he has appropriated for us in our human modes the Truth of God, and perfected in the humanity which he took from us man's knowing of God and speaking of him.⁶² In other words Jesus' growth in wisdom was regarded as opening up a way for man to rise to true knowledge of the Father. Jesus Christ is not only the Truth who has accommodated himself to us in order to reveal himself, not only the Word become flesh, but he is also Man hearing and obeying that Word, apprehending that Truth throughout his life on earth, so that he provides for us in his own obedient sonship within our human nature the *Way* whereby we are carried up to knowledge of God the Father.⁶³

---

60. T. F. Torrance, *Theological Science*, 86.

61. "The fathers have in mind here the Lukan account of the obedience and development of the child Jesus who 'cut his way forward' (*proekopte*) as he grew in wisdom and favor with God and with man." T. F. Torrance, *Theology in Reconstruction*, 38. We shall look at this *prokope* further in the next chapter.

62. T. F. Torrance, *Divine Meaning: Studies in Patristic Hermeneutics*, 250. See the Barthian background here in T. F. Torrance, *Karl Barth: An Introduction*, 104–5. Summarizing, and agreeing with, Athanasius, Torrance says, "in and through Jesus Christ certain forms of human thought and speech are laid hold of and adapted for knowledge of God. . . . In the sanctified and renewed humanity of Christ God has provided for us the source and principle . . . who takes us to the Father." T. F. Torrance, *Divine Meaning: Studies in Patristic Hermeneutics*, 251–52. "Hence God in Christ Jesus took it [the human mind] up into himself along with the whole man, in order to penetrate into it and deal with the sin, alienation, misunderstanding, and darkness that had become entrenched within it. Jesus Christ came among us sharing to the full the poverty of our ignorance, without ceasing to embody in himself all the riches of the wisdom of God." T. F. Torrance, *The Trinitarian Faith*, 187.

63. T. F. Torrance, *Theology in Reconstruction*, 38. See T. F. Torrance, *Theology in Reconciliation*, 240. In the context of a discussion of the hermeneutics of Athanasius, Torrance writes: "He is ὁμοούσιος with the Father. . . . But the Son has taken a human body in and through which he has appropriated human nature for himself, including human life and action and feeling, human thought and speech. In him the *Logos*, the eternal Reason and Word of God, the Son of the Father, is fully incarnate in human life and being, and as such is the source of all our knowledge of God." T. F. Torrance, *Divine Meaning: Studies in Patristic Hermeneutics*, 230.

As Jesus made his advance in the power of the Spirit, "it is through the power of the same Spirit that we participate in *prokope*, and so rise through the Son to true knowledge of, and communion with, God the Father."[64] This communion with God, through Christ in the Spirit, "arises out of the reconciling and healing assumption of our humanity in the incarnation."[65] Thus, Jesus' descent into, and healing ascent within, our carnal and alienated mind is, for Torrance, a crucial part of the epistemological significance of the homoousion.[66] How we know God (participation through the Spirit in the economic descent and corresponding ascent of *prokope*) and what we know of him (real knowledge which terminates on his being) are inseparable.[67]

> There is ... a mutual and exclusive relation between the knowledge of the Father and the knowledge of the Son,[68] but through the Spirit that relation has been inserted, as it were, into human flesh, in the Incarnation so that we through the same Spirit may participate in the relation of the Son to the Father and the Father to the Son, and know and love the triune God as he is in himself.[69]

In this manner "we have a true and faithful knowledge of God when through union with Christ by the power of the Spirit *we receive the mind that was remade and renewed in him.*"[70] Thus, all knowledge of God is unintelligible for Torrance apart from the non-assumptus.

This pattern of knowing extends to our theological statements as well.

---

64. T. F. Torrance, *Theology in Reconstruction*, 39.

65. T. F. Torrance, *The Trinitarian Faith*, 32; T. F. Torrance, *The Mediation of Christ*, 55.

66. In the language from chapter 2, where we looked at Israel as the womb of the incarnation, the removal of estrangement and alienation allows revelation to complete its movement as reconciliation.

67. Torrance calls this part of the "striking ... centrality and epistemological significance of the *homoousion*" in Athanasius' thought. T. F. Torrance, *Theology in Reconciliation*, 239. See T. F. Torrance, *Divine Meaning: Studies in Patristic Hermeneutics*, 259–72.

68. The allusion here is to Matthew 11:27 and Luke 10:22, two passages Torrance often uses in connection with the epistemological significance of the homoousion. See T. F. Torrance, *Incarnation*, 128; T. F. Torrance, *Reality and Evangelical Theology*, 111–12; T. F. Torrance, *Theology in Reconciliation*, 223, 254–55; T. F. Torrance, *The Trinitarian Faith*, 58; T. F. Torrance, *The Doctrine of Jesus Christ*, 1; T. F. Torrance, *The Mediation of Christ*, 53–54.

69. T. F. Torrance, *Theology in Reconciliation*, 240–41.

70. T. F. Torrance, *Divine Meaning: Studies in Patristic Hermeneutics*, 250. Italics mine.

> Jesus Christ supplies the center and basic frame of reference for theological statements, for . . . he is the one place where human forms of thought and speech are secured beyond the infinite hiatus between the creature and the Creator in God himself.[71]

Thus, theology itself is grounded in, and governed by, the epistemological implications of the homoousion. In particular, it is an analogous echo of, and participation in, Christ's movement of descent and ascent (or *prokope*).

> Theological activity is one in which, by the power and communion of the Spirit, we know God through conformity to the economic condescension of his Word and through following the Incarnate Word in his advance up to the Father.[72] The hinge of that movement, and therefore the actual hinge of meaning and apprehension, is the Incarnation and in the Incarnation the identity between the Being of Christ and the Being of God—that is, the *homoousion*.[73]

As it was for the knowledge of God in general, so also in theological activity the non-assumptus must not be dropped out of sight. Speaking of the "profound epistemological implications of this economic condescension which patristic theology was not slow to draw out for biblical interpretation and theological statement," Torrance writes:

> Just as we think of the incarnation as God becoming man in order to become one with man and thereby redeem man within the depths of his human nature, so we may think of the incarnation as God the Word becoming man in order to adapt himself to man in his weakness and lack of ability and to assimilate human modes of thought and speech to Himself, and thereby to

---

71. T. F. Torrance, *Divine Meaning: Studies in Patristic Hermeneutics*, 251. "[W]e can see the immense epistemological import of the *homoousion* for it asserted that theological statements in Christ are rooted in the eternal Word in the Being of God." T. F. Torrance, *Theology in Reconstruction*, 58. Here, in Jesus Christ, genuine theological knowledge arises because "the primary objectivity of God meets us in the secondary objectivities of the given." T. F. Torrance, "Introduction: Theology and Church," 46.

72. T. F. Torrance, *Theology in Reconstruction*, 39. See T. F. Torrance, "Introduction: Theology and Church," 38; T. F. Torrance, *Karl Barth: An Introduction*, 82, 132. Theology must "trace out the order" of this divine economy. T. F. Torrance, *Theological Science*, 128.

73. T. F. Torrance, *Theology in Reconstruction*, 39. See T. F. Torrance, *Theological Science*, 176–77, 276; Lee, *Living in Union with Christ*, 56–57, 64–65.

effect real communication between God and man and man and God.⁷⁴

When we understand the words of Scripture in accord with this economic movement "we receive the mind that was remade and renewed in Jesus Christ."⁷⁵

The Homoousion's Link to the Hypostatic Union

Torrance's language of the Lord's humanity being grounded "in an invisible union with the eternal being of God," and of the "two ends" of the homoousion, does not mean that Christ's human nature is one substance with the divine nature. His point, put more precisely, is that the homoousion, being predicated of the incarnate Christ, implies the necessity of the hypostatic union between our actual condition and the divine nature. That is, the hypostatic union, "the two natures of Christ himself on the horizontal level," must be interpreted in light of the vertical or cross-level reference in the homoousion."⁷⁶ Conversely, the homoousion "is to be taken along with a cognate conception about the indissoluble union of God and man in the one Person of Christ, to which the Church later gave theological formulation as the hypostatic union."⁷⁷ It is the combination which constitutes the "epistemological center in the incarnate Son," and forms the "epistemic bridge" between God and man in Christ.⁷⁸

Put differently, for Nicene theology, "the cardinal point on which everything hinged was the internal relation of Christ to the being of the Father [the homoousion] *and thus* the internal relation of the atonement to the incarnate Person of Christ [the hypostatic union]."⁷⁹ "Hence in Christ the *homoousion* is inseparably bound up with the *hypostatic union*."⁸⁰ Together they give "decisive expression to the supreme truth that God himself is the content of his revelation."⁸¹ The full force of the economy lies in "the

---

74. T. F. Torrance, *Reality and Evangelical Theology*, 108.

75. T. F. Torrance, *Divine Meaning: Studies in Patristic Hermeneutics*, 231, again, citing Athanasius with approval.

76. T. F. Torrance, *The Ground and Grammar of Theology*, 172.

77. T. F. Torrance, *The Christian Doctrine of God*, 94.

78. T. F. Torrance, *The Ground and Grammar of Theology*, 165.

79. T. F. Torrance, *The Trinitarian Faith*, 277. Italics mine.

80. T. F. Torrance, *The Christian Doctrine of God*, 101. See T. F. Torrance, *Transformation and Convergence*, 253.

81. T. F. Torrance, *Trinitarian Perspectives: Toward Doctrinal Agreement*, 104.

inseparability between the life and acts of Christ in the body and the being and person of the eternal Son who is God."[82]

THE HYPOSTATIC UNION

Incarnation and Atonement

For Torrance, following the Greek fathers, incarnation and atonement are "inseparably one."[83] The incarnation is an atoning incarnation, and the atonement is an incarnational atonement. In expounding the Nicene theology of which he is a proponent, Torrance writes:

> The incarnation was seen to be essentially redemptive and redemption was seen to be inherently incarnational and ontological. Union with God in and through Jesus Christ who is of one and the same being with God belongs to the inner heart of the atonement.[84]

Thus, there is a "mutual involution," between the "dual moments in the one movement" of redemption.[85] "The oneness wrought out in atone-

---

82. T. F. Torrance, *Divine Meaning: Studies in Patristic Hermeneutics*, 263.

83. This follows, in part, from the "non-dualist" outlook of Greek patristic theology. T. F. Torrance, *Theology in Reconciliation*, 230. This cardinal principle pervades Torrance's thinking. In the Auburn Lectures, the young Torrance writes: "We cannot therefore properly think of the Incarnation apart from the Atonement, or the Atonement apart from the Incarnation." T. F. Torrance, *The Doctrine of Jesus Christ*, 85. In 1995, at the end of his career, commenting sympathetically on Robert Leighton, he writes: "The Incarnation and the atonement are to be understood together." T. F. Torrance, *Scottish Theology: From John Knox to John McLeod Campbell*, 172. Both citations, virtually bracketing Torrance's work, go on to affirm the cognate concept, which we shall look at shortly, namely, that the person and work of Christ are one.

84. T. F. Torrance, *The Trinitarian Faith*, 159. The fathers "refused to separate incarnation from atonement, or the union of divine and human natures in Christ from his healing and reconciling work." T. F. Torrance, *Karl Barth: Biblical and Evangelical Theologian*, 104. Also, T. F. Torrance, "The Legacy of Karl Barth (1886–1968)," 306. Without this incarnational and ontological grounding, attempts to understand the work of Christ break up into atomistic "'theories of the atonement'—which unfortunately is what has regularly happened in Western Theology." T. F. Torrance, *The Trinitarian Faith*, 159–60.

85. T. F. Torrance, *Conflict and Agreement in the Church: Order and Disorder*, 258. In Irenaeus and Athanasius Torrance finds "a full and satisfying account of the atonement in which incarnation and atonement are very closely associated, and are mutually involved." T. F. Torrance, *Incarnation*, 198. "[I]ncarnation and atonement are regarded as constituting a single, continuous indivisible movement of the redeeming love of God, in which the saving life and passion of Christ as the one Mediator between God and man are understood in the mutual involution of his God-manward and his

ment and reconciliation brings to its perfection or completion the oneness involved in the incarnation."[86] This mutuality means the incarnation cannot be "regarded as merely instrumental and not internally related to atonement."[87]

While this pervasive theme of the interpenetration of incarnation and atonement in Torrance is frequently noted, what is often muted is the fact that it is the non-assumptus which drives the conception. Noting that this incarnational atonement has been derided as the "physical theory of redemption," where the mere physical union of the two natures brings about salvation, Torrance says this "is a serious misrepresentation, for it overlooks the fact that as the incarnate Logos Christ acts *personally* on our behalf . . . from within the ontological depths of our human existence which he has penetrated and gathered up in himself."[88] Commenting on Melito of Sardis's conception of atonement Torrance writes:

> Atonement is something done . . . within the ontological depths of the Incarnation, for the assumption of the flesh by God in Jesus Christ is itself a redemptive act and of the very essence of God's saving work. This takes place, not just in some impersonal physical way, but in an intensely personal and intimate way within the incarnate Lord and his coexistence with us in our fallen suffering condition as sinners. Incarnation is thus intrinsically atoning, and atonement is intrinsically incarnational.[89]

---

man-Godward activity." T. F. Torrance, *Theology in Reconciliation*, 136.

86. T. F. Torrance, *Conflict and Agreement in the Church: Order and Disorder*, 267. "The atonement itself is the at-one-ment inherent in the nature of incarnation and redemption." T. F. Torrance, *Theology in Reconstruction*, 282.

87. T. F. Torrance, *The Mediation of Christ*, 81; T. F. Torrance, "Incarnation and Atonement: Theosis and Henosis," 13. The incarnation and the incarnate life of the Son are not to be treated "only as a prelude or as a necessary means for atonement." T. F. Torrance, *God and Rationality*, 63. This is the root of the notorious "Latin Heresy" in which atonement is construed in predominantly legal, extrinsic and forensic categories. See T. F. Torrance, "Karl Barth and the Latin Heresy." On the humanity of Christ being integral, and not merely instrumental in atonement, see T. F. Torrance, *The School of Faith: The Catechisms of the Reformed Church*, lxxxiii; T. F. Torrance, *Incarnation*, 126, 212; T. F. Torrance, *The Trinitarian Faith*, 150; T. F. Torrance, *The Mediation of Christ*, 81; T. F. Torrance, *Atonement*, 182.

88. T. F. Torrance, *The Trinitarian Faith*, 156. J. N. D. Kelly also calls the label of "physical redemption" a "dangerous half-truth." J. N. D. Kelly, *Early Christian Doctrines*, 173. In Torrance's case, the decisive place he gives to the cross would also mitigate against the charge of physical redemption. For a brief genealogy of the physical theory see Turner, *Patristic Doctrine of Redemption*, 67–74. For an in-depth rejection of the charge of physical redemption, see Hart, "Irenaeus."

89. T. F. Torrance, "Dramatic Proclamation," 155.

Personal action precludes purely physical redemption; but note that this personal incarnate atonement takes place within our fallen humanity. In a revealing passage, Torrance makes the underlying link explicit:

> This means that the incarnation and the atonement are inseparably interlocked throughout the whole life of Jesus from his birth of the Virgin Mary to his resurrection from the dead. It is at this point that the divergence between the East and the West is probably deepest over the issue formulated so succinctly by Gregory the Theologian and Cyril of Alexandria: "the unassumed is the unhealed" / "what Christ has not taken up has not been saved." If the incarnate Son through his birth of the Virgin Mary actually assumed our flesh of sin, the fallen, corrupt and enslaved human nature which we have all inherited from Adam, then . . .[the] incarnating and redeeming events were one and indivisible, from the very beginning of his earthly existence to its end in his death and resurrection.[90]

The incarnational union is an atoning union because in it our lost and damned humanity is "redeemed, healed, and sanctified in Jesus Christ."[91]

There are a number of other ways Torrance expresses the conjunction of incarnation and atonement. Often, as we saw in his Christological reading of Israel's history, he speaks of the inseparability of revelation and reconciliation.[92] Alternatively, with more accent on the ontological nature of this atoning union, Torrance speaks of the oneness of Christ's person and

---

90. T. F. Torrance, "Incarnation and Atonement: Theosis and Henosis," 12. Here we can see the ecumenical significance—"the divergence between East and West"—the non-assumptus is fraught with for Torrance. Robert Walker calls the inseparability of incarnation and atonement, and the assumption and healing of our fallen flesh, "two of the cardinal principles of Torrance's theology." We would add the observation that without the second the first unravels. Walker, "Editor's Introduction to Atonement," lxxii. Speaking of this integration in Barth, Torrance writes: "Atonement is not to be understood, therefore, merely in terms of some external relation between our sins and Jesus Christ, but in terms of his incarnational penetration into the depths of our mortal existence under the judgment of God." He then proceeds to cite the non-assumptus as "the great soteriological principle of the early church." T. F. Torrance, *Karl Barth: Biblical and Evangelical Theologian*, 178–79.

91. T. F. Torrance, *The Mediation of Christ*, 68. In the context of the inseparability of incarnation and redemption, Torrance writes: "For Athanasius, it is everywhere apparent, the incarnational assumption of our fallen Adamic humanity from the Virgin Mary was essentially a sanctifying and redeeming event, for what Christ took up into himself, the whole man, he healed and renewed through his own holy life of obedient Sonship in the flesh, and his vicarious death and resurrection." T. F. Torrance, *Theology in Reconciliation*, 230.

92. We shall consider this below under "The Hypostatic Union in Revelation and Reconciliation."

work. The work of Christ cannot be separated or divorced from his person.[93] In terms of the Old Testament doctrine of redemption, this is another way of saying that the *goel* aspect of atonement, the ontological dimension, provides the overall framework for integrating the priestly and dramatic aspects.[94] While this person-work couplet is essentially synonymous with the incarnation-atonement, and revelation-reconciliation formulas,[95] it does throw into relief the depth of the integration envisioned.

> It is Christ in his person who reveals, atones and reconciles. This unity of person and word, and person and work, and therefore word and work, means that we cannot in any sense think of the work of revelation and reconciliation as a kind of transaction objective to Christ, or simply as an act done by Christ. It is the person of Christ who reveals and atones and thus neither can be separated from his person. Thus, the significance of the cross does not lie simply in the death or the blood shed, it lies in the fact that the person of Christ is the one who sheds his blood—it lies in the identity of his person and work. The atonement is his person in action, not the action by itself.[96]

Again, as with the other couplets, it is the non-assumptus which underlies the conception. "The reconciliation wrought out on the cross is already at work in the person of Jesus Christ, and all his life is the visible working and working out of what took place when the Son of God became man in the midst of our flesh of sin."[97]

This interpenetration means, crucially for Torrance, that atonement is worked out *within* the incarnate constitution of the mediator.[98] Just as the incarnation itself falls within the being and life of God, so atonement is not externally, but internally, related to Christ. It is fulfilled and grounded in his incarnate person.

---

93. T. F. Torrance, *The School of Faith: The Catechisms of the Reformed Church*, lxxxix, cx; T. F. Torrance, *Incarnation*, 37; T. F. Torrance, *Scottish Theology: From John Knox to John McLeod Campbell*, 15; T. F. Torrance, *Preaching Christ Today*, 58–59.

94. T. F. Torrance, *The School of Faith: The Catechisms of the Reformed Church*, lxxxviii.

95. Torrance often uses the couplets synonymously. See T. F. Torrance, *Incarnation*, 296; T. F. Torrance, *The School of Faith: The Catechisms of the Reformed Church*, lxxxix.

96. T. F. Torrance, *Incarnation*, 108.

97. Ibid.

98. "In him the Incarnation and Atonement are one and inseparable, for atoning reconciliation falls within the incarnate constitution of his Person as Mediator." T. F. Torrance, *The Mediation of Christ*, 56, 63, 66; T. F. Torrance, "The Divine Vocation and Destiny of Israel," 100; T. F. Torrance, *Theology in Reconciliation*, 229; T. F. Torrance, "Introduction to Robert Bruce's Sermons," 33.

> Since Jesus Christ is himself God and man in one Person, the atoning mediation and redemption which he wrought for us, fall *within* his own being and life as the one Mediator between God and Man. That is to say, the work of atoning salvation does *not* take place *outside* of Christ, as something external to him, but takes place *within* him, *within* the incarnate constitution of his Person as Mediator.[99]

In accord with this conception, Torrance regularly sees biblical statements in the form of "Christ is X," as meaning "the dynamic atoning union which takes place within the incarnate mediator constitutes X." This is what is in view, for example, in 1 John 2:2: "Christ himself is our propitiation, as St John puts it."[100] A fuller statement is given with respect to John 14:6:

> In the Synoptics, Jesus teaches the truth. In John's Gospel he says, "I am the truth." In the Synoptics, he is set forth as saving man's life. In John's Gospel, he says "I am the life." That is to say, the Act of Christ is Christ, the Work of Christ is Christ; the Word of Christ is Christ; the Truth of Christ is Christ. He is the Way the Truth the Life in Himself. His Being and Life *are* Redemption.[101]

Put differently, "he does not mediate a revelation or a reconciliation that is other than what he is, as though he were only the agent or instrument of that mediation to mankind."[102]

Here, again, the non-assumptus is a corollary. It is a very important aspect of "this interpenetration of incarnation and atonement" that God "has made himself one with us in Jesus Christ in such a way as to take our fallen nature upon himself" to heal and sanctify it.[103] Since atoning reconciliation

---

99. T. F. Torrance, *The Trinitarian Faith*, 155. See T. F. Torrance, "The Legacy of Karl Barth (1886–1968)," 305–6.

100. T. F. Torrance, *Atonement*, 22. "Jesus Christ is Himself the ἱλασμός." T. F. Torrance, *Conflict and Agreement in the Church: Order and Disorder*, 243.

101. T. F. Torrance, *Incarnation*, 109. Similar language is found in T. F. Torrance, *The Doctrine of Jesus Christ*, 150–52. "He *is* the Propitiation for our sins; he *is* our Redemption; he *is* our Justification." T. F. Torrance, "Karl Barth and the Latin Heresy," 476. See T. F. Torrance, *Conflict and Agreement in the Church: The Ministry and the Sacraments of the Gospel*, 69. Robert Walker aptly comments: "The doctrine of the hypostatic union is a theological way of putting what Jesus is saying in his 'I am' statements in the gospel of John, 'I am the resurrection and the life,' 'I am the bread of life,' etc., and what Paul means when he speaks about 'our [your] life in Christ Jesus, whom God made our wisdom, our righteousness and sanctification and redemption.'" Walker, "Editor's Introduction to Incarnation," xxxvi.

102. T. F. Torrance, *The Mediation of Christ*, 56.

103. T. F. Torrance, "The Legacy of Karl Barth (1886–1968)," 306.

is understood to fall within the "personal being of Jesus Christ as the one Mediator between God and Man," it falls "within the ontological roots and actual condition of creaturely existence which he assumed in order to save."[104] This prevents the sacrifice of Christ from being construed as "some kind of superficial socio-moral or judicial transaction between God and mankind which does not penetrate into the ontological depths of human being or bear savingly upon the distorted and corrupt condition of man's actual human existence."[105]

All three couplets, then, require that the hypostatic union, which is the reality within which the integration of the incarnation and atonement, revelation and reconciliation, and person and work occurs, be conceived dynamically from within our fallen flesh. "Hypostatic union and atoning union are held together as the obverse of one another."[106] But, before we look at Torrance's exposition of this we must briefly survey its alleged historical necessity.

Historical Excursus: The Need for Reconstruction

Over against the polarizing tendencies of what are traditionally called the Antiochian and Alexandrian schools of Christology,[107] Torrance sees a "middle stream of development, running from Irenaeus to Athanasius and Cyril, which stressed equally the full humanity and the full deity of Christ," out of which emerged the orthodox doctrine of Christ.[108] This "third school" of Christological development "stressed the vicarious humanity of Jesus along with . . . the Deity and Lordship of Christ."[109] Here "there was a considerable stress upon the obedience of the Incarnate Son and consequently upon the saving significance of the humanity of Christ, both in regard to

---

104. T. F. Torrance, *The Trinitarian Faith*, 158.

105. Ibid.

106. T. F. Torrance, *Scottish Theology: From John Knox to John McLeod Campbell*, 15; T. F. Torrance, *Preaching Christ Today*, 59.

107. Speaking of their general tendencies, Torrance says "the Antiochian school stressed the historical humanity of Jesus, and . . . the Alexandrian school . . . stressed the eternal nature of Christ as divine Logos." T. F. Torrance, "The Place of the Humanity of Christ," 4. For a somewhat fuller summary, along with the caution that this traditional characterization "may be a little too neat," see Crisp, *Divinity and Humanity*, 36–40.

108. T. F. Torrance, *Incarnation*, 198.

109. T. F. Torrance, "The Place of the Humanity of Christ," 4. See Redding, *Prayer and the Priesthood*, 34–40.

Revelation and in regard to Reconciliation," which led to an integrated view of incarnation and atonement.[110]

However, the church councils after Nicea "tended to lose sight of [Christ's] atoning work" in their creedal formulations.[111] Thus, while the church rightly rejected Apollinarianism, the practical impact on her life and liturgy, especially in light of the ongoing battle with Arianism, was to shift the emphasis to Christ's deity and away from his human priesthood and full incorporation into our humanity.[112]

> When Chalcedonian Christology came to be formulated, largely under the guidance of the Epistle of Leo, that is from the church in the West, the doctrine of the person of Christ was carefully and clearly formulated, but in such a way that the atoning work of Christ was not given its proper place.[113]

While "the early church rendered theology magnificent service," it did not adequately relate the hypostatic union to the "historical obedience of Jesus Christ . . . and to his atoning work, and so did not give sufficient attention to the *saving significance of the humanity of Christ.*"[114]

The underlying problem here is explicitly tied to a rejection of the non-assumptus. "In the fourth century there began a revolt against the idea that Christ took our fallen humanity, including our depraved mind, upon himself in order to redeem it from within."[115]

> Thus there developed especially in Latin theology from the fifth century a steadily growing rejection of the fact that it was our alienated, fallen, and sinful humanity that the Holy Son of God assumed, and there was taught instead the idea that it was humanity in its perfect original state that Jesus took over from the Virgin Mary.[116] . . . But in the post-Nicene period, where

---

110. T. F. Torrance, *Incarnation*, 198.

111. Ibid.

112. T. F. Torrance, *Theology in Reconciliation*, 185–204. There was "a tendency to allow the full humanity of Christ to be impaired through absorption into his divine nature. . . . That would appear to be a direct result of the failure to give the atoning work of Christ the mediator its full place in Chalcedonian and subsequent Christology. Whenever the mediatorship of Christ is thrust into the background, as became increasingly apparent in the growth and development of the liturgy in East and West, it is very difficult to stem the tide of monophysite tendencies in Christology." T. F. Torrance, *Incarnation*, 199.

113. T. F. Torrance, *Incarnation*, 198.

114. Ibid., 183.

115. T. F. Torrance, *The Mediation of Christ*, 40.

116. Ibid. "From the fifth century onwards, however, there developed in Latin

that [Anti-Arian] emphasis was carried through, there grew up a shyness of speaking about the assumption by the Son of our flesh of sin, in case that would detract from the perfection of the incarnate Son. And again, when after Chalcedon attacks were launched against the fullness of Christ's human nature, there was no encouragement to take in all its seriousness the fact that he who knew no sin was made sin for us, lest the assumption of the "flesh of sin" should detract from the perfect humanity of Christ.[117]

The result is "it would be very difficult to find in the West, especially after Leo the Great (with whom a distinctly monophysite trend of thought set in), anything comparable to the vigorous stress of Cyril of Alexandria on the saving obedience of Christ."[118]

When it comes to Chalcedon itself, after citing the creedal statement, Torrance appends this sharp criticism:

It does not say that this human nature of Christ was human nature "under the servitude of sin" as Athanasius insisted; it does not say that it was corrupt human nature taken from our fallen creation, where human nature is determined and perverted by sin, and where it is under the accusation and judgment of holy God.[119]

This is no minor defect. It leaves out something essential, "for 'the unassumed is the unhealed,' . . . and it is with and within the humanity he assumed from us that the incarnate Son is one with the Father."[120] We see here, once more, the crucial importance of the non-assumptus for Torrance's

---

theology, an increasing rejection of this teaching in favour of another, according to which it was not our fallen humanity that Jesus took from the virgin Mary, but humanity in its perfect original state. . . . This particular form of the Latin heresy may be traced back to the famous *Tome* of Leo the Great sent to the Council of Chalcedon early in the fifth century, in which a dualist approach to the understanding of the Person and Work of Christ, as God and Man, was set out, which provided the West with its paradigm for a formulation of the doctrine of salvation in terms of external relations." T. F. Torrance, "Karl Barth and the Latin Heresy," 476–77. See also Guthridge, "Christology," 307.

117. T. F. Torrance, *Incarnation*, 199.

118. T. F. Torrance, *Theology in Reconciliation*, 197. However, Torrance's son, Iain, holds that Severus of Antioch, in the sixth century, sought to develop Cyrillian Christology, and taught a more dynamic concept of the union of the natures in Christ. Iain R. Torrance, "Creation and Incarnation," 359; Iain R. Torrance, *Christology After Chalcedon*, 81–105.

119. T. F. Torrance, *Incarnation*, 201.

120. Ibid.

Christology. Not only is Chalcedon censured for ignoring it, even a proper corrective restatement requires it:

> The hypostatic union cannot be separated from the act of saving assumption of our fallen human nature, from the living sanctification of our humanity, through the condemnation of sin in the flesh, and through rendering from within it perfect obedience to the Father. In short, if we think of Christ as assuming neutral and perfect humanity, then the doctrine of the hypostatic union may well be stated *statically*. But if it is our fallen humanity that he sinlessly assumed, in order to heal and sanctify it, not only through the act of assumption, but through a life of perfect obedience and a death in sacrifice, then we cannot state the doctrine of the hypostatic union statically but must state it *dynamically*, in terms of the whole course of Christ's life and obedience, from his birth to his resurrection.[121]

Probing further, Torrance sees Chalcedon's problem as

> speaking of some neutral human nature which we know in some way from our general knowledge of humanity, even though we nowhere have any actual experience of such neutral human nature. Here then, there appears to be a two-fold difficulty. It appears to define the human nature of Jesus in terms of some general conception of human nature, and then to think of Christ's human nature as perfect, or at least neutral, and to that extent unlike our actual human nature.[122]

---

121. T. F. Torrance, *Incarnation*, 201. "When we think of Jesus Christ in Himself, in the mystery of His own Person, the Chalcedonian formula is quite adequate, for it expresses all that we can say, warding off on each side harmful error and reminding us that here we are face to face with a mystery that is more to be adored than expressed. But when, on the other hand, we think of His mission in relation to sinful man, of His Incarnation as the incorporation of Himself into our body of the flesh of sin and the carrying of it to its crucifixion, when we think of His entry into our estrangement in the contradiction of sin, and of His working out, in the midst of our humanity and alienation, reconciliation with God, then the Chalcedonian formula does not say enough, for reconciliation is not something added to hypostatic union so much as the hypostatic union itself at work in expiation and atonement." T. F. Torrance, *Conflict and Agreement in the Church: Order and Disorder*, 240.

122. T. F. Torrance, *Incarnation*, 201. For further polemic against the idea of "some neutral human nature," see T. F. Torrance, "The Goodness and Dignity of Man," 317; T. F. Torrance, *Karl Barth: Biblical and Evangelical Theologian*, 103–4; T. F. Torrance, "The Legacy of Karl Barth (1886–1968)," 306; T. F. Torrance, *Incarnation*, 61; T. F. Torrance, *Conflict and Agreement in the Church: Order and Disorder*, 149.

The Continuous Union 129

We cannot define the human nature of Christ in terms of some preconceived notion of human nature, for he alone is the standard of true human nature.[123] But if we are to judge our human nature in the light of Christ's, and not vice-versa, then we must affirm both the non-assumptus *and* the dynamic conception of the hypostatic union:

> We must also say clearly that he was made in the likeness of our flesh of sin; he assumed sinful flesh, that is, our Adamic fallen human nature, and in sinlessly assuming it began its redemption and healing. He carried that redemption and healing throughout the whole of his life which he lived in perfect obedience, truth and holiness. Throughout, within the poor clay of our corrupt humanity, he showed forth perfect humanity, remaking ours and converting it in himself.[124]

Thus, the hypostatic union, and the redemption it secures in our flesh, is an *achievement* of the whole historical obedient life of the incarnate Christ.

> By living the life which Jesus Christ lived in our midst, the life of complete obedience to the Father and of perfect communion with him, the life of absolute holiness in the midst of our sin and corruption, and by living it through the whole course of our human existence from birth to death, he *achieved within our creaturely being the very union between God and man that constitutes the heart of atonement*.[125]

With the Reformation, Torrance sees a decided shift "in the whole doctrine of God, in a move away from the Latin Stoic conception of God as *deus sive natura* to the living God of the biblical revelation." This change "from a static to a dynamic conception of God" has a "direct bearing on the doctrine of Christ."[126] Thus, more stress is laid on the soteriological significance of the obedience of Christ. "They sought to understand the hypostatic union not simply in terms of a state of union, but in terms of a divine movement of

---

123. T. F. Torrance, *Incarnation*, 201–2. The humanity which Christ has taken from us, healed and sanctified in himself, has "archetypal significance for human beings." T. F. Torrance, "The Soul and Person," 115.

124. T. F. Torrance, *Incarnation*, 204. "Chalcedonian Christology needs to be filled out in accordance with its own fundamental position, in a more dynamic way, in terms of the incorporating and atoning work of the Saviour, for the only account the New Testament gives us of the Incarnation is conditioned by the perspective of the crucifixion and resurrection." T. F. Torrance, *Conflict and Agreement in the Church: Order and Disorder*, 240.

125. T. F. Torrance, *Space, Time and Resurrection*, 47. Italics mine.

126. T. F. Torrance, *Incarnation*, 213. See T. F. Torrance, *The Centrality of Christ*, 27; T. F. Torrance, *Theology in Reconstruction*, 265–66.

grace, which was translated into the *history* of the man Jesus Christ."[127] This entailed looking at "the human nature of Christ . . . from the perspective of his healing and sanctifying assumption of our humanity."[128] Here Torrance attributes his own view of the non-assumptus to the Reformers.[129]

Yet, as we saw in chapter 1, he clearly feels that this affirmation is ambiguous even in Calvin, and it is certainly not carried through in post-Reformation dogmatics.[130] For all its advances, Reformed theology "still tended to be formulated within the parameters of the Latin conception of the incarnation . . . [which] had the effect of undermining and fragmenting the doctrine of atoning reconciliation."[131] It is into this historical situation, following Barth's lead, that Torrance sets forth his dynamic conception of the hypostatic union.

The Hypostatic Union: The Dynamic Conception

The Mystery and Its Projection into Our Existence

If atoning reconciliation takes place within the incarnate Christ, and the whole of his historical life *is* the hypostatic union where person and work are indissolubly one, then we must advance beyond the Chalcedonian formulation.

> We must think of that hypostatic union, however, not in the static categories of patristic thought, but in terms of biblical eschatology, that is, in dynamic categories. As the Captain of our salvation was made perfect through suffering, we must think of that holy union inserted into our flesh and blood at the virgin birth of Jesus as carried through the relativities of history, through the passion and agony of the crucifixion to its transcendent perfection in the resurrection of Jesus from the dead.[132]

---

127. T. F. Torrance, *Incarnation*, 215. See T. F. Torrance, *The School of Faith: The Catechisms of the Reformed Church*, lxxx.

128. T. F. Torrance, *Incarnation*, 215.

129. Ibid., 216.

130. T. F. Torrance, "Karl Barth and the Latin Heresy," 470.

131. Ibid., 478. This Latin conception would seem to be a key reason why the medieval period, with its "Augustinian" dualisms, is skipped in Torrance's exposition of the doctrine of Christ in his Edinburgh Christology lectures.

132. T. F. Torrance, *Conflict and Agreement in the Church: The Ministry and the Sacraments of the Gospel*, 171; T. F. Torrance, *Theological Science*, 216; T. F. Torrance, *The Mediation of Christ*, 64–65.

Torrance expounds the "insertion" of that holy union into our flesh as the product of the eternal counsel of God.[133] He unfolds this in the light of three important New Testament words, μυστήριον, πρόθεσις, and κοινωνία. The mystery, μυστήριον,

> refers to the union of God and man eternally purposed in God now revealed and set forth in Jesus Christ as true God and Man in one Person, a union which creates room for itself in the midst of our estranged humanity and through fellowship or communion gathers men into one Body with Jesus Christ.[134]

This definition actually contains the meanings of the other two cognate terms, the eternal purpose and setting forth (πρόθεσις)[135] of the mystery in Jesus Christ's assumption of our flesh, and the participation or fellowship (κοινωνία)[136] we have in the mystery through the Spirit.

This union is dynamically "inserted" into our knowledge and into our being.[137] With respect to our knowledge, Torrance says:

> But in spite of all the contradiction of sin, the oneness of God and man is inserted into the knowledge of sinners as an essential part of Christ's reconciliation. The teaching of Christ was an essential part of the atonement, and the atonement could not have taken place apart from it.[138]

---

133. "In this respect the doctrine of election, as St. Paul made so clear, is the counterpart to the doctrine of the Incarnation as the projection of God's eternal purpose of Love into our creaturely existence and its embodiment in a unique and exclusive way in Jesus Christ through whom true relations between God and man and man and God are established." T. F. Torrance, *Christian Theology and Scientific Culture*, 133.

134. T. F. Torrance, *Conflict and Agreement in the Church: The Ministry and the Sacraments of the Gospel*, 82. We should conclude from this that the assumption of our estranged humanity is ultimately rooted in the eternal counsel of God.

135. "Through the eternal πρόθεσις actualized in the Incarnation of Christ the mystery of the Kingdom is inserted, so to speak, into our fallen humanity, inserted into the midst of our flesh, into the midst of our choices and decisions, into the midst of our knowledge." T. F. Torrance, *Conflict and Agreement in the Church: The Ministry and the Sacraments of the Gospel*, 89. See T. F. Torrance, *Incarnation*, 171–72; T. F. Torrance, *Theological Science*, 86.

136. T. F. Torrance, *Incarnation*, 171–72; T. F. Torrance, *Conflict and Agreement in the Church: The Ministry and the Sacraments of the Gospel*, 88–90.

137. See the parallel discussion of Christ "clothed with his gospel," where that "clothing" is understood as both ontic and noetic, in T. F. Torrance, *The School of Faith: The Catechisms of the Reformed Church*, lxxxi–lxxxiii.

138. T. F. Torrance, *Incarnation*, 173; T. F. Torrance, *Conflict and Agreement in the Church: The Ministry and the Sacraments of the Gospel*, 90. See T. F. Torrance, *The School of Faith: The Catechisms of the Reformed Church*, lxxxi–lxxxiii. We shall discuss the teaching ministry of Jesus in the next chapter.

This is the noetic dimension of the hypostatic union which entails, in its outworking, Christ's healing of our carnal mind. With respect to our being, Torrance says:

> The oneness of God and Man in Christ is inserted into the midst of our being, into the midst of our sinful existence and history, into the midst of our guilt and death on the Cross. The inserting of the Oneness of God and Man into the deepest depths of man's existence in his awful estrangement from God, and the enactment of it in the midst of his sin and in spite of all that sin can do against it, is atonement. In a profound sense atonement is the insertion of the hypostatic union into the very being of our estranged and fallen humanity.[139]

Torrance has in mind here the more basic and explicitly ontological dimension of the atoning union. Taken together, the insertion of the union into our being and knowledge correspond to the ontological and epistemological significance of the homoousion. Here, as with the homoousion, the non-assumptus plays a decisive role in the formulations. Without it there would be no insertion into *our* being and knowledge.

The Humanity and Deity of Christ in the Hypostatic Union

It is now clear that the hypostatic union cannot be expounded apart from the life of Christ in the midst of our darkness. The fallen humanity which Jesus assumed from us is necessary for both revelation and reconciliation. "The humanity of Christ in its stark actuality is essential to God's *self-revelation*."[140] It guarantees "that God's revelation is revelation to creaturely humanity in the language and life of man, man who is involved within the limitations of time and space, . . . within time and history."[141] Similarly, the humanity of Christ is "essential to God's act of *reconciliation*, for the actuality of the atonement is grounded on the fact that in actual human nature it is God himself acting on our behalf."[142]

---

139. T. F. Torrance, *Conflict and Agreement in the Church: The Ministry and the Sacraments of the Gospel*, 90; T. F. Torrance, *Incarnation*, 173–74. See T. F. Torrance, *The Mediation of Christ*, 65.

140. T. F. Torrance, *Incarnation*, 185.

141. Ibid., 186. See T. F. Torrance, *The Doctrine of Jesus Christ*, 133–34.

142. T. F. Torrance, *Incarnation*, 186. "If he were not man, he would not be our Saviour for only as one with us would God be savingly at work within our human existence." T. F. Torrance, *The Trinitarian Faith*, 114. See T. F. Torrance, *The Doctrine of Jesus Christ*, 135–37.

The deity of Christ is also necessary for both revelation and reconciliation. As we saw when considering the homoousion, Christ's unbroken oneness with the Father guarantees that salvation is the sheer act of God. Concerning the significance of Christ's deity for revelation, Torrance says:

> Certainly revelation would not actually be revelation to us unless it were in our human language and thought . . . but its reality as revelation of God is grounded on the reality of God's presence in it . . . grounded on the identity between revelation and God the revealer. The humanity of Christ guarantees the actuality of revelation, but the deity of Christ guarantees its nature as revelation of *God*.[143]

In the same manner, the deity of Christ, as we saw also with the homoousion, grounds reconciliation in Christ in the very being of God.

Torrance summarizes, again highlighting the non-assumptus: "If the Son was to redeem the whole nature of man, he had to assume the whole nature of man; if in the Son man is to be gathered into the fellowship and life of God, it must be by one who is truly and completely God."[144]

If the hypostatic union is "worked out between estranged man and God, between man's will and God's will in the one person of Christ," this raises the question of the relation between the divine and human natures in the course of the union. Torrance gives a fairly standard summary, from Reformed scholasticism, of the communication of properties, graces, acts, and operations between the natures.[145] Yet, he conceives the dynamic interaction between the natures in the life of Christ in a unique fashion.

Using the four Chalcedonian adverbs, Torrance draws out the implications of the actions of the natures in the union. The extremes in Alexandrian Christology are guarded by "the first two Chalcedonian adverbs, *inconfuse et immutabiliter*, 'without confusion' and 'without change.'"[146]

---

143. T. F. Torrance, *Incarnation*, 188. "If Jesus Christ were not God, he would not reveal God to us for only through God may we know God." T. F. Torrance, *The Trinitarian Faith*, 114.

144. T. F. Torrance, *Incarnation*, 190. See T. F. Torrance, *Theology in Reconstruction*, 129–34. "The saving union between man and God depends on the reality of the oneness between God and man in Christ himself. If the Lord Jesus Christ is not both God and Man, then the gospel of God's revealing and saving acts in Jesus Christ proclaimed by the Apostles is empty of substance." T. F. Torrance, "The Kerygmatic Proclamation of the Gospel," 115.

145. T. F. Torrance, *Incarnation*, 221–27. Though we should note that, even on the Reformed notion of the *communicatio idiomatum* as verbal attribution based on the unity of the natures in the one person, Torrance's Christology, it would seem, would need to "attribute" fallenness to the *person* of the Son.

146. Ibid., 208.

> There can be no intermingling or commingling of the divine and human natures, and no changing of one into the other. But that has to be restated dynamically, and so we must say something like this: in his act of humiliation, in freely uniting himself to our fallen human nature, and in savingly taking its sin and corruption upon himself in order to work out our salvation, the divine nature of Christ suffered no change, but remained truly and fully divine.[147]

In this manner "the divine nature was able to save and redeem that which it assumed into oneness with itself."[148] At just this point, where we might ask how the divine nature communicates with the *fallen* human nature, Torrance does not blink. In his view, both the Fathers and the Reformers stumbled on a Greek conception of the immutability and impassibility of God.[149]

> But if we really take the biblical view of God, then we must think of God the Father as sending the Son into our lost existence, into unutterable humiliation in order to be really one with us. We must think of God as determining himself freely to be our God, directing himself freely to share in the profoundest way in our frail life, in all its limitations and weaknesses, and even in its lostness, all in order to be our God, and to gather us into fellowship with himself.[150]

Here we can see that it is precisely the non-assumptus which, far from causing Torrance to affirm the traditional view of impassibility, provokes

---

147. Ibid., 208.

148. Ibid. This is, not surprisingly in light of the enormous emphasis on the humanity of Christ, one of the few times Torrance ascribes the salvation of our fallen human nature to the divine nature without qualification. This is, of course, implied by the fact that God himself, and not a "third party," steps into the conflict between our sin and his holiness. Yet, in that context Torrance lays great stress on the human action within the divine action.

149. Ibid., 227; T. F. Torrance, *The Ground and Grammar of Theology*, 66. In this they were akin to the docetist Christology from above, which sought to explain "*how* God became man in Jesus Christ in such a way as to give full weight to his divine reality, and yet in such a way as not to compromise his eternal immutability and impassibility through union with the flesh." T. F. Torrance, *The Trinitarian Faith*, 113. For a brief criticism of the idea that the classical formulations of immutability and impassability imply some form of dualism see Muller, "The Barth Legacy," 696.

150. T. F. Torrance, *Incarnation*, 227. "If God is merely impassible He has not made room for Himself in our agonied existence, and if He is merely immutable He has neither place nor time for frail evanescent creatures in His unchanging existence. . . . God is invariant in love but not impassible, constant in faithfulness but not immutable." T. F. Torrance, *Space, Time and Incarnation*, 75.

a reconstruction of the doctrine. It is in the very context of "the atoning exchange," a patristic phrase that, for Torrance, is synonymous with the dynamic hypostatic union where atonement takes place inside the incarnate mediator,[151] that he both reaffirms the non-assumptus and raises the question of impassibility.

> The second implication of the atoning exchange that we must consider is the redemption of suffering. . . . We must also bear in mind . . . that when the holy Son of God took our sinful humanity upon himself, he did it in such a way that instead of sinning himself he brought his holiness to bear upon it so that it might be sanctified in him. He was made sin for us that we might be made the righteousness of God in him. It is along this line, I believe, that we must approach the question of *impassibility*.[152]

If atonement takes place within the incarnate constitution of the mediator, "we cannot think of the sufferings of Christ as external to the Person of the Logos."[153] "God crucified! That is the startling truth of the gospel."[154] Torrance summarizes his dynamic reconstruction:

---

151. "The atoning exchange, then, embraces the whole relationship between Christ and ourselves: between his obedience and our disobedience, his holiness and our sin, his life and our death, his strength and our weakness, his grace and our poverty, his light and our darkness, his wisdom and our ignorance. . . . But all this is worked out within the saving economy of the incarnation, and in the ontological depths of the humanity which he made his own." T. F. Torrance, *The Trinitarian Faith*, 181. In this context, Torrance often cites 2 Cor 8:9: "You know the grace of our Lord Jesus Christ, that though he was rich, yet for your sakes he became poor that you through his poverty might become rich." See T. F. Torrance, *The Christian Doctrine of God*, 250–51 where the atoning exchange is virtually identified with the non-assumptus and, thus, the need to rethink impassibility: "This was the great soteriological principle of sacrificial atoning exchange . . . *the unassumed is the unhealed*, expounded by the Greek fathers . . . since this soteriological exchange takes place within the incarnate constitution of the Mediator . . . we cannot but think of the saving passion of Christ as internal to the Person of God the Son become man."

152. T. F. Torrance, *The Trinitarian Faith*, 184.

153. This is another way of saying that the homoousion guarantees that the incarnate life of Christ falls within the very being of God.

154. T. F. Torrance, *The Christian Doctrine of God*, 247. All that the homoousion was intended to declare "applies even more acutely to the passion of Christ. . . . What would become of our understanding of the Cross if at that supreme point Christ remained ultimately separate from God in being and nature: Christ a mere man on the Cross and God wholly other and alone in his Deity? . . . To leave God in his heaven and put Jesus a man only on the Cross leaves us in utter darkness and despair. But put God on the cross, let Jesus Christ be God himself incarnate, who refused to be alone or without us, but insisted on penetrating into the heart of our sin and violence and unappeasable agony in order to take it all upon himself and to save us, and the whole picture

> The point is this. In Jesus Christ God himself has penetrated into our passion, our hurt, our violence, our condition under divine judgment, even into our utter dereliction, "My God, my God, why hast thou forsaken me?," but in such a profoundly vicarious way that in the very heart of it all, he brought his eternal *serenity* or ἀπάθεια to bear redemptively upon our passion.[155]

Thus, our passion is "exhausted" in his divine impassibility.

> He masters and transmutes it within the embrace of his own immutable peace and serenity. It is an essential aspect of the atoning exchange in Jesus Christ that through his sharing in our passion (πάθος) he makes us share in his own imperturbability (ἀπάθεια).[156]

Thus, Torrance reconceives the action of the divine nature in light of the non-assumptus.[157] The human nature, of course, remains human throughout this process, though the transformation from fallen to healed humanity, as Torrance would grant, is not envisioned by Chalcedon.

On the other hand, the extremes of Antiochene theology are guarded against by "the second two Chalcedonian adverbs, *indivise et inseparabiliter*, 'without division' and 'without separation.'"[158] Torrance's dynamic restatement again is driven by the assumption of our flesh of sin.

> But that must be stated more dynamically. The act of the Son in humbling himself to take upon himself our humanity in the likeness of the flesh of sin and in the form of a servant, without of course sinning himself, and the act of the perfect obedience of the Son to the Father in the whole course of his life in human nature, his whole participation in the life of God, are not two independent acts or events separated from one another. In all their distinctiveness, they are fully and finally and irrevocably

---

is transformed." T. F. Torrance, *The Incarnation: Ecumenical Studies*, xiv–xv.

155. T. F. Torrance, *The Trinitarian Faith*, 185.

156. Ibid., 185–86. Torrance states that this is essentially the same argument, which we discussed above, applied to the exchange between our ignorance and his wisdom.

157. Of course, this is conceived in a Trinitarian framework. See Scandrett, "Suffering Servant." "[F]or it was not the Father or the Spirit who were crucified but the incarnate Son of God, crucified certainly in his differentiation with the Father and the Spirit, but nevertheless in his unbroken oneness with the Father and the Spirit in being and activity." T. F. Torrance, *The Christian Doctrine of God*, 247. See T. F. Torrance, *The Doctrine of Jesus Christ*, 146–47; T. F. Torrance, *The Mediation of Christ*, 113–15.

158. T. F. Torrance, *Incarnation*, 208.

united in being the acts of the one person of the incarnate Son of God.[159]

The Hypostatic Union in Revelation and Reconciliation

As we saw in chapter 2, revelation and reconciliation, which never fully cohere in Israel, are perfectly interlocked in Christ. This occurs in the dynamically conceived hypostatic union.[160]

> If Israel is the sacred story of the penetration of the word of God into the midst of a stubborn and rebellious people, into its very mind and flesh, gathering it into covenanted relation with God, it is here above all that we see the Word made flesh in the unity of person and word, truth and life, word and deed in Jesus Christ.[161]

This unity "means that we cannot in any sense think of the work of revelation and reconciliation as a kind of transaction objective to Christ, or simply as an act done by Christ."[162] Indeed, the essence of the Christian faith "is grounded in the unity of reconciliation and revelation in Jesus Christ, in his unity of word and act, person and work, in the union of true God and true man."[163] In this conception, the incarnate Christ "is both the author and the content of revelation and reconciliation."[164] If it is Jesus Christ himself, the mediator, who is the atonement, then "revelation and atonement are inseparable, Christ revealing and Christ reconciling, for the speaking of

---

159. Ibid., 208.
160. Ibid., 107–8.
161. Ibid., 107.
162. Ibid., 108.
163. Ibid., 296. "This identity of person and word, person and work in Christ is one of the main interests of the fourth gospel . . . the New Testament sums up the whole gospel of revelation and reconciliation in the name *Immanuel, God with us.*" Ibid., 108–9.
164. T. F. Torrance, *Theology in Reconstruction*, 136. Commenting on Irenaeus' theology, Torrance says "this means that Jesus Christ is not only the Agent of our salvation, but its very matter and substance, for God's saving activity has been translated into this-worldly reality in terms of the whole vicarious and sanctifying life of Jesus from his birth of the Virgin Mary to his resurrection from the dead." T. F. Torrance, *Theology in Reconciliation*, 94. Jesus is the one "in whom and through whom and *in the form of whom* divine reconciliation is finally accomplished." T. F. Torrance, *The Mediation of Christ*, 29. Italics mine.

the word and the working out of the atoning deed are done within the one person of Christ."[165]

Revelation does not achieve its end apart from reconciliation, and it does this in the obedience of Christ "within the compass of our sinful flesh."[166]

> Revelation is unthinkable, therefore, apart from the whole movement of divine humiliation from the cradle to the Cross, apart from the grace of the Lord Jesus Christ which means that the Word which was rich with the Wisdom of God for our sake became poor, making our poverty his own, that we through his poverty might be made rich with the wisdom of God. It is only through that atoning exchange that God's revelation achieves its end as revelation to and within a sinful world.[167]

This means Christ's human obedience "was not simply an instrumental but an integral and essential part of . . . divine revelation and reconciliation."[168] In the incarnate mediator alone the revelatory Word of God, and the reconciling action of God, are answered and appropriated by man in the obedient life of Christ within the ontological depths of our darkness.[169]

Again, it is the non-assumptus which makes the dynamic coupling of revelation and reconciliation intelligible:

> Thus God comes himself, freely condescending to enter into our lost and estranged humanity, taking our lost condition upon himself in order to effect, through mercy and judgment, *reconciliation* with himself. . . . In this act of condescension God comes as God the Son and God the Word. He comes as God the Son to enter our rebellious estate in order to effect *reconciliation* by living out his life of filial obedience where we are disobedient, and he comes as God the Word to enter into our darkness and blindness in order to effect *revelation* by manifesting the love of God and by achieving from within humanity faithful appropriation of divine revelation. This is one act; Son and Word, revelation and reconciliation interpenetrating one another.[170]

---

165. T. F. Torrance, *Incarnation*, 37; T. F. Torrance, *Atonement*, 94.
166. T. F. Torrance, *Theology in Reconstruction*, 132.
167. Ibid., 133.
168. T. F. Torrance, *Incarnation*, 126.
169. Ibid.
170. Ibid., 56–57. Italics mine. The concept of the Word made flesh, which accents the revelatory nature of the incarnation, must be supplemented by the concept of the Son made servant, which highlights the reconciling obedience to the Father (and toward men as well). Ibid., 67–76. All of this takes place within the broader framework of the descent and ascent of the Son and Word into our flesh: "It is in that whole movement

This means, correlative to the epistemological significance of the homoousion and the noetic insertion of the mystery, that the hypostatic union is the very substance of *revelation*. In Jesus Christ there is a "hypostatic union between his creaturely language and God's own godly language. It is only in that union in which God's language condescends to take on creaturely form, and human language is joined to God's language, that there is real revelation."[171]

The seriousness with which Torrance takes this issue, and the pervasive nature of the non-assumptus for his thought, is seen in his response to Bultmann's call for a "demythologised reinterpretation of the *kērygma* . . . in which the human language is purified, made perfect through being purged of all improprieties."[172] Torrance replies:

> When the Word was made flesh, was that flesh some immortal perfect flesh, or was it flesh of our flesh? Did the Son of God become incarnate in our fallen humanity . . . or did he assume some kind of pure humanity which we know nothing about? . . . our answer . . . will determine our answer to Bultmann's demand that in the *kērygma* we must find a reinterpretation . . . in some scientifically purified and rarified speech of flesh.[173]

This revelation, wrought within the flesh he assumed from us, is objectively (the Word of God to man, the action of God himself) and subjectively (the answering word of man to God, the human action within the one divine action) fulfilled in Jesus Christ. In this manner our carnal mind is healed and true knowledge of God in human language is secured.

---

of descent and ascent, *katabasis* and *anabasis*, that we are to understand the movement of the Word and Son of God into our human existence, gathering our human existence into oneness with himself, and then the movement of the Word and Son of God from within our humanity back to the heavenly Father. . . . The whole movement of descent and ascent is two-fold in that it is a movement of *revelation through the Word of God* and *reconciliation through the Son of God*." T. F. Torrance, *Incarnation*, 77. This descent and ascent is another way of thinking of the projecting of the mystery into our existence with the goal of creating koinonia between God and man.

171. T. F. Torrance, *Incarnation*, 193. See T. F. Torrance, *Christian Theology and Scientific Culture*, 101–2, 126.

172. T. F. Torrance, *Incarnation*, 288.

173. Ibid., 289. We should note here that Torrance also extends the hypostatic union to include a union between the temporal and eternal, ibid., 273, 335; T. F. Torrance, *Atonement*, 255–56; T. F. Torrance, *Space, Time and Incarnation*, 72–73, and between created rationality and the transcendent rationality of God, T. F. Torrance, *Reality and Evangelical Theology*, 91.

Correlative to the ontological significance of the homoousion and the insertion of the mystery into our being, and with particular forceful emphasis on the non-assumptus, the hypostatic union is also

> the objective heart of *reconciliation*, in atonement. The unassumed is the unhealed, but in the hypostatic union God the Son has sinlessly assumed our flesh of sin into oneness with himself. In so doing he has judged sin in the flesh and made expiation for our sin in his own blood shed on the cross, and so has worked the hypostatic union right through our alienation into the resurrection.[174] The hypostatic union could not have been actualized within the conditions of our fallen humanity without the removal of sin and guilt through atonement and the sanctification of human nature assumed into union with the divine.[175]

This reconciliation is also objectively wrought and subjectively fulfilled in Christ.[176]

The Hypostatic Union: Summary

In this section on the hypostatic union we have covered a number of overlapping, if not virtually identical, constructs in Torrance's Christology. The fact that each conception entails, and may even substitute for, the others makes any linear presentation of Torrance's work challenging. However, we may summarize both the interconnected nature of these ideas, and the utterly decisive role of the non-assumptus, from a remarkably complete passage in *Preaching Christ Today*, where Torrance himself is expounding the hypostatic union.

---

174. T. F. Torrance, *Incarnation*, 195. Italics mine. "Reconciliation is not something added to the hypostatic union so much as the hypostatic union itself at work in expiation and atonement." T. F. Torrance, "Atonement and Oneness," 247. See T. F. Torrance, *Conflict and Agreement in the Church: Order and Disorder*, 240.

175. "The hypostatic union operates as a reconciling union in which estrangement is bridged, conflict is eradicated, and human nature taken from us is brought into perfect sanctifying union with divine nature in Jesus Christ. Embodied within the deep tensions and contradictions of our rebellious humanity, the hypostatic union took on the form of a dynamic atoning union which steadily worked itself out within the structures of human existence all through the course of our Lord's vicarious earthly life from his birth to his crucifixion and resurrection. Incarnation and atonement were internally and essentially intertwined in all he became for our sake and all he underwent in paying the price of our redemption." T. F. Torrance, *The Mediation of Christ*, 65–66. Also, T. F. Torrance, "Incarnation and Atonement: Theosis and Henosis," 12, 17.

176. See the essentially equivalent discussion of objective and subjective justification in T. F. Torrance, *Theology in Reconstruction*, 156–57.

In a single paragraph Torrance makes the following assertions.[177] The hypostatic union "means that in Jesus Christ, God and man, divine and human nature, are indissolubly united in one incarnate person, so that the whole of Christ's life from beginning to end was lived in unbroken relation with God the Father." This means "the saving work of Christ and his incarnate life are inseparable," and that "his humanity is seen to be not just a means to an end." In addition, atoning reconciliation takes "place within the incarnate constitution of the Mediator. His person and work are one . . . , Jesus Christ *is* redemption, he *is* righteousness, he *is* life eternal." Incarnation and atonement, then, must be understood "in terms of their internal relations within the incarnate constitution of Christ." Torrance then draws the following conclusion:

> *If this is the case*[178] we must not flinch from the statement of St. Paul in the Epistle to the Romans (8:3) that the Son of God came among us in the concrete likeness of sinful flesh (ἐν ὁμοιώματι σαρκὸς ἁμαρτίας—cf. Phil 2:7: ἐν ὁμοιώματι ἀνθρώπων), yet far from sinning himself he condemned sin in the flesh. Nor must we try to water down St. Paul's statement that Christ was made sin for us, although he knew no sin (2 Cor. 5:21).[179]

These Pauline assertions are, Torrance continues, simply an affirmation of the patristic non-assumptus. He then asserts that to reject this ancient soteriological principle "is to separate the incarnation from reconciliation, the person of Christ from his saving work."

It is "very crucial for us" to affirm "that the Savior took our fallen Adamic humanity" and healed it throughout the course of his earthly life.

> *Hence we must think*[180] of his incarnating and atoning activities as interpenetrating one another from the very beginning to the end of his oneness with us. Otherwise the humanity of Christ has to be thought of only in an instrumentalist way, and the atonement has to be formulated only in terms of external moral relations or legal transactions. But if the incarnation is itself essentially redemptive and not just a means to an end, then atonement must be regarded as taking place in the ontological depths of Christ's incarnate life, in which he penetrated into the very bottom of our fallen human being and took our disobedi-

---

177. All the citations in this paragraph are from T. F. Torrance, *Preaching Christ Today*, 58.

178. My italics.

179. T. F. Torrance, *Preaching Christ Today*, 58.

180. My italics.

ent humanity, even our alienated mind, upon himself in order to heal it and convert it back in himself into union with God.[181]

Here we have, as the italicized text seeks to indicate, the non-assumptus as both the inescapable conclusion (*If that is the case*) of the other key structures in Torrance's Christology, and the source (*Hence we must think*) of those structures. Thus, all these underlying structures arise and emerge *together* in his thought in such a way that none can stand without the others. The non-assumptus, then, is a fully integrated, indispensable, and formative feature of his whole Christology.

ANHYPOSTASIA AND ENHYPOSTASIA

Introduction and Historical Background

The significance of the anhypostasia-enhypostasia couplet for Torrance is seen in the fact that he uses it as early as 1941.[182] Though he acknowledges that it does not "contain the 'stuff' of Christology," nevertheless as a "disclosure model"[183] or "cognitive instrument," it is a lens "through which we may discern more deeply and clearly the ontological structures of the incarnation."[184] As such, it is found pervasively scattered throughout his thought as a tool for illuminating virtually every aspect of his Christology.[185]

Torrance uses the terms, in dependence on Barth,[186] in whose thought "*anhypostasia* and *enhypostasia* are brought together to give full stress upon

---

181. T. F. Torrance, *Preaching Christ Today*, 59.

182. This is Robert Walker's claim in Walker, "Editor's Introduction to Atonement," lxxviii. The reference is to T. F. Torrance, "Predestination in Christ," 128–29, where the concepts are clearly present but the actual terms are absent. The terms are not used in the even earlier Auburn lectures, but the concepts are present, though underdeveloped. T. F. Torrance, *The Doctrine of Jesus Christ*, 90–91, 114–15, 124.

183. Disclosure models are a more nuanced and complex set of the "conceptual tools" we spoke of in the second chapter. See T. F. Torrance, *Theological Science*, 318; T. F. Torrance, *Transformation and Convergence*, 274–75.

184. T. F. Torrance, *Incarnation*, 233. The couplet is said to be "remarkably fertile in its power to throw light on many difficulties." T. F. Torrance, *Theological Science*, 269.

185. Indeed, it is used to illumine a whole range of doctrines. It is applied, for instance, to the church, T. F. Torrance, "Atonement and Oneness," 255–56, and to theological statements, T. F. Torrance, *Theological Science*, 218. Application is also made, without the express language, to the sacraments and the Christian life. See Colyer, *The Nature of Doctrine*, 170–71; T. F. Torrance, *The Mediation of Christ*, 86–98.

186. Torrance, as Rankin points out, would have been exposed to the doctrine through Mackintosh, who, particularly with respect to anhypostasia, is less enamored of the doctrine than his student. Mackintosh, *Person of Christ*, 205–9, 217–22, 385–90;

the historical Jesus Christ as the very Son of God."[187] He traces the roots of enhypostasia half of the couplet to the sixth-century monk, Leontius of Byzantium,[188] noting however, that in his work, and in John of Damascus following him, the doctrine lacks clarity due to a lack of emphasis on anhypostasia.[189] It was the Reformed scholastics who used the terms together "marking a real advance over the patristic usage of these concepts."[190] It is this patristic and Reformed background, mediated through Barth,[191] which

---

Rankin, "Carnal Union," 75, 284.

187. T. F. Torrance, *Incarnation*, 197. See Barth, *CD*, I.2 163, III.2 70, IV.2 49–50, 91; T. F. Torrance, *Karl Barth: Biblical and Evangelical Theologian*, 125, 199–201. Torrance speaks of being "gripped by the way in which he resurrected and deployed the theological couplet *anhypostasia* and *enhypostasia*." T. F. Torrance, *Karl Barth: Biblical and Evangelical Theologian*, 125.

188. T. F. Torrance, *Incarnation*, 211; T. F. Torrance, *The Christian Doctrine of God*, 160. The nature of what Leontius actually taught concerning enhypostasia is a matter of scholarly dispute. See Davis, *The First Seven Ecumenical Councils (325–787): Their History and Theology*, 233–34. Shults contends that, following the Protestant scholastics, and the nineteenth century work of Friedrich Loofs on Leontius, the modern (i.e., Barth-Torrance) understanding of the couplet is not compatible with Leontius. See Shults, "Dubious Christological Formula." Shults holds that the "en" in enhypostasia, for Leontius, functioned as the opposite of an alpha privative. In this sense, the term meant simply having subsistence, or concrete existence, not, as for Torrance and Barth, having subsistence *in another* hypostasis or nature. Thus, Leontius would not use the term anhypostasia of the human nature of Christ, since it simply meant without subsistence. Loofs' error seems to lie in a conflation of Leontius of Byzantium with his contemporary namesake, Leontius of Jerusalem, who *did* use enhypostasia to mean "subsisting in." Thus, while Shults appears to be correct on the Leontius confusion, the substance of the couplet is not without patristic support. For more background see Rankin, "Carnal Union," 72–75; Davidson, "Theologizing the Human Jesus," 137–41; Crisp, *Divinity and Humanity*, 73; McGuckin, *The Westminster Handbook to Patristic Theology*, 117–18. Our concern here is not with the genetic history of the terms but with Torrance's own usage.

189. Though, previously, Cyril of Alexandria made "illuminating use" of the couplet. T. F. Torrance, "Incarnation and Atonement: Theosis and Henosis," 11–12; T. F. Torrance, *Karl Barth: Biblical and Evangelical Theologian*, 199–200. For Torrance's sources in Cyril see T. F. Torrance, *The Christian Doctrine of God*, 160. Here he credits both Severus of Antioch and John of Damascus with developing the couplet. Torrance credits the couplet with having a mitigating effect on the static conception of the doctrine of Christ in patristic theology. T. F. Torrance, *Conflict and Agreement in the Church: Order and Disorder*, 232.

190. T. F. Torrance, *Incarnation*, 228. Torrance gives Heidegger as an example of the Reformed usage. See Heppe, *Reformed Dogmatics*, 427–28. From early Scottish theology, he also adduces the work of Robert Boyd of Trochrig. T. F. Torrance, *Incarnation*, 197; T. F. Torrance, *Scottish Theology: From John Knox to John McLeod Campbell*, 71.

191. Torrance believes that Barth himself takes the terms primarily from seventeenth century Reformed sources. T. F. Torrance, *Karl Barth: Biblical and Evangelical Theologian*, 200.

provides the framing of the terms which Torrance adopts and extends with great vigor.

Definition of Terms

Torrance insists that anhypostasia and enhypostasia cannot be separated and must be considered together in their complementarity.[192] Let us begin with the basic definitions.

> Anhypostasia asserts: [that] because of the assumption of humanity by the Son, Christ's human nature has its existence only in union with God, in God's existence or personal mode of being (*hypostasis*). It does *not* possess it in and for itself—hence *an-hypostasis* ("*not* person," i.e. no separate person).[193]

Thus, "apart from the incarnation of the Son of God Jesus would not have come into being."[194] The humanity he assumed had no *independent* personality to which a divine person was added.[195] Anhypostasia, then, "stresses the *general* humanity of Jesus" and his ontological solidarity with all men and women. It highlights the fact that he who was *a man* was, at the same time *man*.[196]

> Enhypostasia asserts: [that] because of the assumption of humanity by the Son, the human nature of Christ is given existence in the existence of God, and co-exists in the divine existence or mode of being (*hypostasis*)—hence *en-hypostasis* ("person *in*," that is, real human person *in* the person of the Son). This means that Jesus had a fully human mind, will, and body, and was in complete possession of all human faculties.[197]

---

192. T. F. Torrance, *Incarnation*, 105, 228–29; T. F. Torrance, *Theology in Reconstruction*, 131.

193. T. F. Torrance, *Incarnation*, 84; T. F. Torrance, "Atonement and Oneness," 249. T. F. Torrance, "The Atonement. The Singularity of Christ," 230; T. F. Torrance, "The Place of Christology," 16.

194. T. F. Torrance, *Karl Barth: Biblical and Evangelical Theologian*, 199.

195. "If there had been a human person to whom a divine person was added, there would have been an independent center of personal being in Jesus over against the person of the Son of God." T. F. Torrance, *Incarnation*, 229.

196. Ibid., 230–31.

197. Ibid., 84, 230; T. F. Torrance, *Theology in Reconciliation*, 166–67; T. F. Torrance, "The Atonement. The Singularity of Christ," 230. This personalizing of the humanity of Jesus cannot be considered apart from the Spirit and his "coinherent relation" with the incarnate Son. T. F. Torrance, *The Trinitarian Faith*, 230.

Thus, Jesus "was given a complete human *hypostasis* in, and in perfect oneness with, the divine hypostasis of the Son."[198] Enhypostasia, then, stresses the "*particular* humanity of the one man Jesus, whose person is not other than the person of the divine Son."[199] He who was man (the anhypostatic "many") was also *a man* (the enhypostatic "one").[200] Taken together the terms repudiate any form of adoptionism or Nestorian dualism.[201]

Anhypostasia and Enhypostasia and the Hypostatic Union

The couplet functions in Torrance's Christology as a positive and comprehensive heuristic device. It discloses, or bring into focus, "the inner logic of grace embodied in the incarnation."[202] The once and for all union in the

198. T. F. Torrance, *Karl Barth: Biblical and Evangelical Theologian*, 199. Thus, Jesus has real human personhood in the Son of God. T. F. Torrance, *Incarnation*, 105; T. F. Torrance, *The Ground and Grammar of Theology*, 117–18. "We must assert of the humanity of Jesus that it was given *hypostasis*, reality, real personal being, in the eternal Word, in the eternal Son, in the eternal *hypostasis* of God the Son." T. F. Torrance, *Incarnation*, 177. See Molnar, *Theologian of the Trinity*, 103. For an earlier, and more primitive, assertion of enhypostasia, without the actual term, see T. F. Torrance, *The Doctrine of Jesus Christ*, 132–33.

199. T. F. Torrance, *Incarnation*, 230.

200. T. F. Torrance, *Conflict and Agreement in the Church: Order and Disorder*, 242–43.

201. T. F. Torrance, *Incarnation*, 229. Leontius' intention was also "to give a fuller place to the humanity of Jesus Christ than appeared to be allowed by the rebuttal of Nestorianism." T. F. Torrance, *Incarnation*, 211. Torrance says Barth saw the enhypostasia as a bulwark against "Lutheran" monophysitism as well. T. F. Torrance, *Karl Barth: Biblical and Evangelical Theologian*, 200. Torrance also sees a Nestorian dualism at work among Calvinist theologians "in their doctrine of predestination when election was apt to be read back into the eternal being of God apart from what actually took place in the life, death and resurrection of Jesus, which had the effect of driving a wedge between his divine and human natures." Thus, like the homoousion, "the application of *anhypostasia* and *enhypostasia* to the incarnation, therefore, declares in the strongest way that there can be no thought of going behind the back of Jesus Christ." T. F. Torrance, *Karl Barth: Biblical and Evangelical Theologian*, 200–201. See T. F. Torrance, *The Mediation of Christ*, 100.

202. T. F. Torrance, *Karl Barth: Biblical and Evangelical Theologian*, 125; T. F. Torrance, "The Atonement. The Singularity of Christ," 230. The expression "the logic of grace" is Torrance's shorthand way of saying that the divine action in Christ, far from overwhelming or excluding the human, makes full place for it. All of God does not mean nothing of man, but rather, all of God means all of man. T. F. Torrance, *Theological Science*, 128, 206–7, 214–22; T. F. Torrance, *The Mediation of Christ*, 95–96. Torrance gives us a definition of the logic of grace as "the pattern exhibited by God's grace in the incarnation, life, death and resurrection of Christ." T. F. Torrance, *Christian Theology and Scientific Culture*, 136. "*Anhypostasia* asserts the unconditional priority of grace. . . . But *enhypostasia* asserts that God's grace acts only as grace. God does not override

virgin birth corresponds to anhypostasia, and the continuous union in the life of Christ corresponds to enhypostasia.[203] In light of the action of God in Christ, who steps into our situation "not as a third party," but as a divine actor whose action contains within it full place for the human, anhypostasia accents the divine action,[204] and enhypostasia accents the fully human action within the divine.[205] Together they throw light on, and confirm, Torrance's understanding of the hypostatic union.

> This doctrine of the *anhypostasia* and *enhypostasia* is a very careful way of stating that we cannot think of the hypostatic union statically, but must think of it on the one hand, in terms of the great divine act of grace in the incarnation, and on the other hand, in terms of the dynamic personal union carried through the whole life of Jesus Christ.[206]

Given Torrance's understanding of the hypostatic union, it is not surprising that he applies the couplet to both revelation and to reconciliation, for it is another way of stating their inseparability. Concerning revelation, he says:

> In revelation, therefore, we are not concerned simply with *anhypostatic* revelation and with human response, but with *anhypostatic* revelation and true human response *enhypostatic* in the Word of revelation. We are not concerned simply with a divine revelation which demands from us all a human response, but with a divine revelation which already includes a true and

---

us but makes us free." T. F. Torrance, *Theological Science*, 217. Though Torrance usually speaks of the whole couplet as disclosing the logic of grace, a variation on this entails a distinction between the logic of grace (divine action) and the logic of Christ (divine action translated into human existence). "To use . . . technical terms, we may say that the logic of grace and the logic of Christ are to be related to one another as the doctrines of *anhypostasia* and *enhypostasia*." See the discussions in T. F. Torrance, *Theological Science*, 214–18; Molnar, *Theologian of the Trinity*, 104–5.

203. T. F. Torrance, *Incarnation*, 85, 105. Put differently, anhypostasia correlates to "the transcendent act of grace in the incarnation of the one eternal Son," and enhypostasia, on the other hand, correlates to "the obedient life of the incarnate Son on earth." T. F. Torrance, *Incarnation*, 84.

204. Without anhypostasia the concept that salvation is by the pure grace of God would be lost. T. F. Torrance, *Atonement*, 54.

205. Ibid., 122. "Christ's work is as *enhypostatic* as his person, and thus we must go on to stress that Christ's saving work in atonement is equally *enhypostatic*."

206. T. F. Torrance, *Incarnation*, 84. The couplet *and* the hypostatic union in concert "bring out the essential logic of grace." T. F. Torrance, *Theological Science*, 269.

appropriate and fully human response as part of its achievement for us and to us and in us.[207]

With respect to reconciliation, he writes:

> If anhypostasia alone were to be applied to the atonement . . . that would mean that the deed of atonement would be a pure act of God over the head of man.[208] . . . On the other hand, if enhypostasia alone were to be applied to the atonement without anhypostasia then atonement would be understood as a Pelagian deed placating God by human sacrifice.[209]

As a piece of "theological algebra" illuminating the hypostatic union the couplet is profoundly related to the non-assumptus.

> The doctrine of anhypostasia and enhypostasia (put together as one concept) helps us also to understand or express how God the Son was made in the likeness of our flesh of sin, and yet was not himself a sinner; how he became one with us in the continuity of our Adamic and fallen existence in such a way as to make contact with us in the very roots of our sinning being, and yet did not himself repeat our "original sin" but vanquished it, and broke its continuity within our human nature. He assumed our corrupt and estranged humanity, but in such a way as at the same time to heal and sanctify in himself what he assumed.[210]

Anhypostasia, then, explains Christ's continuity with us in our Adamic existence, and enhypostasia is correlative with the discontinuity of his

---

207. T. F. Torrance, *Theology in Reconstruction*, 131.

208. Here Torrance has Aulen's "Christus Victor" view of the atonement in mind. Aulen, *Christus Victor: An Historical Study of the Three Main Types of the Idea of the Atonement*. "The manhood of Christ was integral and essential and not merely instrumental in atonement, that is to say, in the language that I have been using, that it was enhypostatic and not merely anhypostatic." T. F. Torrance, *Conflict and Agreement in the Church: Order and Disorder*, 244. See T. F. Torrance, *Atonement*, 122. On the need to integrate the anhypostatic ontological (or *goel*) element with the *padah* and *kipper* elements of atonement, and thus with the enhypostatic life of Christ, see T. F. Torrance, *Atonement*, 52–60; T. F. Torrance, *The School of Faith: The Catechisms of the Reformed Church*, lxxxix–xcv.

209. "The inseparability of anhypostasia and enhypostasia in application to the death of Christ is thus supremely important for it means that while atonement is throughout act of God for us, we are to understand it as act of God done into our humanity, wrought out in our place and as our act." T. F. Torrance, "Atonement and Oneness," 250. See T. F. Torrance, *Atonement*, 76–77; T. F. Torrance, *Theology in Reconciliation*, 172.

210. T. F. Torrance, *Incarnation*, 231–32.

personal life of sinless obedience within our flesh.[211] Both ends of the couplet are understood as illuminating, respectively, the assumption and the healing of our fallen flesh.

We must draw attention here to a crucial difference in the two terms of the couplet. Anhypostasia, by stating that the Son did not join himself to an independently existing personality, asserts that "he so took possession of human nature, as to set aside that which divides us men from one another, our independent centers of personality, and to assume that which unites us with one another, the possession of the same or common human nature."[212] Thus, Jesus does not assume our fallen sinful *persons*. It is enhypostasia which, within the ontological solidarity of a common fallen nature, seeks "a solidarity in terms of the interaction of persons within our human and social life, in personal relations of love, commitment, responsibility, decision, etc."[213]

> Thus he, the *enhypostatic* Son of Man, lived out a life of perfect and sinless obedience to the Father in the midst of the fallen human nature which he had *anhypostatically* assumed, and in virtue of which he had entered into solidarity with all mankind.[214]

The couplet, then, corresponds to the two-fold insertion of the union between God and man which we looked at under the hypostatic union. That union is inserted into our being (ontic union, thus anhypostasia), and into our knowledge (noetic union, thus enhypostasia). For if the incarnation were only anhypostatic, it "could only mean a solidarity between Christ and all mankind which was, so to speak, only ontological and therefore physical and mechanical—a causal and necessitarian solidarity."[215] This would, indeed, be "physical redemption."

> The union between man and God in Christ was therefore not just a union in being, else indeed there had been no cross, and

---

211. In the virgin birth the relative stress falls on anhypostasia, yet even there we saw that Torrance taught the "once for all union" involved both continuity and discontinuity with our Adamic existence. Thus, he can speak of the virgin birth as "an act of grace which becomes as such the archetype of all other acts of grace." T. F. Torrance, *Incarnation*, 103, 105. See T. F. Torrance, "Predestination in Christ," 130.

212. T. F. Torrance, *Incarnation*, 231.

213. Ibid. The enhypostatic Son "entered deeply and acutely into personal relations with sinners, so that in personal and responsible ways of the profoundest nature, he might enter within our personal human structure of existence, and assume personally and answerably the whole burden of our sin and guilt upon himself." Ibid., 232.

214. Ibid., 232.

215. Ibid., 231.

the atonement had already been accomplished fully and entirely in the birth of Jesus, in the bare assumption of our human nature into oneness with the Son of God.[216]

Thus, within and upon the ontic union, the noetic union has a crucial place.[217]

The importance of the enhypostatic noetic union lies in the fact that sin is an intensely *personal* matter.

> Because sin has to do with the heart of man, with the roots of the human person, an objective atonement as act of God only upon man is not sufficient of itself if they are to be saved. It must be worked through the heart and mind of men and women, until they are brought to acquiesce in the divine judgment on sin and are restored in heart and mind to communion with God.[218] Reconciliation . . . is not just the clearing up of a misunderstanding, but the eliminating of a lie that has its roots in our nature as fallen and as perverted personal being. Hence the incarnation entailed a physical or ontological union, as well as a Logos-union with man (that is, a union with man in being as well as in word and mind) as the means of reconciliation to God.[219]

Torrance sees this noetic (enhypostatic) union as not simply the Logos uniting himself to, and revealing himself within our humanity, but as enabling our humanity to respond personally in love and obedience.[220] Thus, enhypostasia refers to the conflict with the carnal mind which had already begun in Israel as the pre-history of the incarnation, and which, as we shall see in the next chapter, is carried out in the life of Christ.

216. Ibid., 163.

217. Ibid., 162.

218. T. F. Torrance, *Atonement*, 158. "But if sin is an act of man going down to the roots of human nature and introducing into the very relation with God which constitutes the human person . . . a contradiction . . . then it is in the inner depth of their personal being that humanity must be reconciled to God and we must be healed of our enmity and contradiction to God." Ibid., 159.

219. Ibid., 161. While this citation includes both the anhypostatic ("our nature as fallen") and enhypostatic ("perverted personal being") dimensions, the personal nature of sin involves a certain highlighting of enhypostasia. "God is at variance with humanity in the essential inner relation which constitutes not only their very existence, but the center of the human person . . . it is upon this essential and root personal relation that the emphasis is laid in reconciliation." Ibid., 158. "It was because the inner attitude of man to God which is central to the human person had become perverted, that the incarnation meant the invasion of the Word into that perverted inner attitude of our human being in order to heal and straighten it out into perfect obedience toward the Father." Ibid., 164.

220. Ibid., 162.

Anhypostasia and Enhypostasia and the Creator Logos

Finally, we must look at the crucial matter of how Torrance relates both anhypostasia and enhypostasia to the *creator* Logos, or Word of God. Since Christ is the eternal Son, the creator Word of God who gives all men being, and in whom all men cohere, "there is an ontological relation between the creature and the Creator reposing upon His sheer grace."[221]

In the incarnation of the creator Word, "we have the union of the universal Word and one human creature created by that Word which makes Jesus *at once man, and a man.*"[222]

Thus, an ontological precursor of the anhypostatic relation established in the incarnation exists between Christ and all men by virtue of their creation through the Word.

> The Son and Word of God became man by becoming one particular Man, but because He is the Creator Word who became Man, even as the incarnate Word He still holds all men in an ontological relation to Himself. That relation was not broken off with the Incarnation.[223]

This creational ontological backdrop becomes intensified in the ontological-anhypostatic solidarity that the incarnate Christ shares with our humanity.

> When we remember that Christ is the Incarnation of the Creator-Logos by whom all things have been made and in whom all men cohere, then we can see that this self-giving of Christ to us involves us in an ontological relation with him even in his human nature.[224]

This coming of the Logos "must be regarded . . . as the bringing of his creative activity to bear intensively upon what God has already made, thereby reinforcing its creaturely status, and, in our case, our human status."[225]

---

221. T. F. Torrance, *The School of Faith: The Catechisms of the Reformed Church*, cxii. "He is . . . Head of all creation and . . . all things visible and invisible are gathered up and cohere in Him—from which we cannot exclude a relation in being between all men and Christ." T. F. Torrance, *The School of Faith: The Catechisms of the Reformed Church*, cxiii. See T. F. Torrance, *Reality and Evangelical Theology*, 89–90.

222. T. F. Torrance, *Incarnation*, 231.

223. T. F. Torrance, *The School of Faith: The Catechisms of the Reformed Church*, cxii.

224. T. F. Torrance, *Theology in Reconstruction*, 185. See T. F. Torrance, *Incarnation*, 98.

225. T. F. Torrance, *The Mediation of Christ*, 69. In this connection, Torrance calls Jesus the humanizing Man. See T. F. Torrance, "The Goodness and Dignity of Man,"

The Continuous Union   151

The incarnation "has the effect of finalising and sealing the ontological relations between every man and Jesus Christ."[226] Thus, universal anhypostatic solidarity is grounded in the creative work of the Logos and completed in the Incarnation, whereby the Word has now become flesh in Jesus Christ.

> Since in Jesus Christ the Creator Word of God has become man in such a way that in him Divine Nature and human nature are indivisibly united in his own Person, the humanity of every man, whether he knows it or not, whether he believes or not, is ontologically bound up with the humanity of Jesus.[227]

Torrance regularly, as above, brings the doctrine of Jesus as the creator Logos incarnate to bear on discussions of the universal range, both of his incarnational assumption of our humanity, and of his atoning work.[228] The work of incarnate redemption does not violate, but heals, the rational order with which creation was endowed by the Logos.[229] Thus, the anhypostatic solidarity which all men have with the incarnate Logos entails the universality of his incarnate atoning work.

> To hold that some people are not included in his incarnate and redeeming activity is to cut at the very root of his reality as the Creator incarnate in space and time, as he in whom all things in the universe, visible and invisible, were created, hold together and are reconciled by the blood of his cross (Col. 1:15–20).[230]

318.

226. T. F. Torrance, *The Trinitarian Faith*, 182.

227. T. F. Torrance, "The Goodness and Dignity of Man," 317. The assertion that every man, whether he knows it or not, is ontologically bound up with Christ is common in Torrance. See T. F. Torrance, *The Trinitarian Faith*, 183; T. F. Torrance, *The School of Faith: The Catechisms of the Reformed Church*, cxiv. T. F. Torrance, "Universalism of Election?," 315–16. T. F. Torrance, "Karl Barth and the Latin Heresy," 481. "Moreover if he is both the Image and Reality of God, then he is the unique image-constituting Image of God, and it is by reference to what he is that we must now think of human beings as created in the image of God." Despite sin, "the image of God still remains sealing their human existence through their ontological bond with Jesus Christ the Incarnate Word." T. F. Torrance, "The Goodness and Dignity of Man," 317. For more on the relation of the Word to man's creation in the image of God see T. F. Torrance, *Calvin's Doctrine of Man*, 23–34, 52–60.

228. T. F. Torrance, "The Atonement. The Singularity of Christ," 244–45, 249–50. We shall discuss this further when we look at the cross of Christ in chapter 6.

229. T. F. Torrance, *The Christian Frame of Mind*, 40–41.

230. T. F. Torrance, "The Atonement. The Singularity of Christ," 245. Rankin argues that this construal of anhypostasia introduces an element of contingent necessity into the incarnation. "Thus, the extent of the incarnation was a contingent necessity for the Logos. Because of the universal range of anhypostatic solidarity, Christ must—by

Christ's role as creator Logos is also critical in construing the enhypostasia end of the couplet. Not only is the incarnate Christ the anhypostatic many, he is the enhypostatic one.

> [T]he true secret of our humanity is lodged in the Word. In the incarnation of this Word, Christ became the "proper man," as Luther called him, the true man, and because that Word made flesh is the creative source and true secret of our humanity, because in him our humanity is lodged, because all mankind consist in him, he is the only one who can really represent all men and women from the innermost center and depth of human being.[231]

As the Son of God made flesh, "Christ the Mediator is the *personalising Person*."[232] Torrance uses this concept expressly in connection with avoiding Nestorian dualism on the one hand, or making Christ's "human person . . . an empty mask of the divine Person," on the other.[233]

> Thus, far from depersonalising human being, or overriding the human person, the coming of Jesus Christ has the effect of personalizing human being in a profounder way than ever before. With the Incarnation there took place an acute personalising of all God's interaction with us, so that the Incarnational union of the Person of the Son with our human nature must be regarded as the most intensive personalising of it that could have taken place. In Jesus Christ we have embodied in our humanity personalising Person and personalised person in one and the same being, in whom the personalised person is brought to its fullest reality. Thus far from being emptied or overpowered by the divine Person, the human person is reinforced and upheld in its indissoluble oneness with the divine.[234]

---

contingent necessity—represent and be carnally united to all human beings in his person and work." Rankin, "Carnal Union," 290–91.

231. T. F. Torrance, *Atonement*, 126.

232. T. F. Torrance, *The Mediation of Christ*, 67.

233. "[I]n virtue of the fact that the Person who became incarnate in Jesus Christ is the creator Word of God by whom all men are made and in whom they consist, and is therefore the Person from whom all creaturely personal being is derived, the incarnation must be regarded as creative, personalizing activity. As the incarnate Son of God Jesus Christ is Person in His own divine Being, but we are all created persons. He is the personalizing Person, and we are personalized persons." T. F. Torrance, *The Mediation of Christ*, 67–68; T. F. Torrance, *The Christian Frame of Mind*, 39; T. F. Torrance, *The Christian Doctrine of God*, 161; T. F. Torrance, *Theological Science*, 207.

234. T. F. Torrance, *The Mediation of Christ*, 68. See T. F. Torrance, *The Trinitarian Faith*, 230; T. F. Torrance, "The First-Born of All Creation," 14. This personalizing

Torrance's expression "personalizing person and personalized person," existing in indissoluble unity, functions as equivalent to the humanity of Jesus being given enhypostatic reality in and with the person of the Logos-Son.[235]

This personalizing of our humanity in Christ has decidedly social implications. Enhypostasia, as we saw, entails a healing penetration into the social and personal life of men and women. He personalizes our humanity and, consequently, personalizes others who come into contact with him.[236] Thus, this aspect of enhypostasia is profoundly related to the non-assumptus.

> However, we must not forget at this point that the incarnational union was also an atoning union, in and through which our lost and damned humanity is redeemed, healed and sanctified in Jesus Christ. That means that the broken state of human *personal* being, resulting from the alienation of humanity from God and the conflict between them that has became embedded within its very existence, is brought within the redeeming, healing and sanctifying activity of God in Jesus Christ.[237]

Our human personality "suffers from a . . . schizoid condition" which "gives rise to insincerity and hypocrisy" due to "estrangement from the personalising source of our being." The result is "we become imprisoned in a self-centered individualism which cuts us off from genuine relations with others, so that the very personal relations in which persons subsist as persons are damaged and twisted."[238]

> That is the state of affairs in which the personalizing Person of the Son of God became incarnate, but, instead of becoming insincere and hypocritical himself, he healed the ontological split in human being through the hypostatic and atoning union which he embodied within it. . . . It is in this sense also that Jesus Christ is personalizing Person, for he redeems us from

---

activity of the incarnate Son rests on the fact that "in the strict sense God only is Person, for he is in himself the fullness of personal Being—he is personalising Person." T. F. Torrance, "The Goodness and Dignity of Man," 318; T. F. Torrance, "The Soul and Person," 116; T. F. Torrance, "Predestination in Christ," 117, 123–25; T. F. Torrance, *Christian Theology and Scientific Culture*, 70–71.

235. Notice enhypostasia allows Torrance to speak of Jesus as a human person or, as we saw earlier, as having a human hypostasis.

236. T. F. Torrance, "The Soul and Person," 116.

237. T. F. Torrance, *The Mediation of Christ*, 68. Italics mine.

238. Ibid., 68–69.

thralldom to depersonalizing forces, repersonalising our human being in relation to himself and to other human beings."[239]

The result is "that Jesus Christ is now the fount of all that is truly personal among us[;] . . . we are not personal in virtue of some personal substance inherent in ourselves, but only through what we receive from Jesus Christ[;] . . . to be personal, therefore, is to be in Christ."[240]

We may summarize the various overlapping correspondences Torrance employs as follows:

Anhypostasia: divine action, virgin birth, once for all union, ontic union, Christ as the "many," Christ as man, incarnate Logos as ground of ontological solidarity.

Enhypostasia: human action, life of Christ, continuous union, noetic union, Christ as the "one," Christ as *a* man, incarnate Logos as personalizing person.[241]

ANALYSIS AND CRITIQUE

In examining the deep Christological structures that shape, and are shaped by, Torrance's conception of the non-assumptus, a number of strengths emerge. Surely, the immense stress laid on the homoousion answers to its epochal significance. Particularly helpful is Torrance's unfolding of the evangelical, or ontological, significance of the Nicene term. In reminding us that the term was developed in response to, and predicated of, the incarnate Christ, and that it occurs in a soteriological context in the creed, Torrance's pervasive teaching that all Jesus says and does God says and does is salutary. While the term was developed to ground the *being* of the Son in oneness with the Father, Torrance is surely correct that it also entails, with the Trinitarian caveats, a oneness in *agency* as well. The divine validity of the gospel does indeed rest on the homoousion. The immense ontological significance

---

239. T. F. Torrance, *The Mediation of Christ*, 69. See T. F. Torrance, *The Trinitarian Faith*, 230, where our becoming personalized persons is explicitly linked to Jesus' enhypostatic human nature. By the "ontological split," Torrance means the difference, created by the depersonalizing effects of sin, between the image we present of ourselves and the reality.

240. T. F. Torrance, "The Goodness and Dignity of Man," 318.

241. In terms of Israel, we could see her corporate election (the community of reciprocity) as correlated to anhypostasia, and the nucleus of individual prophets as correlated to enhypostasia. The covenanted way of response, first in the cult and then "hypostatized" in the Servant of the Lord, would entail the couplet in its complementarity.

of the term is never to be detached from its economic and soteriological significance.

Yet ambiguity arises when Torrance says this means that God *is* eternally in himself what he *is* toward us in Jesus Christ. On the one hand this notion, along with its concomitant idea that "there is no God behind the back of Jesus," would seem to point to an identity of the ontological and economic Trinities. Torrance, however, holds that they "overlap" and are not "disparate." He affirms that the "temporal and causal connections that obtain in our creaturely existence"[242] may not be read back into the eternal being of God. He makes it clear that the ontological Trinity is not "constituted by or dependent upon the economic Trinity," and that we may not speak of the oneness between them "without distinguishing and delimiting" the economic from the ontological.[243] We only desire to point out that the stress on oneness and fidelity between God in his eternal being and God in Jesus Christ, admirable as it is, can often appear absolute in Torrance. Once one takes his own qualifications into account it would seem that there must be some way of speaking, without the dark and sinister overtones he often attaches to it, of a God who is "behind the back" of Jesus Christ.

In the context of the ontological significance of the homoousion we explored the fact that this implied that there is "no third party" in the conflict between God and man. Rather, in Jesus Christ, we have God acting *as* man and sharing in the conflict from both sides. Torrance's conception of a single divine atoning action which, within it, is also a fully human action is immensely helpful. While it does not eliminate all the temptations to Nestorianism (two actors), those temptations are not unique to Torrance, but inhere in the whole history of Christology. The formulation, "God as man," enables him to give full range to the action of Jesus in our flesh without positing another actor.

This fully human action requires seeing the homoousion as a bi-polar construct. Here Torrance, controversially, asserts that the homoousion was intended to ground the reality of the Lord's humanity in oneness with ours. While Gorringe *may* be correct that, in light of the threat of Apollinarianism, by "Constantinople the homoousion is a bi-polar formula—Christ is of one substance with both God and man,"[244] Muller is surely correct in asserting that "the Christological issue, the consubstantiality of the Word Incarnate with our humanity, was only given confessional formulation at

---

242. T. F. Torrance, *The Christian Doctrine of God*, 97. It remains unclear how the incarnation can be "new" to God and fall "within his life" without, in some manner, reading temporal and causal connections back into the ontological Trinity.

243. T. F. Torrance, *The Christian Doctrine of God*, 108–9.

244. Gorringe, "Not Assumed Is Not Healed," 487.

the Council of Chalcedon in 451 AD."[245] While the historical pedigree for speaking of the homoousion as applying to Jesus' humanity seems dubious, this way of speaking can also give the impression that the humanity of Jesus is of one substance (homoousion) with the divine nature. James Cassidy makes just this accusation when speaking of "the fundamental flaw" in Torrance's formulation of the homoousion:

> Nicea does not identify the substance of Jesus Christ, in his divine-human hypostasis, with God. . . . The divine nature [of] the person of the *Logos* is of the same substance as of the Father and the Spirit, not the divine and human person of the hypostasis. . . . This way of stating things is extremely problematic . . . it makes both natures of Christ of one nature with God. . . . For Torrance Jesus Christ, in both his human and divine nature is of the divine *ousia*.[246]

Understandable as this is, it is a serious misreading of Torrance. He makes it clear, as we have shown, that the union of the two natures of Christ on the horizontal level (hypostatic union) is to be interpreted in light of the "vertical" reference of the homoousion. The two concepts are cognate, but they are not confused in Torrance's thought. When he speaks of the homoousion as applying to Jesus' humanity, he means simply that he was fully man.

In this context, we saw that the non-assumptus is crucial in giving integrity to the full humanity of Jesus' actions. Here Torrance asserts that the assumption of some "neutral human nature" by the divine person, "who could not choose to sin any more than he could choose not to be God," entails making the humanity merely instrumental in the hands of God. But he also asserts that in assuming our sinful flesh, it was not possible for God in Christ to sin. Thus it would appear that the question of peccability is, even on his own terms, independent of the status of the nature assumed. This casts some ambiguity over the notion of the "instrumentality" of Christ's humanity which is so prominent in Torrance, and repeatedly coupled with the non-assumptus.

Torrance's rigorous integration of incarnation and atonement, person and work, while we believe it is often overstated,[247] is salutary in its giving

---

245. Muller, "The Barth Legacy," 688. "Athanasius never so much as dreamt of applying the Nicene language of *homoousios* to the doctrine of the person of Christ." By "person of Christ," Muller is referring to the Christological usage of the term, especially its human pole, by Torrance.

246. Cassidy, "Soteriological Objectivism," 179.

247. For example, when Jesus says, "I judge you not, but the word that I have spoken

full, and not merely "instrumental," place to the human obedience of Jesus. However, we point out that, even on the "Westminsterian" theology which Torrance rejects, the human obedience of Christ is not *merely* instrumental to the atonement. His active obedience is imputed to believers and, while the framework is "merely legal and forensic," it remains a crucial part of his saving work. Indeed, one could argue that a human nature that is corrupt and depraved would be even *more* instrumental in the hands of God, since the only nature (or will) which can act freely to save it would be the divine.[248]

With respect to the epistemological significance of the homoousion, Torrance is on more tenuous ground than he is with respect to its unquestioned ontological and evangelical significance. Here we can also distinguish the historical and the theological questions. Muller states the historical objection plainly: "It was surely not, moreover, either the intention of Athanasius and the Council of Nicea or of the Fathers of Chalcedon to use the *homoousion* as an epistemological or heuristic principle for all theology."[249] Theologically, the issue lies in Torrance's presentation (following Barth) of Christ as the exclusive place for knowledge of God. Muller contrasts a *soteriological* Christocentrism with the Barth-Torrance *principial* Christocentrism, and highlights the role of the *extra-Calvinisticum* in allowing for genuine revelation outside of the incarnation.[250] The debates at Nicea, and subsequently at the Reformation, were soteriological and not about the identity of God with his revelation.[251] This raises the vexed and difficult area, not only of natural theology in general, but of Torrance's com-

---

to you, that shall judge you at the last day" (Torrance's paraphrase of John 12:47–48, see T. F. Torrance, *Atonement*, 406), he is surely distinguishing, though not separating, his person from his word, and thus his work. See a similar distinction between Jesus and his works in John 10:38 and 14:11. Thus, it is the precise nature of the integration that is in question. Is it, as Torrance often asserts, sheer identity, or is it some other type of interlocked relation? Since Torrance's presentation of the oneness of incarnation and atonement depends critically on the non-assumptus, that is where we will focus our attention.

248. This raises the issue, again, of the actual status of this assumed humanity, and to this we will return shortly. We note as well, that even ascribing the healing of sinful flesh to the work of the Spirit does not mitigate the *prima facie* claim that a fallen human nature would be more instrumental in the hands of God than a "neutral" humanity.

249. Muller, "The Barth Legacy," 689. Luoma agrees that Torrance's reading of Athanasius as denying the possibility of revelation outside the incarnation is "a slight overinterpretation." Luoma, *Incarnation and Physics*, 37. The charitable adjective, slight, is used since both Torrance and Athanasius agree that all revelation comes through the Word of God.

250. Muller, "The Barth Legacy," 685–87. See Calvin, *The Institutes of the Christian Religion*, 2.13.4.

251. Muller, "The Barth Legacy," 676, 689, 699.

plex reformulation of natural theology wherein it is a kind of prolegomenon *within* theology proper.[252]

Untangling the issues involved here is not our present concern. However, it must be seen that the non-assumptus is largely responsible for the epistemological exclusivity which Torrance ascribes to the incarnation. It is precisely because Christ descends into *our* ignorance, *our* alienated mind, and gathers up *our* human through forms, speech and rationality, restructuring them within himself, that Torrance can posit the incarnate Word as the *only* place where a bridge has been forged in *our* humanity to genuine knowledge of God. Couple this with a kind of substance ontology[253] wherein human nature is seen as an assumable entity, and the conclusion is hardly avoidable. Without the non-assumptus, some other "bridge" would have to be forged between the depths of our being and the being of God.

Leaving the question of exclusivity aside, it is far from clear that the homoousion can carry the full epistemological weight Torrance places on it. Even given his conception of a single "carnal" union in which we participate, a real distinction must be made between the minds of Christians and the mind of Jesus of Nazareth. Whatever the nature of our pneumatic participation in the one union is, it is clear that the minds of Christians are not hypostatically united to the Logos. Thus, it does not appear that using the homoousion as a bridge between our human knowledge and God is entirely unproblematic, since it requires an "additional" or, in Torrance's conception, a "participatory" pneumatic bridge between believers and Christ. This highlights a fundamental problem with the non-assumptus. It is designed to bridge the gap between God and man, to enable God to reach us in our actual condition, yet, the absolute uniqueness of the God-man (homoousios with the Father, enhypostatic in the Logos) *guarantees* a gap of some sort between Christ and believers.[254] Torrance, of course, grants this, but still

---

252. See T. F. Torrance, *The Ground and Grammar of Theology*, 75–109; T. F. Torrance, *Karl Barth: Biblical and Evangelical Theologian*, 136–59; T. F. Torrance, "The Problem of Natural Theology"; McGrath, *Intellectual Biography*, 174–94; Colyer, *How To Read T. F. Torrance*, 192–207; T. F. Torrance, *Reality and Evangelical Theology*, 30–34; T. F. Torrance, *Reality and Scientific Theology*, 32–61. Colyer calls Torrance's reconstruction of natural theology one of the most difficult aspects of his theology. Colyer, *How To Read T. F. Torrance*, 192.

253. Rankin, "Carnal Union," 278.

254. "I have ventured to suggest that in stressing the absolutely unique character of the God-man relationship in Christ, orthodox incarnational theology has (unconsciously) been going against the leading of this principle." Wiles, *Working Papers in Doctrine*, 120. The principle in view is the non-assumptus. On the necessity of some sort of a gap between Christ and believers despite the non-assumptus see Wiles, *The Making of Christian Doctrine*, 108–13.

argues for the necessity of the non-assumptus. However, it seems that necessity would have to be rephrased more loosely as "suitability or fittingness."[255]

Turning now to the hypostatic union proper, there are also historical and theological concerns. Torrance's reading of the historical need to reconstruct Chalcedon is of a piece with his general reading of church history which we surveyed in the opening chapter. Muller calls Torrance's whole reading of the Barth legacy as the way back to Nicea, and thus, we would add, to a proper understanding of the non-assumptus, "a massive misrepresentation of the history of the church and an egregious falsification of our theological heritage."[256] Whether one agrees with Muller or not, certainly seeing the "Latin heresy" as the main stream of the church's post-Nicene (and especially post-Chalcedonian) development is an idiosyncratic reading. However, our concern lies with the theological issues. Let us highlight four of them.

First, there is a pervasive and underlying question of conceptual clarity. Kelly Kapic notes that this whole issue of the assumption of our fallen humanity has been plagued by a lack of definitional clarity.[257] He concludes, "progress on this issue will only occur when definitions of sin, guilt and vicarious are agreed upon."[258] To this, we would add that "human nature" itself needs clearer formulation. This is a question that quickly becomes exquisitely complex.[259] Yet, Torrance appears to take no position on just what constitutes Christ's human nature. It appears to be a substance, the assumption of which includes every instance of the substance in every human being, without, as both Torrance and classical Christology affirm, the assumption of a human *person*.[260] This is far from clear, but how else could

---

255. Wiles, *The Making of Christian Doctrine*, 112–13. Wiles claims the non-assumptus should be generalized as: "You can't do anything effective about something without entering into some sort of relation with it." Wiles, *Working Papers in Doctrine*, 115. For a more robust affirmation of what Wiles is after, yet still denying the non-assumptus, see Crisp, *Revisioning Christology*, 128.

256. Muller, "The Barth Legacy," 684. "Vincent of Lerins has been stood, like Marx's Hegel, on his head: the universal right teaching of the church has been identified as what has been believed in a few disparate places, sometimes, and by no more than three or four select theologians."

257. Kapic, "The Son's Assumption of a Human Nature."

258. Ibid., 166.

259. See a small sampling of the options regarding Christ's human nature in Crisp, *Divinity and Humanity*, 34–71.

260. "If there is believed to be a single reality—humanity—such that both Christ and we share (albeit in different ways) in the same reality, the principle [the unassumed is the unhealed] appears more plausible than if we do not hold such a belief." Wiles, *Working Papers in Doctrine*, 117.

the actual humanity of every human being be ontologically assumed and healed, and not "merely" represented, in the hypostatic union? What does seem clear is that Jesus can only be *an instance* of fallen humanity.[261] He is male, not female, Jewish, not Gentile, Jesus of Nazareth, not Paul.[262] Only his human nature is hypostatically united to, and personalized by, the Logos. This does not mean he cannot represent or substitute for us, even from within a fallen human nature like ours, but it does seem to require moving the whole conception in a more forensic and covenantal direction.

Second, Torrance sees a large part of Chalcedon's problem as defining the human nature of Jesus in terms of some neutral, general conception of which we have no actual experience. Human nature is not to be defined in abstraction from the humanity of Christ. The problem with this way of putting the matter is twofold. First, to speak at all of Christ assuming *our* human nature, fallen or unfallen, is intelligible only on some kind of distinction between human nature as it is in us and as it is in him. Second, the humanity which Christ assumes, that is, our fallen, twisted humanity, abstracted from concrete sinful persons[263] and hypostatically united to the Logos, is also a humanity with which we have no experience. Again, the God-Man's uniqueness casts a shadow over the goal the non-assumptus is intended to achieve.

Third, in re-conceiving the hypostatic union dynamically, an ambiguity about its status arises similar to the ambiguity about the status of the humanity of Christ after the "sanctifying" union of the virgin birth. Surely, there is a hypostatic union between God and man from the very beginning of Jesus' life, but if that is so,[264] how is the hypostatic union also an achievement of the whole historical life? If, as Torrance asserts, reconciliation is not an addition to the hypostatic union, but the hypostatic union at work in expiation and atonement (a statement fully compatible with the traditional view he is critiquing) then surely the union, in a fundamental way, precedes the work of atonement. Of course, it is the non-assumptus that

---

261. This is true whether one views the human nature of Jesus as a set of properties or as a concrete particular. See Crisp, *Revisioning Christology*, 124–27. Crisp is critiquing Kathryn Tanner's conception of incarnate atonement, but the conclusions apply to Torrance's conception of "human nature" as well. On Tanner, see Tanner, *Christ the Key*.

262. See Ho, *A Critical Study on T. F. Torrance's Theology of Incarnation*, 75. We are not denying that Jesus is the one who stands in the place of the many. The question is whether he can ontologically *be* one and many simultaneously.

263. We refer to the fact that enhypostasia entails no assumption of our fallen personalities. We shall explore this further below.

264. Torrance also speaks of the union as "holding" or being dynamically upheld, throughout the course of Christ's agonizing obedience, a conception which would also be acceptable on the traditional view.

drives the need for dynamic reconstruction, and what Torrance seems to be saying is that we have a hypostatic union between the divine nature and sinful human nature at the beginning which, through the course of Christ's obedience, becomes a hypostatic union between the divine nature and purified human nature at the end. Yet, he never quite puts the matter this way, insisting (generally) rather on a once for all *and* a dynamic construction of the *union itself*. This raises the question, analogous to the status of the post virgin birth humanity, of the precise status of the hypostatic union, and thus of Christ's humanity, in the interim.

Fourth, we saw that Torrance conceives of a hypostatic union between creaturely language and God's language. He extends this to a union in Christ between the temporal and the eternal, and between created and divine rationality. Leaving aside the fact that this is hardly within the purview of Chalcedon, it would seem to require moving the whole conception in a more representative and "forensic" direction since Jesus could only unite one human language, or one period of time, with the divine. We shall address this elastic inclusivity of the hypostatic union further after we see it worked out in the historical life of Christ in the following chapter.

Turning to Torrance's exposition of anhypostasia and enhypostasia, we find a pervasive use of the terms which seems to go well beyond the historical meanings. However, its is important to recognize that Torrance is using the terms as lenses which "do not contain the stuff of Christology," thus, the various correlations he provides need to be seen in this light. With that caveat, nonetheless, it is clear that Torrance takes the correlations very seriously. The terms, apparently, help us get at "the stuff of Christology."

Anhypostasia, at least with respect to the definition, Torrance takes in its traditional sense. The humanity of Jesus has no independent personal existence apart from the incarnation. But it is highly doubtful whether the various correlations (divine action, once for all ontic union, Christ as man, or "the many") can really be wrung out of the term itself.[265] The common thread here, which moves Torrance's correlations beyond the traditional definition, is that of universal ontological solidarity with all men. This is, as we have seen, driven by the non-assumptus which, in Torrance's hands, leads to (or, perhaps, is preceded by) the notion of human nature as a single assumable entity. While Torrance seeks to work from Christology outward, and thus would eschew the idea of a prior ontology, it is difficult to see how Christology itself must entail this conception of anhypostasia. The fact that the creator Logos has an ontological relation with all men does not, of

---

265. This is a point we are sure Torrance would grant. The *term itself* does not entail the profuse set of correlations Torrance makes.

itself, imply that the incarnation of that Logos entails the realist ontological assumption of human nature we find in Torrance. Jesus is indeed a man, a concrete human being, *and* man, in the sense that he is fully human, but by "man" Torrance means the one in whom the common fallen nature of all men has been realistically assumed. Even if we could make sense of the ontology involved here, the universality he ascribes to anhypostasia would need to be established on exegetical grounds, and not simply by an appeal to the creator Logos.[266]

With enhypostasia, again we have a traditional definition and a unique set of correlates drawn from it. Yet, the way Torrance elaborates the definition itself raises questions. He can say that the humanity of Jesus is given real personhood in the eternal Son, that no independent center of personality is assumed, and that the person of Jesus "is not other than the person of the divine Son." However, he can also speak of Jesus as "personalizing person" and "personalized person" in unity, and in this very context speak of the divine person not overwhelming the human person. The result is that a personalized human *nature* bleeds over into what appears to be a second *person* in union with the divine Son. The ambiguity is seen when, speaking of the act of incarnation, he says:

> Far from the presence of the Deity of the Son overwhelming or displacing the rational *human person* in Jesus, his human mind and human soul, the exact opposite took place. And so it must be said that no human being has such a full and rich personal *human nature* as Jesus.[267]

Admittedly, the problematic issue of expressing the full personal reality of Jesus without lapsing into Nestorianism is not unique to Torrance. Neither would we want to press this critique, but we have seen that there are numerous phrases he uses which, in conjunction with the enormous stress on the human action of Jesus, lend an apparent Nestorian coloring to his Christology. For example, in a context where he is repudiating Nestorianism, he can still say it makes Jesus' human *person* "an empty mask" of the divine person.[268] A full and charitable reading of Torrance would require us to take the language of "human person" as equivalent to "the human nature given full personal existence in the Logos," yet his terminology can be, at the very least, confusing.

---

266. We shall discuss the range of the atonement when we look at the work of the cross in the final chapter.
267. T. F. Torrance, *The Trinitarian Faith*, 230.
268. T. F. Torrance, *The Mediation of Christ*, 67.

Definitional ambiguity aside, Torrance's use of enhypostasia has far-reaching ramifications for the non-assumptus. Since no person, or personal center of consciousness, is assumed, this means, in Torrance's words, that the incarnation sets aside what divides us, namely our sinful human personalities. Thus Christ, while assuming what unites us (our common natures: anhypostasia), does not assume our fallen human persons. This is devastating for the non-assumptus. It means that no concrete *personal* instance of fallen humanity is assumed, only fallen human "nature"—whatever that is—dissociated from fallen human persons. Surely, this humanity is, to use Torrance's description of "neutral" humanity, one of which we know nothing. So we have a split in the heart of the non-assumptus: fallen human nature is assumed, fallen human persons are set aside. Thus, it is not only the uniqueness of the God-Man which creates a "gap" with humanity, it is the nature of the non-assumptus itself.

It is apparent that Torrance is aware of this issue, and that his whole notion of the Logos as the "personalizing person" who "acutely personalizes" human nature in the incarnation is designed, in part, to deal with the problem. However, we fail to see how this heals the basic split. The acute personalization of human nature in Christ does not compensate for the non-assumption of our fallen human personalities. Even on Torrance's own reading of enhypostasia, this personalization yields precisely one unique (composite) person, the Logos made flesh. Enhypostasia, after all, tells us that Jesus is *a man*, the one and *not* the many. This requires conceiving of the union Christ has with our human *persons* in a much more representative and covenantal framework. If this is so, then the split in the non-assumptus creates a critical tension between anhypostatic ontological solidarity and enhypostatic representation.

Torrance, of course, believes Christ represents us, but because he is the Word "in whom the secret of our humanity is lodged," he represents us "from the innermost center and depth of human being." But we fail to see how this can be the case if our fallen and twisted persons are not assumed. We surveyed a range of Torrance's thought on the personal nature of sin lodged in the roots of the human person, of reconciliation as dealing with perverted personal being, and of the Son's invasion into this state of affairs in order to heal and bend back our nature into obedience to the Father. This invasion, it turns out, is into something called "fallen human nature" from which our independent fallen personalities have been abstracted.

This invasion into our personal existence was also given a social dimension. Jesus enters into relations with others so that the structures of our social life might be brought within the sphere of his healing and atoning work.[269] This appears to create yet another split related to the non-assumptus. However atonement takes place in the internal constitution of the mediator, it cannot be of one piece with his extrinsic healing penetration into society. According to his (correct) understanding of enhypostasia, the persons Jesus encounters *ad extra* are not assumed within the healing embrace of the hypostatic union. Thus, the redemption of our inter-personal societal lives must also be construed along a much more forensic conception of representation. The combination of both of these splits (fallen nature but no fallen persons, and *ad intra* versus *ad extra* working of the hypostatic union) gives us reason to doubt the coherence of the non-assumptus which underlies them.

Two issues remain, both of them related to enhypostasia. First, we must ask about the fallenness of a humanity which has been fully personalized in the Logos. Jesus' person is divine and, thus, not sinful. But does the Son enhypostatically personalize the assumed and fallen humanity of Jesus in such a way that the resultant personalized humanity is still fallen? If no fallen persons are assumed, from whence does the *personal* character of sin in the assumed humanity come? The second issue is closely related and can be stated as a question. *Who* is doing the resisting, *who* is personally opposing the bending back of our corrupt natures which takes place in the agonizing obedience of Jesus? If our fallen humanity opposes the work of atoning mediation, it must *personally* oppose it. Torrance's presentation, as we shall see in the next chapter, everywhere assumes this and often states it explicitly. Yet, there is only one person in the union. Here, again, is the specter of a latent Nestorianism.

---

269. We shall discuss this further in the conclusion to the next chapter after seeing how this societal penetration works itself out in the historical life of Christ.

5

THE CONTINUOUS UNION
The Life of Perfect Faithfulness

HAVING EXAMINED THE ONCE for all union of God and man in the virgin birth, and having looked at the fundamental structures of Torrance's Christology which underlie his conception of the life of Christ, we come in this chapter to an exposition of the "continuous union" in the historical life of Christ up to, but not including, his death. We shall do this under two headings. First, we shall look at Torrance's conception of Christ's condemning sin in the flesh. This is a matter which extends throughout the whole life of Christ and thus pertains to the whole of the continuous union. Secondly, we shall look at various "focal" aspects in the life of Christ. In this manner we shall see how the assumption of our fallen flesh plays a determinative role in Torrance's narration of the atoning life of Christ in the Gospels.

CONDEMNING SIN IN THE FLESH

Torrance affirms without equivocation the utter sinlessness of Jesus. In language borrowed from the Reformed tradition, yet with transformed content, he speaks of Christ's passive obedience "in which he submitted to the divine judgment upon us," and his active obedience "in which he took our place in all our human activity before God the Father."[1] The active obe-

---

1. T. F. Torrance, "The Distinctive Character," 6–7. Lee sees a correlation here between passive obedience and anhypostasia on the one hand, and between active

dience means "from the very beginning to the very end, he maintained a perfect filial relation to the Father in which he yielded to him a life of utter love and faithfulness." This entailed "his loving self-offering to the Father in our name and on our behalf, and also his own loving appropriation of the Father's word and will in our name and on our behalf."[2] By passive obedience "is meant the submission of Jesus Christ to the judgment of the Father upon the sin which he assumed in our humanity in order to bear it in our name and on our behalf." This includes both his passion and his "willing acceptance of the divine verdict" upon our sin.[3] It is important to see that the passive obedience, for Torrance, extends throughout the whole of Christ's life.

> The passive obedience is manifested above all in the obedience of Jesus unto the death of the Cross, but that was a passion that began with his very birth, for his whole life, as Calvin says, was in a real sense a bearing of the Cross, but it was in the Cross itself that it had its telos or consummation.[4]

The active and passive obedience do not differ with respect to their subject—they are both aspects of the Son's obedience—nor with respect to time, since they both belong to the whole life of Christ. "They are set in mutual unity in the *whole life of Christ*. Since this is so we may speak of the active obedience as an *actio passiva* (passive action), and the passive obedience as a *passio activa* (active passion)."[5]

---

obedience and enhypostasia on the other. Lee, *Living in Union with Christ*, 188.

2. T. F. Torrance, *Incarnation*, 80; T. F. Torrance, *The School of Faith: The Catechisms of the Reformed Church*, lxxxiv; T. F. Torrance, *Theology in Reconstruction*, 154.

3. T. F. Torrance, *Theology in Reconstruction*, 154; T. F. Torrance, *Incarnation*, 80–81; T. F. Torrance, *The School of Faith: The Catechisms of the Reformed Church*, lxxxiv. In the last citation the verdict is said to be rendered upon "our rebellious humanity."

4. T. F. Torrance, *Theology in Reconstruction*, 154; T. F. Torrance, *Incarnation*, 81. Torrance places great weight on the cross, nevertheless, the atoning passion extends across the whole of Christ's life. "The twofold work of the cross was already revealed as active in the earthly ministry of Jesus: that is the divine exposure of and judgment upon our sin, and yet the divinely given provision in Jesus, within our humanity, of atonement for sin. His activity is at every point proleptic of the cross, or to put it the other way around, it is atoning mediation at work before the cross." T. F. Torrance, *Incarnation*, 148. See T. F. Torrance, *The School of Faith: The Catechisms of the Reformed Church*, lxxx–lxxxiv. Alternatively, "From the beginning to the end of his life, he submitted our fallen humanity with our human will to the just and holy verdict of the Father, freely and gladly yielding it to the Father's judgment, and was therefore obedient unto the death of the cross." T. F. Torrance, *Incarnation*, 205.

5. T. F. Torrance, *Incarnation*, 81; T. F. Torrance, *Theology in Reconstruction*, 155.

In very traditional language, which shows Torrance's willingness to stress the place of the cross in the passive obedience,[6] he writes:

> This mutuality of Christ's active and passive obedience is important for it means that in our justification we have imputed to us not only the passive righteousness of Christ in which, in suffering his death on the Cross, he satisfied and atoned for our sins, but the active righteousness of Christ in which he positively fulfilled the Father's will in an obedient life. In other words justification means not simply the non-imputation of our sins through the pardon of Christ, but positive sharing in his human righteousness.[7]

Yet, this traditional affirmation is not set in the context of classical federal theology. Because of the non-assumptus, it is given an ontological frame of reference. Torrance insists that we cannot consider the active and passive obedience apart from the "*holy union* he wrought out in his birth, life, death, and resurrection between our fallen human nature and his divine nature."[8] This ontological dimension is essential, Torrance claims, because without it "the active and passive obedience fall apart," and "we are unable to understand justification in Christ as anything more than a merely external forensic non-imputation of sin."[9] Thus, the assumption of our fallen humanity, and the "saving and sanctifying union" it effects, is something that "belongs to *the very substance of our faith.*"[10]

---

6. "In Christ God Himself was among men and women judging sin in the flesh, but it was on the cross above all that we find a complete judgment enacted." T. F. Torrance, *Atonement*, 120.

7. T. F. Torrance, *Incarnation*, 81; T. F. Torrance, *The School of Faith: The Catechisms of the Reformed Church*, lxxxv–lxxxvi; T. F. Torrance, *Theology in Reconstruction*, 155.

8. T. F. Torrance, *Incarnation*, 82; T. F. Torrance, *The School of Faith: The Catechisms of the Reformed Church*, lxxxv; T. F. Torrance, *Theology in Reconstruction*, 155. Torrance also finds this relation of active and passive obedience to incarnational union in Robert Bruce. T. F. Torrance, "Introduction to Robert Bruce's Sermons," 35.

9. T. F. Torrance, *Incarnation*, 82; T. F. Torrance, *The School of Faith: The Catechisms of the Reformed Church*, lxxxvi; T. F. Torrance, *Theology in Reconstruction*, 156. This claim is clearly false. The majority reading of the Westminster theology of justification, for example, while it may be extrinsic and forensic, sees justification as the fruit of union with Christ, though it does this under the rubric of "effectual calling." See *The Westminster Shorter Catechism*, Q. 29–33; *The Westminster Larger Catechism*, Q. 66–72; *The Westminster Confession of Faith*, XI.1. Also, justification is not construed as mere non-imputation of sins. In addition to pardon for sin, it includes the imputation of "the obedience and satisfaction of Christ." *The Westminster Confession of Faith*, XI.1.

10. T. F. Torrance, *Incarnation*, 82. See also T. F. Torrance, *The School of Faith: The Catechisms of the Reformed Church*, lxxxvi; T. F. Torrance, *Theology in Reconstruction*, 156.

This saving union, as the ontological frame of the active and passive obedience, is associated with the removal of our *original* sin, while the combination of active and passive obedience themselves deal with our *actual* sins.

> If we are to think of the active and passive obedience of Christ as dealing with our actual sin and its penalty, we are to think of the Incarnational union of the Holy Son with our unholy nature as dealing with our original sin,[11] or sanctifying our human nature, through bringing it into a healing and sanctifying union with his own holy nature.[12]

Thus, the flawless perfection of Jesus' obedience is wrought from within our actual condition.

> He has come to live out in our inhumanity the life of true humanity, in the midst of our disobedience a life of obedience, and so to live the perfect life in communion with the perfect God.... In the sheer perfection of His humanity in all its absolute purity and sinlessness He offered the Amen of Truth from within our humanity to the Word and Will of God's eternal Truth.... He stood in the gap created by man's rebellion and reconciled man to God by living the very life He lived ... within the limitations of our humanity in the house of bondage.[13]

---

11. As we saw in chapter 3, this "dealing with our original sin" is affirmed, ambiguously we believe, as beginning, or even as happening, in the virgin birth.

12. T. F. Torrance, *Theology in Reconstruction*, 156; T. F. Torrance, *Incarnation*, 82; T. F. Torrance, *The School of Faith: The Catechisms of the Reformed Church*, lxxxvi; T. F. Torrance, *Preaching Christ Today*, 59. "It was not only our actual sins, but it was original sin and original guilt that the Son of God took upon himself in incarnation and atonement, in order to heal, convert, and sanctify the human mind in himself and reconcile it to God." T. F. Torrance, "The Reconciliation of Mind," 4–5. This distinction between active and passive obedience being associated with actual sins, and incarnational union dealing with original sin can be confusing since Torrance frequently speaks of the union itself as wrought out in the whole life of (active and passive) obedience. The point is simply that without the ontological grounding in our fallen humanity our original corruption remains untouched by the life of Christ. In classical Reformed soteriology our fallen nature is transformed by the work of the Spirit in regeneration and sanctification. This is inadequate for Torrance, since it is not grounded in the prior action of Christ *in the depths of our actual humanity*. See T. F. Torrance, "The Atonement. The Singularity of Christ," 238.

13. T. F. Torrance, "The Atoning Obedience of Christ," 75; T. F. Torrance, *Incarnation*, 123. "What is it that the servant-Son does here within our humanity? Here within our fallen and disobedient humanity, where we are less than human because of our sin, here where we have dehumanized ourselves in our rebellion, here where we, the sons and daughters of God, have become bastards and not true sons and daughters, he the Son of God becomes true Son of Man, true man for the first time in utter obedience."

The full picture, then, includes three interpenetrating factors: solidarity with our fallen humanity, an active life of holiness to the Father's will, and a lifelong passion of submission to the verdict of God on our corruption.[14] In this manner, Jesus "condemns sin in the flesh" by his very sinlessness.[15]

The reference to condemning sin in the flesh brings us to one of Torrance's crucial texts for the obedient work of Christ in our humanity.

> God sent his Son in the concrete likeness of sinful flesh, *en homoiomati sarkos hamartias*, an expression which is used in Romans, "For God has done what the law, weakened by the flesh, could not do: sending his own Son in the likeness of sinful flesh and for sin, he condemned sin in the flesh."[16]

Torrance says it is the non-assumptus, the "realist approach to the fact that in Jesus Christ God the Son has united himself to our actual existence," in conjunction "with the view that atonement takes place within the incarnate life and being of the Mediator," which led Nicene theology to take seriously the teaching of the apostle on the Son of God coming in the likeness of sinful flesh.[17]

Torrance's use of the phrase "the concrete likeness of sinful flesh" is significant. It indicates that he understands ὁμοιώματι not in the sense of difference, or even difference within likeness, but rather as a concrete instantiation of our sinful flesh.[18] For Torrance, the difference lies in what

---

T. F. Torrance, *Incarnation*, 73.

14. T. F. Torrance, "The Goodness and Dignity of Man," 317. Here all three elements are brought together nicely: "It was not by assuming some neutral human nature but by assuming our actual fallen human nature, thereby taking our place under the judgment of God's Holiness and Love, that he effected our salvation and transformed our human being in himself, bringing it into conformity with his own perfect obedience as incarnate Son of the Father."

15. T. F. Torrance, *Incarnation*, 63.

16. Ibid., 63. Romans 8:3.

17. T. F. Torrance, *The Trinitarian Faith*, 161.

18. This places Torrance with a small minority of interpreters. The necessity of understanding ὁμοωμάτι as full identity has been argued by Vincent Branick, in reliance upon Ugo Vanni's study of the term in the LXX. Branick, "Sinful Flesh." Florence Gillman, while arguing against the necessity of the term as implying full congruence, nevertheless gives exegetical reasons as to why it may mean identity in Rom 8:3. Gillman, "Another Look at Romans 8:3." Gillman lists Barrett, Jewett and Dunn as commentators holding that ὁμοωμάτι means identity in Rom 8:3. Cranfield takes the term to mean likeness, but holds that "the intention is not in any way to water down the reality of Christ's fallen nature, but to draw attention to the fact that, while the Son of God truly assumed fallen human nature, He never became fallen human nature and nothing more, but always remained Himself." Cranfield, *Romans: A Shorter Commentary*, 176. The young Torrance, anticipating his later understanding of Rom 8:3, says ἐν ὁμοιώματι

Christ does, or more accurately, does not do, in our flesh. In his complete identification with us in the concrete likeness of sinful flesh, Jesus is also completely unlike us in that he does not do what we sons of Adam do in the flesh, namely, sin.

> On the other hand, we must say that he was completely unlike us in that by taking our fallen human nature upon himself, he condemned sin in it; he overcame its temptations, resisted its downward drag in alienation from God, and converted it back in himself to obedience toward God, thus sanctifying it. . . . In all this the Son is wholly like us, in that he became what we are, but also wholly unlike us, in that he resisted our sin, and lived in entire and perfect obedience to the Father.[19]

It is important to grasp the conjunction of holiness and judgment at work here. Christ's holiness, his whole self-sanctification, which includes, but is not reducible to, the aspect of submission to the Father's judgment,[20] is what "condemns sin in the flesh." Salvation is wrought through the sanctifying judgment which is the life of Christ.[21] "By His obedience He

---

ἀνθρώπων in Philippians 2:7 "does not mean 'in the appearance or superficial likeness,' but in the *concrete likeness* of men." T. F. Torrance, *The Doctrine of Jesus Christ*, 109.

19. T. F. Torrance, *Incarnation*, 205. "Christ took from Mary a corruptible and mortal body in order that he might take our sin, judge and condemn it in the flesh, and so assume our human nature as we have it in the fallen world that he might heal, sanctify and redeem it." Ibid., 62. "He enters into Adam's rebellious existence and ranges himself among sinners wearing their flesh of sin, standing with them under the divine judgment, and there he, unlike them, acknowledges God's just judgement on sin and so condemns sin in our flesh. By his obedience he is the amen to God's word of truth against our flesh. He accepts the verdict upon sinful man . . . and so is obedient where Adam and all the Adamic race are disobedient, obedient even unto the death of the cross. Within our flesh of sin Jesus is sinless, not in spite of being within the flesh of sin, but because he is within it the amen of obedience to God." Ibid., 73. "Far from sinning himself or being contaminated by what he appropriated from us, Christ triumphed over the forces of evil entrenched in our human existence, bringing his own holiness, his own perfect obedience, to bear upon it in such a way as to condemn sin in the flesh." T. F. Torrance, *The Trinitarian Faith*, 161.

20. Of course, since we are talking about *condemning* sin in the flesh, the aspect of standing under the Father's verdict, the passive obedience, receives a certain prominence here. "He entered our human existence . . . ranged Himself beside sinners and stood with them under judgment. By his obedience He acknowledged God's judgment on sin and so condemned sin in the flesh." T. F. Torrance, *Conflict and Agreement in the Church: Order and Disorder*, 253.

21. "The very forgiveness which he proclaims in word carries at its heart a judgment upon sin, but in that the Word is made flesh, the forgiveness enacted in the flesh involves the ultimate action of condemnation of sin in the flesh." T. F. Torrance, *Incarnation*, 111.

acknowledged God's judgment on sin and so condemned sin in the flesh."[22] Describing Athanasius's understanding of Romans 8:3, Torrance writes:

> That is to say, Athanasius sought to take with full seriousness the fact that Christ was "made sin" and "made a curse," the just for the unjust, and so bore upon himself and in himself for our sakes "the whole inheritance of judgment that lay against us," but he did that in such a way that instead of being overcome by evil he overcame it, instead of sinning in the flesh he condemned sin in the flesh *through his self-sanctification on our behalf.*[23]

There is, thus, a mutual involution where the Word made flesh, "God's word of truth and grace ... in the flesh of our sin and ungodliness ... at once exposes and condemns our sin and untruth in the flesh, and sanctifies our humanity."[24]

This condemnation of sin, then, is coordinate with the great *paliggenesia*, the conversion of our humanity back from its disobedience, or in other language crucial for our purposes, the "bending back" of our fallen will into conformity with the will of God.[25]

> In Jesus Christ the Son of God entered into our rebellious humanity, laid hold of the human nature which we had alienated from the Father in disobedience and sin, and by living out

---

22. T. F. Torrance, "Atonement and Oneness," 260.

23. T. F. Torrance, *Theology in Reconciliation*, 153. Italics mine. See T. F. Torrance, *The Mediation of Christ*, 41. Torrance finds the same doctrine in the Cappadocians. See T. F. Torrance, *Theology in Reconciliation*, 154–56.

24. T. F. Torrance, *Atonement*, 107.

25. With particular emphasis on the healing of our alienated mind and effecting reconciliation "deep within the rational hegemony of human being ... [where] sin had entrenched itself inextricably in human existence," Torrance summarizes what he takes to be the view from Irenaeus to Cyril of Alexandria: "[I]nstead of sinning like all other human beings, he condemned sin in our flesh by living a life of perfect holiness within it, and through his obedient Sonship he converted our disobedient human being back into true filial relation to the heavenly Father." T. F. Torrance, "Karl Barth and the Latin Heresy," 476; T. F. Torrance, *Karl Barth: Biblical and Evangelical Theologian*, 104. The various issues we are discussing are often telescoped together. "In his incarnation Christ not only took upon himself our physical existence from God, but in taking it into himself he at the same time healed it, sanctified it, and changed it, bending our will back to agreement with the divine will, and bringing our human mind back into agreement with the divine mind—and so in the innermost being of the incarnate Son, throughout the whole course of his life, Jesus Christ converted the mind and will of estranged humanity back to the Father. That was the great paliggenesia." T. F. Torrance, *Atonement*, 70.

from within it the life of the perfectly obedient Son he bent our human nature in himself back into obedience to the Father.²⁶

The bending back of our wayward and alienated will highlights the interior hostility which
Jesus faced in his historical life. He enters our existence and orders it "from within *against* our human nature, that is, against the consequences of sin in all its disorder, chaos, and lawlessness, entrenched in fallen human nature."²⁷ We can see the depths of the realism this "bending back" entails in Torrance's understanding of Christ's prayer, "not my will, but thy will be done." "'Not my will. . . ,' that is, your will and my will, our human self-will, which Jesus appropriated and bent back in the agony of Gethsemane in total obedience to the will of the Father."²⁸

Thus, Christ's obedience was "not light or sham obedience;" it was "a battle." "It was agonizingly real in our flesh of sin."²⁹ In this connection, Torrance often refers to προέκοπτεν in Luke 2:52 as meaning Jesus "beat his way forward by blows."³⁰ In doing so he opens up a way from within our flesh for us to rise to the knowledge of the Father.³¹ This "cutting his way forward" is necessitated by the non-assumptus.

> As the Son of Adam he was born into our alienation, our God-forsakenness and darkness, and grew up within our bondage and ignorance, so that he had to beat his way forward by blows, as St. Luke puts it. . . . He learned obedience by the things which he suffered, for that obedience from within our alienated humanity was a struggle with our sin and temptation. . . . Throughout the whole course of his life he bent the will of man in perfect submission to the will of God, bowing under the divine judgment against our unrighteousness, and offered a perfect obedience to the Father, that we might be redeemed and reconciled to him.³²

---

26. T. F. Torrance, *Theology in Reconstruction*, 126, 157.

27. T. F. Torrance, *Conflict and Agreement in the Church: The Ministry and the Sacraments of the Gospel*, 15.

28. T. F. Torrance, *The Mediation of Christ*, 79–80.

29. "It was in agony of blood, 'with strong crying and tears' in the things that he suffered that Jesus learned obedience." T. F. Torrance, *Incarnation*, 64. "It had to be fought out with strong crying and tears and achieved in desperate anguish and weakness under the crushing load of the world's sin and the divine judgment." T. F. Torrance, *Theology in Reconstruction*, 132.

30. T. F. Torrance, *Incarnation*, 64, 106. The word is rendered "increased" or "grew" in virtually all English translations.

31. T. F. Torrance, *Theology in Reconstruction*, 38.

32. Ibid., 132.

This is a movement, we have noted, which "gathered intensity until it reached decisive enactment in the crucifixion."[33] Christ's whole life is one of increasing solidarity with sinners. "Throughout that growing interpenetration of the Son of Man with sinful man, the intensity of battle within the person of Christ increases, reaching its culmination in Gethsemane."[34] Let us now examine this intense movement of obedience which condemns sin in the flesh by focusing on key aspects of Christ's historical life.

FOCAL ASPECTS OF THE CONTINUOUS UNION

The Baptism of Jesus

Torrance lays immense stress on Jesus' baptism at the hands of John in the Jordan river. It belongs "to the great redemptive events of the gospel."[35] It was the baptism of Jesus "which transformed John's rite of baptism into Christian baptism."[36] In addition to the public acknowledgement by the Father of his beloved Son, Jesus' baptism is "his solemn anointing or consecration as the servant who in obedience to God is to be led as a lamb to be the sacrifice for the sins of the world."[37] This means that the passion into which he was born, the passion which is his whole life, is the passion into which "he was solemnly and lawfully consecrated at his baptism."[38]

It is the baptism of Jesus which, marking the beginning of his public ministry, causes the conflict which he bore throughout his life to intensify.

> His whole life, particularly after his baptism among sinners, was a life of intervention in our conflict with God, in which he penetrated into the depths of our personal existence and human

---

33. T. F. Torrance, *Conflict and Agreement in the Church: Order and Disorder*, 240–41.

34. T. F. Torrance, *Incarnation*, 106–7, 110; T. F. Torrance, "The Atoning Obedience of Christ," 71.

35. T. F. Torrance, *Theology in Reconciliation*, 85; T. F. Torrance, *Conflict and Agreement in the Church: The Ministry and the Sacraments of the Gospel*, 112.

36. "The Christian rite of baptism derives from John the Baptist, but the form of that rite is determined by the event that took place in the baptism of Jesus." T. F. Torrance, *Conflict and Agreement in the Church: The Ministry and the Sacraments of the Gospel*, 108, 165; T. F. Torrance, *Theology in Reconciliation*, 84–85; T. F. Torrance, *The Trinitarian Faith*, 293; The Church of Scotland, *Interim Report*, 7–9; The Church of Scotland, *Biblical Doctrine of Baptism*, 18–19.

37. T. F. Torrance, *Incarnation*, 69.

38. Ibid., 70. "He goes forth from his baptism as the lamb of God to bear and bear away the sins of the world." Ibid., 135.

society in sin, taking the conflict into his own innermost being, and suffering it in his heart, from the wilderness of temptation right through to the Garden of Gethsemane.[39]

Jesus' baptism, then, is telescoped into the cross. The baptism in water and the Spirit is locked into the baptism in blood in the long atoning passion that is the life of Christ.[40] In this connection, Torrance refers to Luke 12:50[41] as a "very pregnant and significant passage in which Jesus speaks of the baptism with which he is being baptized, that is the passion which he was undergoing in the continuous present."[42] Thus, "Jesus linked his baptism in the Jordan with his death on the cross, and interpreted his whole life and ministry as the baptism with which he was being baptized, identifying its completion with his passion."[43] This holistic conception of Christ's passion and "baptism" necessarily means that the great event in the Jordan not only points forward to the cross, but points "back to His own birth from above of the Spirit,"[44] which is itself a redeeming and atoning action upon our humanity.

---

39. Ibid., 112. "Beginning with his baptism among sinners at the Jordan . . . we see the person of Christ in a movement of increasing solidarity . . . with sinners." Ibid., 106–7.

40. "It was thus into the cross that He was baptized, so that His baptism came to fulfillment in His crucifixion. But between His baptism in water in the Jordan and His baptism in blood on the cross His whole servant-existence and active obedience was His baptism." T. F. Torrance, *Conflict and Agreement in the Church: The Ministry and the Sacraments of the Gospel*, 112.

41. "I have a baptism to be baptized with, and how great is my distress until it is accomplished."

42. T. F. Torrance, *Incarnation*, 70. The mention of baptism here, as in Mark 10:38, is generally taken as metaphorically referring to the cross, without reference to Jesus' baptism. Torrance mentions, and expressly rejects, this position: T. F. Torrance, *Conflict and Agreement in the Church: The Ministry and the Sacraments of the Gospel*, 112–13. Green sees a possible reference to Jesus' baptism: "The whole of v. 50—with its three elements: baptism + being consumed + completion—should be understood along these lines as well [as a statement of mission]. That is, Jesus' reference to 'baptism' might serve less as a metaphor for judgment and more as a reference to this event in his own life, since Luke presents Jesus' baptism, in part, as an episode of commissioning." Green, *The Gospel of Luke*, 510.

43. T. F. Torrance, *Theology in Reconciliation*, 85; T. F. Torrance, *Conflict and Agreement in the Church: The Ministry and the Sacraments of the Gospel*, 71, 113; T. F. Torrance, *The Trinitarian Faith*, 293; T. F. Torrance, *Conflict and Agreement in the Church: Order and Disorder*, 241; The Church of Scotland, *Biblical Doctrine of Baptism*, 17–18.

44. T. F. Torrance, *Conflict and Agreement in the Church: The Ministry and the Sacraments of the Gospel*, 112, 129; T. F. Torrance, *Theology in Reconciliation*, 85. The effect of this forward and backward interlocking is that Christian baptism "is into the name of the whole Christ; not just into the name of the dying and rising Christ, but the Christ

Christian baptism, then, is grounded in Christ's birth, as well as his death and resurrection. Torrance says, "what binds these two aspects together is the simple but often neglected fact that our incorporation into Christ is grounded entirely and primarily upon His incorporation into us."[45] Tellingly, he continues:

> It is, moreover, just because He incorporated Himself into our estranged humanity under the divine judgment, and through that incorporation fulfilled that judgment both in His holy life in condemning sin in our flesh and by submitting and offering our humanity in Himself to the final judgment of God, that Baptism also has an aspect as baptism into judgment and into repentance.[46]

The truth of our baptism is "lodged in Jesus Christ himself and all that he has done for us within the humanity he took from us and made his own, sharing to the full what we are that we may share to the full what he is."[47]

Not surprisingly, this understanding of the baptism of Jesus and, by implication, Christian baptism, rests on the ontological foundation of the assumption of our fallen humanity. In submitting to John's baptism, Jesus "identified himself with the people of God concluded under sin that through union with them in one body he might make their sin his own."[48]

---

who was born of the Virgin Mary, who was baptized at the Jordan, in fact the whole historical Jesus." T. F. Torrance, *Conflict and Agreement in the Church: The Ministry and the Sacraments of the Gospel*, 128. "[T]he Sacrament of Baptism has very definite relation to the birth of Jesus Christ from above by the Holy Spirit, and is concerned with His growth in wisdom and grace into the full stature of manhood before God and men." T. F. Torrance, "The Place of the Humanity of Christ," 5. See T. F. Torrance, *Conflict and Agreement in the Church: The Ministry and the Sacraments of the Gospel*, 118.

45. T. F. Torrance, *Conflict and Agreement in the Church: The Ministry and the Sacraments of the Gospel*, 119. Thus, it is impossible to understand Torrance's doctrine of the sacraments apart from the non-assumptus. Our incorporation into his prior incorporation into our humanity is what leads Torrance to say there is "one baptism common to Christ and the church." T. F. Torrance, *Theology in Reconciliation*, 82–105. "His baptism set forth the fact that it was our humanity in him that was baptized and anointed." T. F. Torrance, *Theology in Reconstruction*, 200; See T. F. Torrance, *The Trinitarian Faith*, 292–94.

46. T. F. Torrance, *Conflict and Agreement in the Church: The Ministry and the Sacraments of the Gospel*, 119–20. Here "baptism" has a double reference to our baptism and, behind that, Christ's baptism.

47. T. F. Torrance, *The Trinitarian Faith*, 294.

48. T. F. Torrance, *Theology in Reconstruction*, 198. "The first thing He did as He entered upon His active ministry was to be baptized in a crowd of sinners—that was His identification in the body of His flesh with the whole mass of sin and death. By Baptism He made Himself one with us all." T. F. Torrance, *Conflict and Agreement in the Church:*

His being made in the likeness of sinful flesh, under our curse and judgment, is something we see vividly

> already in his baptism where he identifies with sinners, is baptized with the baptism of repentance, and immediately is driven by the Spirit into the wilderness where he fasts and is tempted in immediate fulfillment of his mission as made flesh of our flesh, and as identified with sinners from whom repentance is required, in complete solidarity with them.[49]

Finally, Torrance teaches, that from his baptism onward, Jesus lived only as the Son of Man. In a discussion of the *communicatio gratiarum* (communication of graces), he says:

> What is meant is that from the first moment of his life, his properties as God and man, and the communication of the properties of his divine and human natures, effectively entered into operation step by step with his developing human life—and here we think especially of the graces of knowledge, will and power in which Jesus increased and grew, growing in knowledge, and learning obedience. It is at the baptism of Jesus, when he was anointed for his ministry and consecrated for his sacrificial life and death as the suffering servant, that we are surely to think of this growth and increase as reaching its culmination.[50]

Thus, from his baptism onward, "within our condition, within our weakness and frailty, within our house of bondage—and though acknowledged by the Father as His beloved Son at Baptism, He lived only as the Son of Man."[51]

The point Torrance is making is not that the one divine-human action, or the divine action within which the human has full place, is negated after the baptism, but rather that Jesus lived "not simply as Son of God but as Son of God become *man*. . . . For Jesus, therefore, the life of the perfect and true man in the midst of our sinful humanity was the life of man in perfect and absolute fidelity to his vocation as Son of Man."[52] He resisted the temptation

---

Order and Disorder, 241.

49. Torrance, *Incarnation*, 62. "He received the baptism meant for sinners. In our human nature he received the divine judgment upon sin. . . . For Jesus, baptism meant . . . that he became one with us, taking upon himself our unrighteousness." T. F. Torrance, *Theology in Reconciliation*, 86–87.

50. T. F. Torrance, *Incarnation*, 225.

51. T. F. Torrance, "The Atoning Obedience of Christ," 76; T. F. Torrance, *Incarnation*, 124.

52. T. F. Torrance, *Incarnation*, 123.

not to be man. "The devil assaulted him with the temptation simply to be what he was, and to live the life of who he was, the mighty omnipotent Son of God."[53] But Jesus refused:

> not by acts of open divine majesty and compelling power but, Son of God though he was, by acts of humble service, in which he ranged himself with sinners in their weakness and lostness and bondage under the tyranny of evil and under the judgment of God, acting from their side toward God and only as such acting as God in their midst to save and deliver them.[54]

Vicarious Repentance and Confession

The baptism of Jesus, being a baptism into the depths of our sinful condition, means Jesus lived a life of vicarious repentance for our sins.

> Jesus was baptized "into repentance" (*eis metanoian*), for as the Lamb of God come to bear our sins he fulfilled that mission not in some merely superficially forensic way . . . but in a way in which he bore our sin and guilt upon his very soul which he made an offering for sin. That is to say, the Baptism with which he was baptized was a Baptism of vicarious repentance for us which he brought to its completion on the Cross where he was stricken and smitten of God for our sakes.[55]

Because we are "unable to repent and have to repent even of the kind of repentance we bring before God," and "we are quite unable through our own free will to escape from our self-will," Christ, in his holy vicarious repentance,

> laid hold of us even in the depths of our human soul and mind where we are alienated from God and are at enmity with him, and altered them from within and from below in radical and

---

53. T. F. Torrance, *Incarnation*, 124; T. F. Torrance, *Atonement*, 213–14.

54. T. F. Torrance, *Theology in Reconstruction*, 200–201. The last phrase is important. It is only as God acting from the human side, as man in the midst of our sinful flesh, that Jesus acts to save us. Torrance is emphatic that not even Jesus' miracles indicate a calling on the divine nature in his life of obedience. "Although he wrought miracles as signs of the kingdom, as part of his revelation in act and word, he did not call in supernature to help himself, but lived and worked within the nature, weakness and limitations of the creature, to the very end." T. F. Torrance, *Atonement*, 307. This would seem to leave only the Spirit, and not the divine nature of the Son, as the means by which the human will of Jesus is "bent back" into obedience.

55. T. F. Torrance, *The Mediation of Christ*, 84–85.

> complete *metanoia*, a repentant restructuring of our carnal mind, as St. Paul called it, and a converting of it into a spiritual mind.[56]

Of course, Torrance does not believe that Christ was a sinner, nor that he needed personally to repent.[57] However, since he takes our place as man, and not simply as God, "he must be recognised as acting in our place in *all* the basic acts of man's response to God: in faith and repentance . . ." The liberal and evangelical objection to this, in attempting to preserve a realm of "personal decision of faith and repentance" where God has not acted for us, means "they will have nothing to do with the concept of *total substitution*."[58]

The concept of vicarious repentance, then, includes two basic elements. Penitence or *metanoia*, through which he heals our alienated mind, and the bearing of the penalty for our sin. Torrance correlates these with the Latin terms *poena* and *poenitentia*, meaning "penalty or satisfaction, and repentance or penitence," respectively.[59]

> He wrought out in our human nature and in our human soul complete agreement with the Father in his righteous condemnation of our sin, his grief and sorrow over our rebellion and alienation. In vicarious penitence and sorrow for the sin of mankind, Christ met and responded to the judgment and vexation of the Father, absorbing it in his own being.[60]

---

56. T. F. Torrance, *The Mediation of Christ*, 85. The repentant restructuring of our carnal mind is also called, in this context, the *paliggenesia*. See also T. F. Torrance, *Atonement*, 70.

57. "H. R. Mackintosh used to remind his students that 'Jesus was not a Christian.' A Christian is a sinner whose sins have been forgiven. . . . But Christ was not a sinner who needed forgiveness." T. F. Torrance, *Incarnation*, 11; T. F. Torrance, *Theology in Reconstruction*, 135–36. Interestingly, the young Torrance eschews the notion of vicarious repentance: "Jesus ever preached repentance but never for a moment suggested any aligning of himself with men in that respect. In his own soul there was no state of repentance and absolutely no conviction of sin." T. F. Torrance, *The Doctrine of Jesus Christ*, 28.

58. T. F. Torrance, "Karl Barth and the Latin Heresy," 479–80; T. F. Torrance, *Theology in Reconciliation*, 136. The latter source adds "confession, penitence, sorrow, chastisement, and submission to the divine judgment," to the vicarious responses of Christ.

59. T. F. Torrance, *Scottish Theology: From John Knox to John McLeod Campbell*, 305–6. "*Poena* could be used of external infliction, but *poenitentia* of its internal counterpart in the soul. Christ endured both *poena* and *poenitentia* . . . for us and in our place. . . . In that sense the notion of vicarious repentance is understandable." *Poena* would correlate to Torrance's concept of passive obedience and *poenitentia* would correspond to active obedience. See the discussion of these terms, with the helpful editorial footnote from Walker, in T. F. Torrance, *Atonement*, 69–70.

60. T. F. Torrance, *Atonement*, 70.

For his basic understanding of vicarious repentance, Torrance is heavily dependent on the work of John McLeod Campbell.[61] Campbell speaks of Christ's "perfect repentance ... perfect sorrow ... perfect contrition"[62] in relation to his confession of our sins.

> The noble words of McLeod Campbell are: "That oneness of mind with the Father, which towards man took the form of condemnation of sin, would in the Son's dealing with the Father in relation to our sins, take the form of a perfect confession of our sins. This confession as to its own nature, must have been a perfect Amen in humanity to the judgment of God on the sin of man."[63]

Speaking of Campbell, in words equally applicable to Torrance, Trevor Hart says:

> The oft made complaint that the notion of a sinless Christ "repenting" for others is meaningless fails to see that for Campbell Christ's sinlessness, far from disqualifying him from "repentance," is actually that which *enables* him to confess the sins of the race, and that this "repentance" culminates precisely in a

---

61. The primary work Torrance is engaging is Campbell, *Atonement*, 114–26. See T. F. Torrance, *Scottish Theology: From John Knox to John McLeod Campbell*, 305–12. This whole chapter is a deeply appreciative appraisal of Campbell's theology. For an earlier, and more critical, appraisal see T. F. Torrance, *The Doctrine of Jesus Christ*, 166–74. The early Torrance feels there is not enough stress on "the conception of forensic satisfaction of divine justice" in Campbell's conception of vicarious repentance. T. F. Torrance, *The Doctrine of Jesus Christ*, 166. Though a "great work ... moving and deeply devotional," Campbell's *The Nature of the Atonement* "fell down rather badly both in its failure to appreciate the element of judgment in atonement and also in a fundamentally Pelagian element in its conception of the vicarious penitence and priesthood of Christ." T. F. Torrance, "The Place of the Humanity of Christ," 8. See T. F. Torrance, *Royal Priesthood: A Theology of Ordained Ministry*, 40. Notably, these criticisms are absent from the later appraisal in *Scottish Theology*. In fact, Torrance urges us to see "the supreme importance of John McLeod Campbell and his great book *The Nature of the Atonement*, in which he rightly warned us against thinking of the atonement in purely penal terms." T. F. Torrance, *Atonement*, 72. See the discussion of Torrance's interaction with Campbell in Rankin, "Carnal Union," 59–67.

62. Campbell, *Atonement*, 118.

63. T. F. Torrance, *The Doctrine of Jesus Christ*, 173; Campbell, *Atonement*, 118. Here we see the interlocked nature of *poena* and *poenitentia*. Campbell "did wrestle very seriously, as no one else in his generation, with the saving significance of the human obedience of Jesus as the *Amen* of truth to the Divine Will." T. F. Torrance, "The Place of the Humanity of Christ," 8. On Christ as our perfect Amen to God see: T. F. Torrance, *Conflict and Agreement in the Church: The Ministry and the Sacraments of the Gospel*, 68–70; T. F. Torrance, "The Atoning Obedience of Christ," 76; The Church of Scotland, *Interim Report*, 48–51.

oneness of mind with the divine judgment on sin, and a submission to the sentence of death.[64]

Torrance also speaks of this priestly penitence or confession in terms of ὁμολογία as used in the epistle to the Hebrews.[65]

> In each case it sets forth primarily the confession made by the High Priest as he enters within the veil. It is the confession of our sin before God and the confession of God's righteous judgment upon our sin. As Apostle Christ bears witness for God, that He is Holy. As High Priest He acknowledges that witness and says Amen to it. . . . But this confession and intercession are not to be understood in terms of word only, but in terms of the actual historical events of the life and passion of Christ.[66]

In conjunction with the texts from Hebrews, Torrance appeals to David's confession in Psalm 51 to elucidate the nature of this confession.

> There we have a confession of a divine righteousness and judgment, and of human sins deserving judgment, confession in which there is no resentment against God's righteousness or against its judgment on us. Confession in holiness is the supreme act of confession in which there is enshrined a perfect oneness between the mind of God and the mind of man.[67]

---

64. Hart, "Anslem and Campbell," 329. Cited in Redding, *Prayer and the Priesthood*, 199.

65. Hebrews 3:1, 4:14, 10:23. T. F. Torrance, *Atonement*, 69, 88–89; T. F. Torrance, *Royal Priesthood: A Theology of Ordained Ministry*, 12, 14.

66. T. F. Torrance, *Royal Priesthood: A Theology of Ordained Ministry*, 12. See also T. F. Torrance, *Atonement*, 89. "That confession was the translation of the Word or truth of God into our flesh and blood in the whole life of Jesus, and the whole life of Jesus was at the same time his answering confession of that divine truth . . . he was the truth of God done into our flesh, which condemned sin in the flesh. But he was also the obedient answer of humanity to that truth, and so from beginning to end when he witnessed a good confession before Pontius Pilate he was 'the true and faithful witness, the amen.'" In this context Torrance also asserts: "In the three instances of *homologia* or 'confession' in the epistle to the Hebrews what is set forth is primarily the confession made by the high priest as he enters within the veil into the holy presence of God. It is the confession of our sin and the confession of God's righteous judgement upon our sin." Yet, it is clear that in all three passages it is the church's confession, not Christ's, which is in view.

67. T. F. Torrance, *Atonement*, 89. "In the words of the 51st Psalm it was an acknowledgement before God of our sin, and of sin as against God only, that God might be justified in his word against us and be supreme in his judgment . . . and so Christ descended into the deepest depths of our guilt and submitted to the complete judgment of God upon it." T. F. Torrance, *Atonement*, 121.

Thus, this confession, and the vicarious repentance of which it is an indispensable part, extends across the whole life of Christ. It is "an enacted acknowledgement . . . a complete acknowledgement and a complete acquiescence in complete judgment."[68]

Jesus As Believer: Vicarious Faith

If Christ substitutes and acts for us in all our human responses, then it follows that he also exercised a vicarious faith. All of these vicarious responses are intelligible in Torrance's theology only on the premise of Christ's assumption of our fallen humanity. In this case that entails stepping into our condition of infidelity.

> We must think of Jesus as stepping into the relation between the faithfulness of God and the *actual unfaithfulness* of human beings, actualizing the faithfulness of God and restoring the faithfulness of human beings by grounding it in the incarnate medium of his own faithfulness so that it answers perfectly to the divine faithfulness. Thus Jesus steps into the *actual situation* where we are summoned to have faith in God, to believe and trust in him, and he acts in our place and in our stead *from within the depths of our unfaithfulness* and provides us freely with a faithfulness in which we may share. He does that as Mediator between God and man, yet precisely as man united to us and *taking our place at every point* where we human beings act as human beings and are called to have faith in the Father, to believe in him and trust him, That is to say, if we think of belief, trust or faith as forms of human activity before God, then we must think of Jesus Christ as believing, trusting and having faith in God the Father on our behalf and in our place.[69]

There is, then, a two-fold faithfulness at work in the incarnation. "Jesus Christ is thus not only the incarnation of the divine *pistis*, but He is the embodiment and actualization of man's *pistis* in covenant with God."[70]

---

68. T. F. Torrance, *Atonement*, 121; T. F. Torrance, *Incarnation*, 123.

69. T. F. Torrance, *The Mediation of Christ*, 82–82. Italics mine.

70. T. F. Torrance, *Conflict and Agreement in the Church: The Ministry and the Sacraments of the Gospel*, 80. "All that is remarkably summed up in 2 Cor. 1:18 f., according to which Jesus Christ is not only the faithful Yes of God to man, but is also the faithful Amen of man to God." T. F. Torrance, *Conflict and Agreement in the Church: The Ministry and the Sacraments of the Gospel*, 81. See The Church of Scotland, *Interim Report*, 47–48. "Jesus Christ is the Truth of God actualized in our midst, the incarnate faithfulness of God, but He is also man keeping faith and truth with God in a perfect

The concept of vicarious faith deals with this polarity from the human side. "Jesus Christ is not only Word of God to man, but Believer."[71] This means that Jesus lived the life of "the perfect believer, who believed for us, and who yielded to God's faithfulness the perfect response of trust and faith."[72] In this manner "he became at once the author and perfecter of faith."[73]

This conception of Jesus' faith does not preclude the necessity, or the reality, of a response from believers.[74] Rather, human faith is grounded upon the faithfulness of God.

> Rom. 1:17: "The righteousness of God is revealed from faith (*pisteos*) to faith (*pistin*)." That is to say, the righteousness of God is revealed from God's *pistis* to man's *pistis*, but man's *pistis* is his implication in the divine *pistis*. God draws man within the sphere of His own faithfulness and righteousness and gives man to share in it, so that his faith is embraced in God's faithfulness.[75]

More precisely, our faith is implicated in "the faithfulness of Christ Jesus (*pistis Christou Iesou*) of which St. Paul speaks so often."[76] Torrance reads a host of texts, generally interpreted as speaking of faith *in* Christ, as referring in a dual manner to first, and primarily, the faith (or faithfulness) *of* Christ, and secondarily, to our human acts of believing.[77]

---

correspondence between His life and activity in the flesh and the Word of God." T. F. Torrance, *God and Rationality*, 154. See T. F. Torrance, *Theological Science*, 50. Here the Truth of God "condescends to us . . . stoops down in pity and mercy to reveal Himself to us in our lowliness and brokenness and earthiness." In Christ God enters "into the midst of our hostility to the Truth . . . to be the Truth of God to man and the Truth of man toward God." T. F. Torrance, *Theological Science*, 188, 190.

71. T. F. Torrance, *Theology in Reconstruction*, 131, 159–60. "If it was in his humanity in entire solidarity with us that Jesus Christ stood in our place . . . then this includes the fact that He believed for us, offering to God in His vicarious faithfulness, the perfect response of human faith which we could not offer." T. F. Torrance, *God and Rationality*, 154. In equivalent "Torrancian" language, Jesus' faith is part of the divinely provided way of covenant response.

72. T. F. Torrance, *Incarnation*, 125. "He is also Believer, but Believer for us, vicariously Believer, whose very humanity is the embodiment of our salvation." T. F. Torrance, *Conflict and Agreement in the Church: The Ministry and the Sacraments of the Gospel*, 81.

73. Hebrews 12:2, T. F. Torrance, *Incarnation*, 138. See The Church of Scotland, *Interim Report*, 50.

74. See Torrance's denial of such an implication in T. F. Torrance, *The Mediation of Christ*, xii, 81–84.

75. T. F. Torrance, *Conflict and Agreement in the Church: The Ministry and the Sacraments of the Gospel*, 79.

76. Ibid., 78.

77. Included are: Rom 3:22; Gal 2:16, 20; 3:22. See T. F. Torrance, *Conflict and*

In most of these passages the *pistis Iesou Christou* does not refer only either to the faithfulness of Christ or to the answering faithfulness of man, but is essentially a polarized expression denoting the faithfulness of Christ as its main ingredient but also involving or at least suggesting the answering faithfulness of man, and so his belief in Christ, but even within itself the faithfulness of Christ involves both the faithfulness of God and the faithfulness of the man Jesus.[78]

Torrance's thought here comes out most forcefully in "those striking words of St Paul in his Epistle to the Galatians, 2:20, which give succinct expression to the evangelical truth which we have been trying to clarify."

> "I am crucified with Christ: nevertheless I live, yet not I but Christ lives in me; and the life which I now live in the flesh I live by faith, the *faithfulness* of the Son of God who loved me and gave himself for me." This is surely the insight that we must allow to inform all our human responses to God, whether they be in faith, conversion and personal decision, worship and prayer, the holy sacraments. or the proclamation of the Gospel: "I, yet not I, but Christ." This applies even to faith.[79]

Agreement in the Church: The Ministry and the Sacraments of the Gospel, 79–80.

78. T. F. Torrance, *Conflict and Agreement in the Church: The Ministry and the Sacraments of the Gospel*, 80. "Faith is thus a polar concept that reposes upon and derives from the prior faithfulness of God which has been permanently translated into our actual human existence in Jesus Christ." T. F. Torrance, *Theology in Reconstruction*, 159. Also, T. F. Torrance, *The School of Faith: The Catechisms of the Reformed Church*, cviii–cix.

79. Torrance continues: "I am convinced that the peculiar expression which St Paul used to express the faith-relationship with Christ should be translated as I have rendered it, but even if it is translated as 'by faith in the Son of God,' the self-correction made by St Paul applies, 'not I but Christ.' That is to say, when I say 'I believe' or 'I have faith,' I must correct myself and add 'not I but Christ in me.' That is the message of the vicarious humanity of Jesus Christ on which the Gospel tells me I may rely: that Jesus Christ in me believes in my place and at the same time takes up my poor faltering and stumbling faith into his—'Lord, I believe, help my unbelief'—embracing, upholding and undergirding it through his invariant faithfulness." T. F. Torrance, *The Mediation of Christ*, 98. This means there are two "I's," or two natures, in the Christian. He is perfect in Christ, yet in his "visible psychological personality" he is still peccator. The two natures exist in a "quasi-hypostatic or eschatological relation." T. F. Torrance, *Conflict and Agreement in the Church: Order and Disorder*, 47. For additional uses of Gal 2:20 in the sense of "the faithfulness of Jesus Christ" see T. F. Torrance, *The Christian Doctrine of God*, 154; T. F. Torrance, *Incarnation*, 28; T. F. Torrance, *A Passion for Christ*, 24–25; T. F. Torrance, *Preaching Christ Today*, 31; T. F. Torrance, *Scottish Theology: From John Knox to John McLeod Campbell*, 19.

Vicarious Reception of the Spirit

As the eternal Son of God in communion with the eternal Spirit, Jesus did not need the Spirit, "but his baptism set forth the fact that it was our humanity in him that was baptized and anointed."[80] This vicarious reception of the Spirit precedes his baptism and extends across the whole of his life.

> Jesus Christ was born of the Virgin Mary into our human nature through the power of the Spirit; at his Baptism the Holy Spirit descended upon him and anointed him as the Christ. He was never without the Spirit for as the eternal Son he ever remained in the unity of the Spirit and of the Father, but as the Incarnate Son on earth he was given the Spirit without measure and consecrated in his human nature for his mission as the vicarious Servant. He came through the temptations in the wilderness clothed with the power of the Spirit and went forth to bring in the Kingdom of God by meeting and defeating the powers of darkness entrenched in human flesh. He struggled and prayed in the Spirit with unspeakable cries of agony, and bore in his Spirit the full burden of human evil and woe. Through the eternal Spirit he offered himself without spot to the Father in sacrifice for sin; according to the Spirit of Holiness he was raised from the dead, and ascended to the right hand of the Father to receive all power in heaven and earth. There he attained the ground from which he could pour out the Spirit of God upon all flesh.[81]

In this manner, through the atoning union, the Spirit has been "adapted" to dwell in our human nature, and our human nature has been "adapted" to receive the Spirit.[82] This is, as we have come to expect, both a

---

80. T. F. Torrance, *Theology in Reconstruction*, 200. "It behooved Christ also to be man that he might receive the Spirit of God in our human nature and mediate it to his brethren through himself." The world cannot know or receive the Spirit "apart from Jesus Christ and what happened to our human nature in him." T. F. Torrance, *Theology in Reconstruction*, 245–46. See T. F. Torrance, *Conflict and Agreement in the Church: The Ministry and the Sacraments of the Gospel*, 113–14; T. F. Torrance, "The Atoning Obedience of Christ," 77; T. F. Torrance, *The Christian Doctrine of God*, 148.

81. T. F. Torrance, *Theology in Reconstruction*, 246. See T. F. Torrance, *The Trinitarian Faith*, 61; T. F. Torrance, *Incarnation*, 135–36.

82. "Hence in the union of divine and human natures in the Son the eternal Spirit of the living God has composed himself, as it were, to dwell with human nature, and human nature has been adapted and become accustomed to receive and bear that same Holy Spirit." T. F. Torrance, *Theology in Reconstruction*, 246; T. F. Torrance, *The Trinitarian Faith*, 32. "[T]hrough the incarnate life of the Son the Holy Spirit, who in the eternal God is the consubstantial communion between the Father and the Son, has accustomed

sanctifying action and one which, due to the non-assumptus, precipitates judgment. "This immanence of the Holy Spirit inevitably means that the Holiness of God is brought to bear upon the ontological roots of our sinful being in fearful judgment which we are quite unable to bear."[83] And it is precisely there, "in the ontological depths of human existence," "making our lost and damned condition his own," that Jesus "has made himself the dwelling place of Holy Spirit."[84]

This means that it is in the power of the Spirit that Christ makes his agonizing advance in our flesh. Alluding to Basil, Torrance adds the Lukan προέκοπτεν to the vicarious reception of the Spirit in the life of the incarnate Son. "Christ became incarnate through the operation of the Holy Spirit, and it was through the power of the Spirit that he made that advance or *prokope*, as it was through the power of the Spirit that he wrought miracles, and was raised from the dead."[85]

> It was only at infinite cost that Jesus Christ gained for us the gift of the Holy Spirit, receiving him in all his consuming holiness into the human nature which he took from our fallen and alienated condition. We shall never fathom the depth of

---

himself, as Irenaeus once expressed it, to dwell with man and adapted human nature to receive him and be possessed by him." T. F. Torrance, *Theology in Reconciliation*, 102. Torrance cites Athanasius to the same effect, see T. F. Torrance, *The Trinitarian Faith*, 190. This is a significant part of the "blessed exchange," whereby Christ assumes our "sinful and dying humanity," and transfers to us his filial life and purity. See Colyer, "Holy Spirit," 162.

83. T. F. Torrance, "The Goodness and Dignity of Man," 320. "But that is the Spirit in which Jesus emitted his cries of anguish as he healed the sick and groaned as he raised Lazarus from the dead, for it was already an offering of himself through the Spirit in atonement for Lazarus.... All through his life and ministry, from the baptism to the cross, he was at work in holy atonement, bearing the sins of the world on his spirit, and through the Spirit offering himself in sacrifice to God." T. F. Torrance, *Incarnation*, 136.

84. T. F. Torrance, "The Goodness and Dignity of Man," 320–21. "Through the reconciling sacrifice of Christ the profound ontological tension between our human being and the Holy Spirit has been healed." Also, T. F. Torrance, *Theology in Reconstruction*, 237: "It is only with the reconciliation of the world, and the removal of the enmity between man and God, that the Spirit of God may be poured out upon his creatures without consuming them in judgment."

85. "That operation of the Spirit is what we see taking place in the *prokope* of Jesus Christ, for since he came to share our human nature and we are united to him through the Spirit which he gives us, it is through the power of the same Spirit that we participate in *prokope*, and so rise through the Son to true knowledge of, and communion with, God the Father." T. F. Torrance, *Theology in Reconstruction*, 39. Thus, through the vicarious reception of the Spirit "upon our humanity which he wears ... the doors of heaven are opened and the divine blessings are poured out." T. F. Torrance, "The Atoning Obedience of Christ," 77.

> the humiliation and passion that were his or the indescribable tension into which he entered for our sakes. . . . Until he had sanctified himself and perfected in our human nature his one offering for all men . . . the Kingdom of Heaven could not be opened to believers and the blessing of the divine Spirit could not be poured out upon human flesh.[86]

This vicarious reception of the Spirit is what we, in our subjective appropriation of the Spirit, are given to share.

> Our receiving of the Spirit is objectively grounded in and derives from Christ who as the incarnate Son was anointed with the Spirit in his humanity and endowed with the Spirit without measure, not for his own sake . . . but for our sakes, and who then mediates the Spirit to us through himself.[87]

This reception "is not independent of or different from the vicarious receiving of the Spirit by Christ himself but is a sharing in it."[88] Thus, the Spirit actualizes in us what has been accomplished once for all in the incarnate Christ's healing assumption of our fallen flesh.[89] The mystery of our participation, and its express connection to the Spirit in the life of Christ, is affirmed in yet another citation of Galatians 2:20:

> How the "I" of the human believer and the "I" of Christ are related to one another, expressed for example in the Pauline statement, "I, yet not I but Christ," is a miracle of the Spirit, and is ultimately as inexplicable as the miracle of the Virgin Birth of Jesus which for me is the unique God-given pattern of unconditional grace.[90]

---

86. T. F. Torrance, *Theology in Reconstruction*, 247.

87. T. F. Torrance, *The Christian Doctrine of God*, 148.

88. Ibid. "In the activity of the Spirit . . . God unites us with Christ in such a way that his human agency in vicarious response to the Father overlaps with our response, gathers it up in its embrace, sanctifying, affirming and upholding it in himself." T. F. Torrance, *Theology in Reconciliation*, 103. The epistemological relevance of the Spirit's work in uniting us to Christ is discussed in T. F. Torrance, *God and Rationality*, 165–92.

89. T. F. Torrance, *The School of Faith: The Catechisms of the Reformed Church*, cvi–cix. Here Torrance, relying on Craig's Catechism of 1581, asserts that there is only one union of God and man, the one wrought in the incarnate life of Christ. Our "spiritual union" is not another union, but a participation in this one "carnal union." For critical interaction see Rankin, "Carnal Union," 119–45.

90. T. F. Torrance, *The Mediation of Christ*, xii. This reception of the Spirit, already vicariously received by Christ, is another instance of "the logic of grace."

The Temptations of Jesus

Although Christ endured temptation throughout the whole of his life, it is immediately after his baptism that the situation intensifies. In the Synoptic Gospels we see that

> he was immediately thrust into the wilderness where he, who had just been baptized in solidarity with sinners with the Baptism into repentance … was tempted and entered upon His redemptive work, being obedient to the Will of God where we were disobedient.[91]

He was born into his passion, and "into that passion he was thrust right away in his temptations when he was tempted to evade the cross."[92]

These temptations involve a number of interlocked factors. First, there is the temptation not to be man.

> With what force the temptations came as He exposed Himself to our weakness and frailty after forty days fasting, temptations to live after all as Son of God and not as Son of Man in all the weakness and frailty of man. "If Thou be the Son of God, command these stones to be made bread." And so one after another the Devil assaulted Him with the temptation simply to be what He was, and to live the life of who He was, the mighty omnipotent Son of God.[93]

Second, there is a ferocious attempt to divide the Son from the Father.

> The forces of darkness did their utmost to divide the Son from the Father by breaking his trust in God and diverting him from the way of the Cross, through temptations that were all the more fearful as they were put to him on the very ground of his divine Sonship, temptations to which he was subjected not only in the wilderness immediately after his Baptism or throughout his earthly ministry, but above all in Gethsemane and even on the Cross itself.[94]

---

91. T. F. Torrance, *Conflict and Agreement in the Church: The Ministry and the Sacraments of the Gospel*, 107–8 See T. F. Torrance, *The Mediation of Christ*, 36–37.

92. T. F. Torrance, *Incarnation*, 70. "[H]e was driven by the Spirit like a scapegoat into a waste land where under the burden of our sin he became the prey of the forces of darkness which sought to wrench him away from his mission as the Servant of the Lord." T. F. Torrance, *The Mediation of Christ*, 36–37.

93. T. F. Torrance, "The Atoning Obedience of Christ," 76. See T. F. Torrance, *Incarnation*, 72, 124; T. F. Torrance, *Theology in Reconstruction*, 200–1.

94. T. F. Torrance, *The Mediation of Christ*, 65. "Therefore all the powers of evil

Third, as the last sentence above shows, these temptations, like the conflict within the incarnate person of the mediator generally, become increasingly more intense as Jesus progresses toward the cross.[95]

Finally, Torrance is emphatic on the role of the non-assumptus in providing realism, depth, and integrity to the temptations of Jesus.

> [U]nless we take seriously at this point the fact that Christ assumed our will, the will of estranged man in an estranged Adamic human nature, in order to suffer all its temptations and to resist them and to condemn sin in our human nature, and then to bend back the will of man into oneness with the divine will, it is difficult to give the temptations of Christ their full place, and therefore the human obedience of Christ in struggle against the onslaught of evil and sin its full and proper place in atoning reconciliation.[96]

Thus, Jesus' obedience "from within our alienated humanity was a struggle with our sin and temptation."[97]

The Prayer Life of Jesus

Jesus' prayer life is also an integral part of his redeeming activity. His "holding fast to God in prayer" against the dark powers, "the fearful struggles of prayer with strong crying and tears, 'not my will but Thine be done,' all that

---

launched their attack upon Jesus; fearful temptations and assaults fell upon Him, all in order to isolate Him from God, to break the bond of fellowship between them, to snap the life of prayer and obedient clinging to the heavenly Father, to destroy the life of obedience to God's Will and Word, and so to destroy the ground of reconciliation, to disrupt the foundation of atonement being laid in the obedient and prayerful life of the Son of Man." T. F. Torrance, "The Atoning Obedience of Christ," 70. See T. F. Torrance, *Atonement*, 216; T. F. Torrance, *Incarnation*, 119.

95. T. F. Torrance, "The Atoning Obedience of Christ," 71; T. F. Torrance, *Incarnation*, 119; T. F. Torrance, *Conflict and Agreement in the Church: Order and Disorder*, 240–41.

96. T. F. Torrance, *Incarnation*, 212.

97. T. F. Torrance, *Theology in Reconstruction*, 132. From the perspective of our alienated mind and Christ's assumption of it, Torrance criticizes Apollinarius: "By eliminating from Jesus what corresponds to 'the inward man' in us, and replacing it by a divine Mind or Spirit, which by definition is immutable and unchangeable and sinless, it deprives Jesus of fully human experience, and therefore of sharing with us our experience to the full, our birth, growth, death, our pain, anguish, distress, agitation, and what is more our incapacity and temptation, and our human existence in a condition of servitude and humiliation." T. F. Torrance, *Theology in Reconciliation*, 147–48.

belongs to the innermost heart of the reconciling and atoning life of Jesus."[98] Indeed, Jesus' whole life is construed as redemptive prayer. His perfect obedience is called "the prayer which is the whole assent of Jesus to the will of God as it confronts the will of man."[99]

Thus, Jesus' life of prayer is brought into the closest connection to his passion. Alluding to Calvin, Torrance says, "Christ in his intercession joined to the shedding of his blood prayers that our sins may be pardoned."[100] In reference to the prayer of John 17, Torrance writes:

> added to his vicarious passion set forth in the supper, he presented himself before the face of the Father and presented us to the Father as included in himself who had come just for this purpose to stand in our place. Then he went forth to Gethsemane and to the cross, where in high priestly intercession and sacrifice he fulfilled in deed and in death the prayer of his whole incarnate life.[101]

All of this takes place in the depths of our fallen humanity. Jesus offers "from within man's alienated life, a truly childlike and filial obedience in prayer and petition to the heavenly Father."[102] We have already seen that the "not my will" in Gethsemane is taken by Torrance to mean "not the fallen will I have assumed." In that context, Torrance puts the assumption of our fallen humanity in relation to Christ's vicarious prayer life vividly.

> It is in our place that Jesus prays, standing where we stand in our rebellion and alienation, existing where we exist in our refusal of divine grace and in our will to be independent, to live our own life in self-reliance. In that condition, Jesus prays against the whole trend of our existence and against all the self-willed movement of our life.[103]

---

98. T. F. Torrance, "The Atoning Obedience of Christ," 70–71; T. F. Torrance, *Incarnation*, 119. In this context Torrance speaks of the "great paliggenesia" as the fruit of the "worshipping and praying obedience" of Jesus.

99. T. F. Torrance, *Royal Priesthood: A Theology of Ordained Ministry*, 13; T. F. Torrance, *Atonement*, 275.

100. T. F. Torrance, *Incarnation*, 120; T. F. Torrance, *Scottish Theology: From John Knox to John McLeod Campbell*, 306.

101. T. F. Torrance, *Incarnation*, 120.

102. Ibid., 118. "In his steadfast obedience and life of prayer, Jesus penetrated into our life and recreated the bond between man and God, and therefore also between human beings." Ibid., 120.

103. Ibid., 117.

Thus, praying "from within our alienation and in battle against our self-will . . . we are given to overhear: 'Not my will (that is, not the will of the alienated humanity which Jesus has made his own), but thy will be done.'"[104] A similar understanding prevails with respect to the Lord's prayer. It is first Christ's prayer "which he prayed with us in our flesh,"[105] and thus it becomes our prayer. "Therefore, he also puts *his own prayer* in our unclean mouth that on the ground of his obedience and prayer, we may pray *with him*, 'Our Father who art in heaven.'"[106] His life is the fulfillment of the first three petitions of the Lord's prayer, "and also the redemption of mankind as the second half of the Lord's prayer makes clear."[107]

This means that Christ himself *is* our prayer. He is "the one, all sufficient and eternal oblation of mankind," who "lifted up our human nature in worship and prayer and adoration to God."[108] He is the vicarious prayer with which we respond to the Father.[109] This means, of course, that our prayers are not an independent offering, but a participation in the prayer that is Christ's life.

> Our prayer in Christ which is directed through him and with him and in him to the Father is prayer in which we rely on Christ's prayer offered on our behalf, for in Christ we are turned away in our praying from resting on ourselves to rest on his vicarious prayer, which he prayed not only in word but in life, in complete self-offering to the Father.[110]

The Teaching Ministry of Jesus

The teaching ministry of the Word made flesh, which Torrance associates with his office as prophet,[111] "is an essential element of His atoning work, in-

---

104. Ibid., 117–18.

105. T. F. Torrance, *Atonement*, 275.

106. T. F. Torrance, *Incarnation*, 120. Italics mine. See T. F. Torrance, "The Atoning Obedience of Christ," 72; T. F. Torrance, *Atonement*, 274; T. F. Torrance, *Space, Time and Resurrection*, 116.

107. T. F. Torrance, *Incarnation*, 122.

108. T. F. Torrance, *Theology in Reconstruction*, 248. See T. F. Torrance, *God and Rationality*, 156–58.

109. T. F. Torrance, *The Mediation of Christ*, 88; T. F. Torrance, *Royal Priesthood: A Theology of Ordained Ministry*, 14.

110. T. F. Torrance, *Theology in Reconciliation*, 141, 109–10; T. F. Torrance, *The Mediation of Christ*, 88–89.

111. T. F. Torrance, *Atonement*, 59, 265, 277.

asmuch as revelation and reconciliation cannot for a moment be separated from one another."[112] This follows from the deepest structures of Torrance's theology. We recall here that the prophets of Israel insisted that the law and cult be "done into the flesh." This entails a primacy of the Word which accents the importance of Jesus' teaching ministry.

> Jesus steps into the tradition of the cult prophets and it is primarily as Word of God that He approaches the Cross, but it is the Word made flesh. He is at once the Word of God to man and for the first time a real word of man to God.[113]

In the oneness of his person and work he *is* the truth. Thus, the person of Christ and his teaching are inseparable.[114] Put in the noetic categories we examined earlier, "in spite of all the contradiction of sin,"[115] the mystery of the union of God and man in Christ is "inserted into the midst of our knowledge."[116] Thus, his incarnate existence is "the redemption of man's estranged and rebellious mind."[117]

The fact that "the self-revelation of Jesus is given as much through the unfolding drama of his life . . . as by word"[118] means that his teaching has a dynamic movement akin to his life. "He deliberately holds back revelation by word so that it may *keep pace* with revelation through the dynamic movement of his advance to the hour of eschatological completion on the cross."[119] This means that the revelatory atoning ministry of Christ is not simply something which happens *ad intra* upon our assumed and alienated mind, it also has a profound *ad extra* dimension.

---

112. T. F. Torrance, *The School of Faith: The Catechisms of the Reformed Church*, lxxxix "[H]is teaching and praying . . . his miracles and parables, are an integral part of his atonement." T. F. Torrance, *Theology in Reconstruction*, 202. "The teaching of Jesus was an essential part of the atonement, and the atonement could not have taken place without it." T. F. Torrance, *Conflict and Agreement in the Church: The Ministry and the Sacraments of the Gospel*, 90; T. F. Torrance, *Incarnation*, 173.

113. T. F. Torrance, *Royal Priesthood: A Theology of Ordained Ministry*, 8. See T. F. Torrance, *Atonement*, 66–67; T. F. Torrance, *Incarnation*, 64.

114. T. F. Torrance, *Conflict and Agreement in the Church: The Ministry and the Sacraments of the Gospel*, 69.

115. T. F. Torrance, *Incarnation*, 173.

116. T. F. Torrance, *Conflict and Agreement in the Church: The Ministry and the Sacraments of the Gospel*, 90; T. F. Torrance, *Incarnation*, 172–73; T. F. Torrance, *Atonement*, 162–63.

117. T. F. Torrance, *The Trinitarian Faith*, 166.

118. T. F. Torrance, *Incarnation*, 21.

119. Ibid.; T. F. Torrance, *Theology in Reconstruction*, 120.

> Thus the faithfulness of Jesus to the word of the Father in hearing and receiving it within our frail humanity and his faithfulness in teaching it *and imparting it to those whom he had made his fellows in human weakness,* forms an essential part of his reconciling work in reinstating mankind in fellowship and communion with the living and true God.[120]

As we have seen, Torrance refers to these two dimensions as the ontic and noetic, respectively, with the ontic being primary.[121] The ontic is internal, and the noetic includes Jesus' external interactions with others. Thus, his solidarity with us rests

> not only on assumption of our humanity into oneness with himself, but on the interpenetration of Jesus into the lives of people, of men and women through his personal relations, in which he entwined himself more and more with them in their lives, burdens, sins and weaknesses, all in the most acutely personal fashion that led directly to the crucifixion.[122]

Jesus As the Good Shepherd

Taking Mark 6:34[123] as his primary text, in conjunction with his acts of feeding the multitudes, and "the great parables of the shepherd and the sheep in the Synoptics and the fourth Gospel," Torrance concludes that the image of a compassionate shepherd "was one of the major ways in which Jesus regarded his own ministry to lost and damned humanity."[124] In often moving and graphic terms, Torrance describes the sympathy involved:

> Jesus looks upon the multitudes of men and women as the disinherited and lost, and he pours out his life in compassionate

---

120. T. F. Torrance, *Atonement*, 163. Italics mine. Thus, the atoning healing of the mind of man is construed as happening both in the incarnate humanity of the mediator, and in his personal interaction with others.

121. The ontic corresponds to anhypostasia and the noetic to enhypostasia. See T. F. Torrance, *The School of Faith: The Catechisms of the Reformed Church*, lxxxi–lxxxii; T. F. Torrance, *Atonement*, 161–64.

122. T. F. Torrance, *Atonement*, 161–62. "He penetrated into the depths of our personal existence *and human society in sin*, taking the conflict into his innermost being." T. F. Torrance, *Incarnation*, 112. Italics mine.

123. "As he landed he saw a great throng, and he *had compassion* on them, because they were like sheep without a shepherd; and he began to teach them many things." Torrance's translation and italics.

124. T. F. Torrance, *Incarnation*, 129–30.

service for them, standing in the gap where there is no shepherd, and taking their hurt and their troubles to himself. He lays all their guilt and need upon himself, bearing it in his mercy, shepherding the flock in spite of all that they do to him, even when they turn round and smite the shepherd and cry 'crucify him, crucify him.'[125]

When the Gospels speak of Jesus having compassion on the multitude, the word they use "is one of the most pregnant and profound in the whole of the New Testament"[126]—ἐσπλαγχνίσθη.[127] Torrance relates this to the visceral bowels of the mercy of God.

> What Jesus does then is described by this word, *splagchnizesthai*. He has made himself one body with sinners and feels for them as a mother toward her unborn baby, and he pours himself out in love for them; his whole inner self is poured out for men and women in their weakness and need and sin.[128]

In Jesus, "God has bound himself with our flesh, and as such, one body with us, he penetrates into our weakness and need with his indescribable compassion."[129] This compassion came at great cost and was accompanied by interior anguish which "was evident in the way in which Jesus groaned in agony as he forgave and healed. It cost him infinite anguish. It was only by that kind of *splagchnizesthai* that he could heal and forgive, by bearing the awful burden of our *astheneia*[130] upon himself."[131] He "seeks to be yoked together with people in their awful burdens of sin and guilt that he may bear them."[132] The result is that Jesus forgave and healed "only as he bowed himself to receive the just judgment upon our human sin and guilt."[133]

This entry into our need as shepherd also partakes of the dynamic of increasing intensity which we have seen in the other aspects of Christ's earthly

---

125. T. F. Torrance, *Incarnation*, 131.

126. Ibid., 132.

127. See Mark 6:34, Matt 9:36.

128. T. F. Torrance, *Incarnation*, 132.

129. Ibid., 133–34.

130. Weakness or infirmity, cf. Matt 8:17.

131. T. F. Torrance, *Incarnation*, 134–35. Torrance cites a number of incidents from the Synoptics where Jesus either groaned or sighed in healing.

132. Ibid., 135. Behind this "lies the idea of the high priest in the Old Testament liturgy who bore on his shoulders and breast the names of the twelve tribes of Israel, who had them written on his heart, as he entered within the veil of the holy of holies with the blood of sacrifice in order to intercede for them." Ibid., 133.

133. Ibid., 136.

life. Referring to Hebrews 2:10, Torrance says, "'making perfect' refers to his ordeal of consecration when before the cross he entered more and more into compassionate and sympathetic solidarity with lost and guilty sinners, bringing his relation of solidarity with them to its purposed end in the cross."[134]

Jesus as King of the Kingdom

Jesus' role as king has a strong affinity with his active obedience. It is "the way in which Christ broke into our captivity to redeem us and save us, but 'the mighty act' of God here is the holiness of Jesus' life, for it was through his holy life within our alienated humanity that he broke the thraldom of evil and emancipated us from its power."[135] The kingdom which Jesus manifests, and which provokes the crisis of increasing intensity, is the divine instrument whereby he penetrates into our lost estate.

> It was in that perfect holy obedience of his life as true man in the midst of sinful men and women that Jesus collided with the dark forces of evil which had entrenched themselves in the flesh (*sarx*) of humanity. The sovereign presence (*parousia*) of this king is everywhere characterized by divine authority or *exousia*, for in the coming and presence (i.e. *parousia*) of Jesus, the mighty Son of God and the holy one of Israel, the heavenly power of God himself impinges upon the fallen world in direct challenge and conflict, in struggle with the powers of darkness and in victory over all the forces of evil.[136]

The incarnation is an "invasion of the mighty Son of God into our domain where evil has come to exercise its sway, in order to break its bonds and deliver us from its captivity."[137]

---

134. Ibid., 137.

135. T. F. Torrance, *Atonement*, 60. Thus, it corresponds to the *padah* aspect of redemption, namely, redemption by the mighty act of God. See T. F. Torrance, *The School of Faith: The Catechisms of the Reformed Church*, xci–xcv. In the latter, and much earlier (1955), citation Torrance correlates the kingly office to the active *and* passive obedience of Jesus. "Here the mighty hand of God was the weakness of Jesus, His passive as well as his active obedience, in which he submitted to all that evil could do to him, and broke its power by a meekness and obedience unto the death of the cross." T. F. Torrance, *The School of Faith: The Catechisms of the Reformed Church*, xciii.

136. T. F. Torrance, *Incarnation*, 236. In the power of the Spirit he "went forth to bring in the Kingdom of God by meeting and defeating the powers of darkness entrenched in human flesh." T. F. Torrance, *Theology in Reconstruction*, 246.

137. T. F. Torrance, *Atonement*, 31. "The Son of God become man is the strong man of Jesus' own parable who invades the tyrant's house, and by his power subdues him, binds him, and spoils him of all he has unjustly usurped." T. F. Torrance, *Incarnation*,

Thus, this aspect of Christ's ministry highlights, not only the assumption of our fallen nature, but the full social and cosmic dimensions of the evil which needs to be confronted.

> Thus it was not only into our contingent and finite condition that the Word of God had to penetrate, but into our sin and alienation where we are subject to the thraldom of evil power, into our guilty existence under the sentence of divine judgment, and into the disintegration of our human being in death. He came, therefore, to share our lost and enslaved existence where it was breaking up under the corrosion of sin and guilt, disease and want, death and judgment, and to enter into the disordered state of our created rationalities in which finite distinctions are damaged and distorted into contradictions, in order to engage with the inhuman forces of darkness that had encroached upon the bodies and minds of men, to struggle with the perverse nature of an alienated creation, to meet the full hostility of evil by accepting and bearing it in Himself, and to make an end of it in His own vicarious life and death.[138]

This conflict comes into sharp relief in Jesus' confrontation with evil men, disease, and the demonic.[139] "By the finger or Spirit of God he brings the power of God to bear upon the whole realm of evil and asserts the sovereignty of God's grace over and in it all."[140] Here the "flesh of sin" is extended beyond the actual human nature of Jesus.

> The battle was joined, the battleground was 'the flesh of sin,' and the enemy was the devil. Jesus invaded the terrain occupied by the enemy and by his authoritative divine presence, his *exousia* in grace and holiness, he laid claim upon it for God the Father ... in order to restore alienated humanity to the ownership of God.[141]

78, 155. See T. F. Torrance, *The Doctrine of Jesus Christ*, 112.

138. T. F. Torrance, *God and Rationality*, 142–43.

139. "Wherever Jesus went, his presence brought conflict with the authorities or powers (*exousiai*) of this world wherever they were found, in the synagogue, in the hearts of rulers, and in the poor bodies of the sick and possessed, the demoniacs and maniacs." T. F. Torrance, *Incarnation*, 237.

140. T. F. Torrance, *Incarnation*, 236. See T. F. Torrance, *The School of Faith: The Catechisms of the Reformed Church*, xcvi–xcviii.

141. T. F. Torrance, *Incarnation*, 237. "[T]here takes place *a struggle with evil will*, a struggle which is waged between God and evil not only in the sinner's heart, not only in their thoughts and desires, but in their bodily and spiritual existence, for the whole creaturely realm is the sphere of this struggle." T. F. Torrance, *Incarnation*, 241.

This is accomplished in Christ's role

> as the lowly one who breaks into the hearts of men and women through submitting to the violence of the violent and thereby storming his way by meekness and passion into the ultimate citadel of evil in order that by atonement he might bring about redemption and emancipation.[142]

This intensifying movement,[143] akin to the sighing and groaning by which he healed and forgave, is provoked by Jesus himself and, in some manner, involves "shouldering" or "absorbing" the evil he confronts.

> Our words and concepts ultimately fail us here, but even if we cannot state it with precision, it is clear in the Gospels that Jesus used the developing situation more and more to enable him to lay hold upon humanity and to shoulder the full load of the world's need and guilt—but to do that he had to exert constant pressure on men and women in order to force them to declare themselves to be toward him what they really were in their hearts, and all the time he was stooping to shoulder their full burden of sin and guilt.[144]

Finally, we must see all of this as an intensely *personal* battle with personal forces of evil.

> [T]herefore even when Jesus heals people of physical distress he does so only through a struggle with evil will. Nowhere does Jesus heal as a human doctor, but always he heals as one who wrestles personally with evil and overcomes it through the conflict of his own holy will with the unholy powers of evil spirit.[145]

---

142. T. F. Torrance, *Incarnation*, 236.

143. This intensification is a matter of necessity because "the will that God opposes and struggles with is so interwoven with the will of man in alienation from God that it is with man that God struggles, but here man under the judgment of God is given by that very judgment an obdurate and brazen character in sin." Ibid., 243.

144. Ibid., 154. "Thus by taking our flesh on himself the Son of God exposed himself to the fearful assault of Satan, and evil and sin; he advanced to meet it at the very summit of its wickedness in crucifying him, drew it all upon himself and slew it as he submitted to the divine judgment upon it." Ibid., 78.

145. Ibid., 241. "The innermost constitution of sin is double—characterized by the act of human rebellion and by the act of divine judgment. In both cases it is personal act. God personally resists sin—that is why God's opposition to sin and his judgment upon is called 'wrath'; for sin is a personal act against the very person of God. It is met in personal relation and is judged in personal action." Ibid., 252.

ANALYSIS AND CRITIQUE

Torrance's presentation of the union between God and man wrought out in the historical life of Christ has a number of compelling features. His account of the baptism of Jesus at the hands of John makes clear that some notion of vicarious repentance and confession is a crucial part of the messianic mission of the Servant of the Lord. His integration of this baptism with the "baptism in blood" on the cross gives depth, unity, and coherence to the historical obedience of Christ. This insight makes clear that the passion was, at the very least, proleptically anticipated in the suffering life of the incarnate mediator. Closely related to this is Torrance's robust doctrine of the active obedience of Christ. While it is not worked out in a bi-covenantal framework, it is, we believe, *mutatis mutandis*, something which the traditional view could appropriate with benefit. In addition, Torrance's contention that, without assuming our fallen and depraved humanity, the temptations of Christ cannot be given their full force and integrity, is a claim any sensitive reader should appreciate. Even if Christ's unyielding obedience, in contrast to our capitulation, makes his experience of temptation more intense than ours, without the non-assumptus there would seem to be a large class of human temptations from which he is immune. Here, the deeply pastoral question of whether God has come all the way into our situation in Christ becomes acute.

Torrance's presentation of the compassion of Jesus, the Good Shepherd, and his mighty kingship in confronting evil and disease, is full of holy pathos and helpful insights. Finally, while it has been a source of contention in Torrance scholarship, his thoroughgoing emphasis on our response to the gospel reposing on Christ's prior work has many helpful features. Our obedience rests on (is "enfolded" in) his obedience, our faith on his prior faithfulness, and our prayer rests on his intercession. There is a deep, albeit provocative and controversial, integration of the work of the Spirit *in* us and the prior work *of* Christ for us.[146]

We turn now to some broad critical questions which must be put to Torrance's presentation. First, on the matter of Jesus' temptations, it would appear that the utter uniqueness of the God-man, which we discussed at the end of the previous chapter, would mitigate the force of Torrance's

---

146. The underlying issue here is whether Torrance leaves any place for real human response to the gospel. Since he conceives of only one union between Christ and us, how is our "spiritual" union with him through faith to be construed as "contained," or "embraced," in his prior "carnal" union with us? See the various views in Smail, *The Giving Gift*, 109–12; Kettler, *Vicarious Humanity*, 138–42; Rankin, "Carnal Union," 14, 285–89. There are important issues at stake here, but our focus is on the life of Christ, and this controversy, we believe, rests on whether or not Torrance has made the non-assumptus intelligible.

argument. He affirms, on the basis of the hypostatic union, not merely the sinlessness, but the impeccability of Christ. While this need not mitigate the reality of the temptations, it does mean that Jesus' confrontation with them is *sui generis*.[147] In addition, the assumption of a fallen nature without the assumption of a fallen person would preclude the presence of past personal sinfulness. Leaving aside the question of the intelligibility of how a fallen nature personally resists, it appears that the temptations of Christ would need to be seen in a more representative manner.

Second, we saw that Torrance, in the context of the *communicatio gratiarum*, speaks of the divine communication of knowledge, will, and power as ceasing at Jesus' baptism.[148] Thenceforth, he lived "only as Son of Man." This does not mean that there is no divine actor, simply that the divine actor takes the form of the meek and obedient humanity of Jesus. The fundamental point is that Jesus did not use the divine majesty to aid himself, or avoid his mission. But, is it credible not to ascribe his miracles, healings, and exorcisms, to his divine power?[149] We detect here, and this is not a charge, a squinting towards the Nestorianism that seems to tempt advocates of the fallen nature view.[150] The actor here is always divine and, thus, never lives only as the Son of Man, even with the qualifications Torrance makes. In his own words, "in the indissoluble fusion of his human life with his divine activity, his vicarious representation of us was backed up by his divine life."[151]

Third, Torrance's assertion of the sinlessness of Jesus needs to be buttressed with an explanation of precisely how it is maintained. It is not clear that his doctrine *must* result in construing Jesus as sinful,[152] but without a definition of "fallen human nature" which excludes sin, there is a cloud of suspicion which looms. Some clarity may be provided by distinguishing sinfulness

---

147. For a defense of impeccability over against mere sinlessness that attempts to give the temptations of Jesus full range, see Crisp, *God Incarante*, 122–36.

148. Despite his denial of a kenotic theory of the incarnation, there appears to be a mild form of it here. See T. F. Torrance, *Incarnation*, 74–76.

149. Even if we ascribe these things to the Spirit, it is still the divine Spirit, received by the divine Son into his humanity, who is the actor. For Trinitarian completeness, we recall that Jesus says it is the Father who is at work in him and he only does what the Father does (John 5:17–19). Note, the Johannine text refers not simply to mighty acts, but all the Son does.

150. See Kapic, "The Son's Assumption of a Human Nature," 162. The tendency exists because somehow this "corruption" must not taint the divine nature. This is not an acute problem for Torrance given the way he reconceives the interaction of the natures. We looked at this in the previous chapter when we examined his view of impassibility.

151. T. F. Torrance, *Atonement*, 274.

152. Though on a classical Reformed notion of original sin there seems to be no way for Torrance to avoid this charge.

as a property of the *hypostasis or person*, and fallenness as a property of the *nature* assumed.[153] Then, since the person of Jesus never sins in the corrupted nature he assumed, perhaps his sinlessness would be intelligible. Torrance is working with this distinction when he says that Jesus does not do what we do in sinful flesh, namely, sin. But problems remain. Torrance affirms that Christ was "made sin" and was yet "without sin."[154] He affirms that he "condemned sin in the flesh" throughout the whole course of his life. It would appear that a definition of sin which excludes the presence of a sinner is also needed.[155] This becomes all the more acute, because Torrance speaks of sin as a personal act which God personally opposes.[156] Another way this surfaces is in the manner Torrance can speak of the nature which Jesus assumed as if it were a fully self-conscious *actor*. It resists, it becomes increasingly recalcitrant, its mind wars against the repentant restructuring it is undergoing. Jesus obeys, Torrance repeatedly asserts, *in the midst of* our disobedience, our "untruth," our rebellion and infidelity. He steps into the *conflict* between God and man. One can be left wondering just how this fallen nature stops short of a full fallen person. Classical Christology holds, and Torrance surely affirms, that natures do not act. Persons act by means of, or through, their natures. In the case of Christ, the Logos acts in and through the (fallen) human nature. In Torrance, this language is probably a function of trying to define the mystery of the battle within Christ, but the lack of a crisp definition of "fallen human nature" does not help the matter.[157]

Fourth, the exegesis Torrance does in connection with our topic seems to yield conclusions which are, at best, merely possible and, at worst, highly unlikely. We have already seen that, with respect to the key text, Romans 8:3, Torrance's reading is in the decided minority.[158] Also, we have noted previously

---

153. See McFarland, "Fallen or Unfallen?"

154. 2 Cor 5:21 and Heb 4:15, respectively. Torrance takes 2 Cor 5:21 to refer to the whole incarnate economy and not a forensic transaction at the cross.

155. Torrance seems to be working with something like the following definition: A malevolent and evil disposition, an alienation of mind and affection, an impurity and rebellion which is bent away from God, under his just wrath and condemnation, which nonetheless, in the life of Jesus, never actually manifests itself in disobedience through the actions of his human will.

156. T. F. Torrance, *Incarnation*, 252.

157. As we asked at the end of the previous chapter: If the sin which God opposes in the flesh Jesus assumed is personal, *who* is the person to whom it belongs and how is that person not a sinner?

158. Even here, assuming that ὁμοιώματι means a concrete instantiation of sinful flesh, one would need a definition of the, admittedly complex, σαρκὸς ἁμαρτίας, which is compatible with "sinful *nature* united to the sinless Logos." On 2 Cor 5:21, Branick, with Torrance and against the virtually unanimous consensus, sees Christ's being

that his understanding of προέκοπτεν in Luke 2:52 is not followed in any English translation, and his understanding of παλιγγενεσια in Titus 3:5 does not refer primarily, if at all, to what happened to our humanity in Christ. The same thing can be said of ὁμολογία in Hebrews, which is not a reference to the High Priest's confession of our sins. When we look at Torrance's claim that the Lord's prayer is Jesus' own prayer, we are confronted with two immediate difficulties. First, it is clearly a prayer he taught to his disciples (this Torrance, of course, also grants), and second, it includes a petition for forgiveness.[159] Again, his understanding of the Lord's petition in Gethsemane, "not my will . . . but thy will be done," as meaning "not my fallen will which I assumed," is far from certain. Even the oft cited texts in the form of Christ is X (e.g., He is the propitiation for our sins, 1 John 2:2), can be read, not as affirming an identity of person and work, but simply as affirming that "Christ is the one who accomplished X." On a matter so controversial and crucial to his overall theology, we would expect exegetical work which entailed more compelling conclusions. However, the main force of Torrance's narrative presentation lies in its overall theological structure. To that subject we now turn.

First, we begin with what might be called the psychological, or anthropological, believability of the portrayal of the inner life of Christ. Atonement takes place *within* the incarnate constitution of the mediator, and it is the product of a fierce internal war. Christ is in an agonizing battle to heal our carnal mind and bend back our wayward will. But if we think, for instance, of Jesus' teaching ministry, this would entail that before he taught, e.g., the Sermon on the Mount, he had to first vigorously resist an interior disposition to teach falsehood. Is this a believable psychological portrait of the teaching ministry? Does Jesus, as the Good Shepherd, have to first "bend back" and overcome our interior lack of compassion before he has compassion on the multitudes? Does he have to resist an indifference toward, or a desire not to heal, the sick and lame before he acts on their behalf?

Second, and more to the heart of our concern, is the state of the humanity of the incarnate Christ throughout the one continuous act of atonement as narrated by Torrance. As with our critique of the once for all union in the virgin birth, here we also lack clarity as to what state the humanity

---

"made sin" (ἁμαρτίαν εποιησεν) as referring to the whole incarnate economy, and not simply the cross. Branick, "Sinful Flesh," 256.

159. Torrance takes this as part of Christ's vicarious confession of our sins, and thus his whole atoning life. "Christ's life of obedience is a hallowing of the Father's name and a fulfilling of his will on earth as it is in heaven, and that is the coming of God's kingdom, and also the redemption of mankind as the second half of the Lord's prayer makes clear, all to the eternal glory of God." T. F. Torrance, *Incarnation*, 122. Thus, though Torrance often calls it the Lord's "own prayer," he does not "pray" the petition for forgiveness as we do. Nevertheless, it is an idiosyncratic reading.

of Christ is in throughout his life. If Jesus is, as Torrance insists, a believer, then his humanity, it would seem, must be compatible with the humanity of a believer. But, if this is the case, his humanity cannot be, *at any point, simply* our lost and damned and alienated humanity. Of course, Torrance affirms that, in the very act of assuming our humanity, Christ also sanctified it. He also affirms that he sanctified it throughout the long course of his obedience. Torrance approvingly notes, "Calvin, following Irenaeus and others, held that our birth is sanctified by the birth of Jesus, our infancy by His infancy, our youth by His youth, and our manhood by His manhood."[160] This means that the healing of our original sin, which Torrance associates with the lifelong union, is a progressive affair. The lifelong obedience "bends back" our enslaved will into obedience to the will of God.

If we focus our concern here on the state of the human *will* of Christ, and incorporate the full scope of Torrance's presentation, we have the following situation:

a) The human will of Christ is under God's just condemnation since, throughout the whole course of his life, Christ "condemned our sin in the flesh," and confessed our sinful will before the Father.

b) The human will of Christ is also perfectly obedient, since Christ is the perfect Amen of man to God's judgment on our wayward will. It is his obedient will which "condemns sin in the flesh," and confesses our sin (including the sins of our wayward will).

c) The human will of Christ is being progressively sanctified, since the atoning union is wrought through all the stages of the Lord's life. The "bending back" of our will is not instantaneous, but it does indeed occur in the life of Christ.

d) The human will (as an aspect of the sinful flesh) becomes increasingly brazen and obdurate, since the situation within the incarnate mediator is one of increasing conflict and intensification.

To say this is an anomalous situation would be an understatement. The *same will* is perfectly obedient, and progressively sanctified, and under just condemnation (construed, we might add, ontologically and not merely

---

160. T. F. Torrance, "The Place of the Humanity of Christ," 5. "[T]hat union with human being was worked out through the whole personal life and growth of man, worked through the growth of Jesus from infancy to adulthood." T. F. Torrance, *Atonement*, 163. Atoning obedience includes "the whole our Lord's incarnate life from his cradle to his grave in which, as one of us and one with us, he shared all our experiences, overcoming our disobedience through his obedience and sanctifying every stage of human life." T. F. Torrance, *The Trinitarian Faith*, 166–67.

forensically), and increasingly hostile, *at every point in the incarnate life of Christ before the cross.*

Now it is possible to bring *some* clarity to this by considering the reality of a believer's struggle with sin. Torrance does this by drawing an analogy between David's confession in Psalm 51 and Christ's perfect confession of our sins. Here we have an act of holy repentance which is, at the same time, an agreement with (an "Amen" to) the judgment of God on one's sin.[161] Thus, we can sense some congruity in the act of a single will obediently confessing its sinfulness, and thus, "condemning sin in the flesh."

Three points are in order here. First, this is intelligible for a believer, a person like David, in covenant with God. Since Jesus is a believer, Torrance would need to construe his post virgin birth humanity as akin to our redeemed, but sub-eschatological, humanity for the analogy to hold. It is not clear that he is willing to do this. Second, Torrance speaks of the struggle between the two natures of the believer, which he says exist in a "quasi-hypostatic or eschatological relation," as having some analogy to the hypostatic union.[162] While this is helpful, it is far from clear how much light it can shed on the unique situation of the human will of Christ. This is especially true when one considers that, for Torrance, the hypostatic union itself is to govern the downstream analogies rather than the reverse. Third, in believers, the progressive sanctification of the will does *not* lead to its progressive hardening.

We conclude this examination of the internal state of Christ's will by affirming that a will which is perfectly obedient, perpetually condemned, progressively sanctified, and increasingly in conflict with the will of God, is not coherent. It is surely out of accord with the Sixth Ecumenical Council (AD 680–681), which declared that the "two natural wills and two natural operations" in Christ "are not contrary to one another . . . but his human will follows *and that not as resisting and reluctant*, but rather as subject to his divine and omnipotent will."[163]

Our final consideration of the continuous union concerns what we have called the *ad extra* dimension of Christ's incarnate ministry. Much of what Torrance affirms here can be viewed in a quite traditional manner. Jesus enters into our need, shoulders our burden, groans and sighs in compassion as he heals and pardons. Yet, Torrance presses this language into a quasi-hypostatic

---

161. See T. F. Torrance, *Atonement*, 89; Ibid., 121.

162. T. F. Torrance, *Conflict and Agreement in the Church: Order and Disorder*, 47.

163. Davis, *The First Seven Ecumenical Councils (325–787): Their History and Theology*, 283; Crisp, *Divinity and Humanity*, 47. Italics mine. Torrance says that, while third Constantinople "marked a considerable advance" in Christology, it failed to take seriously Christ's assumption of our estranged will. T. F. Torrance, *Incarnation*, 212.

mold. Jesus' interaction with people (the noetic dimension), with "human society in sin," with rulers and principalities, is all of one piece with his *ad intra* atoning work on our human nature (the ontic dimension).[164]

Jesus is in anguish as he forgives and heals, and does so only as he bows to receive judgment. In the confrontation with the demonic, the "flesh of sin" is now the flesh of all humanity where the forces of evil have entrenched themselves. Into this social and cosmic situation, Jesus "penetrates," he "absorbs" evil, and "bears it" in his own being. Again, we have deep reservations about the cogency of this picture. Does Jesus absorb demonic forces as he performs exorcisms? How does one account for the casting of "Legion" into the swine on this model?[165] Does he absorb the diseases of those he heals into his own being? How does Torrance account for the myriad of healings, exorcisms, and acts of human compassion which are *not* accompanied by sighs and groaning and tears? Does not this conception entail a hypostatic union, not only with our fallen nature, but with all fallen *persons*, and indeed with all of fallen human *society*?[166]

Torrance, of course, does not hold that Jesus assumed all (or any) fallen human personalities in the hypostatic union. Yet, he construes the *ad extra* human and personal interaction in hypostatic terms. Here the hypostatic union appears to become something of a vortex into which all human and social evil and disease is sucked. The underlying issue here is this: if the way Jesus heals and restores human beings *ad extra* is fundamentally different from the way he heals our fallen nature *ad intra*; which it surely is,[167] then one has good reason to question the *ad intra* conception and, thus, the non-assumptus.

---

164. T. F. Torrance, *Atonement*, 163. The reconciling life and death of Christ was an insertion "into the midst of our perverted attitude of heart and mind toward God as well as toward our fellow human beings."

165. Mark 5:1–17.

166. We saw an example of the "elasticity" of the hypostatic union in Torrance's contention that there is a hypostatic union between creaturely language and God's language. Even if granted, this union, it appears, could only "heal" one language—the one Jesus spoke. This would then have to stand in a representative relation to all other languages. See T. F. Torrance, *Incarnation*, 193.

167. For example, surely the way Jesus enlightens and heals the alienated minds of those he instructs, is not of one piece with his own internal, hypostatic healing of the human mind he assumes.

6

THE CROSS OF CHRIST

THE JUDGMENT OF THE CROSS[1]

Since atonement is incarnate atonement, and the passion extends across the whole life of Christ, what we are to examine in this chapter stands in essential continuity with, and acts as the consummation of, all that has gone before. The condemning of sin in the flesh "takes place supremely on the cross, but the cross reveals what was taking place all the time in the incarnate life of the Son."[2] He brings "his holy relation with sinners to its perfection and completion at last on the cross,"[3] for "it is on the cross that at last all the sin of humanity is finally laid upon him."[4] Thus, "it was on the cross above all that we find a complete judgment was enacted."[5] All of this means that the realities involved in the non-assumptus are acutely present at this culminating point of judgment.

---

1. We shall end our narrative description of the fallen humanity of Christ in Torrance with the cross. The primary reason for this is that the humanity which is raised is no longer, in any sense, fallen. Secondarily, we have already, representatively, covered the relation of the non-assumptus to the post-resurrection situation by looking at how our knowledge, faith, regeneration, etc., repose on what Christ has accomplished in our fallen flesh.
2. T. F. Torrance, *Incarnation*, 112.
3. Ibid., 64.
4. Ibid., 136.
5. T. F. Torrance, *Atonement*, 120.

That assumption of our fearful and lost condition reaches its supreme point in the cross where the Son freely assumes our damnation and final judgment, freely assumes our God-forsakenness in the *Eli, Eli, lama sabachthani* of death on the cross under judgment. And so he achieves our assumption into oneness with himself, and because that assumption is maintained even in the hell into which the Son descended, it achieves its end in the resurrection of man out of hell and the exaltation of man in Christ to the right hand of God.[6]

Particularly, it is the personal and two-sided nature of sin, referred to at the end of the previous chapter, which comes into focus here.

> Sin is not simply the perversion of man's mind and attitude toward God but affects man in the ontological depth of his being; and it also entails a real "change," as it were, in God's mind and attitude towards his disobedient and rebellious creatures . . . and it is that which constitutes the innermost nature and therefore the gravity of sin.[7]

Thus, man's personal resistance of God is met by a reciprocal divine and personal resistance.[8] The nature of sin means "God is at variance with humanity in the essential inner relation which constitutes not only their very existence, but the center of the human person," and "it is upon this essential and root personal relation that the emphasis is laid in reconciliation."[9] Reconciliation, then, is an "onto-personal" affair: "it is in the inner depth of their personal being that humanity must be reconciled to God."[10] It is the fact that the resistance of this holy love, this wrath, penetrates into the depths of our fallen and twisted humanity which makes the cross so terrible.[11] The enmity which exists on *both sides* of the relation between God and man must be done away with if there is to be peace.[12]

> The cross is the point at which the dehumanisation of humanity by sin and sin's isolation of humanity is effectively overcome, and the means by which the impersonalisation in human thought

---

6. T. F. Torrance, *Atonement*, 150.

7. T. F. Torrance, *The Doctrine of Jesus Christ*, 160. See T. F. Torrance, *Incarnation*, 248–54.

8. Indeed, "sin gains part of its character as sin from the divine resistance to it." T. F. Torrance, *Atonement*, 110.

9. Ibid., 158.

10. Ibid., 159.

11. T. F. Torrance, *The Doctrine of Jesus Christ*, 161, 163.

12. T. F. Torrance, *Atonement*, 153.

> and practice is broken down, because here we are set on a new and acutely personal relationship to God, that is, reconciled to God in Jesus Christ.[13]

Christ, as we have seen, participates in this conflict from both sides. He is the God who judges and the man who, in accord with his human righteousness, submits himself to the judgment.[14] Thus, "he is in himself propitiation acutely personalised in both its Godward and manward aspects."[15] This two-sided drama plays itself out in the theatre of our fallen flesh and culminates in the cross.

> While sin is the double fact of man's opposition to God and God's opposition to man, Christ came in the concrete likeness of our flesh of sin, as St. Paul expressed it, condemning sin in the flesh, numbering himself with the transgressors and submitting himself to the judgment of God upon our sin.[16]

As it was with his life of obedience in general, so the sacrifice of Christ "is to be understood both in a passive and an active sense." The passive obedience of suffering our judgment, and the active obedience of fulfilling the holy will of God for us, both reach their apex here.[17]

Though he participates in both sides of the conflict, it is not, as we have seen, as a third party. The atoning action of the cross is also anhypostatic act of God and enhypostatic act of man (or act of God from the side of man).[18] In coordinate terms, it is ontic and noetic.[19] Within the compass of the ontic-anhypostatic, Torrance lays great stress on the human enhypostatic (or noetic) dimension of atonement.[20] It is in this context that he stresses the working out of the hypostatic union through the whole personal life on

---

13. Ibid., 166.

14. Ibid., 124. "The atoning death of Christ is justification in that here God is just against sin, justifies himself in the judgment of sin, and it is also justification in that here there is offered to God a righteousness, a holiness, a perfect obedience, completely in accord with God's own righteousness." Ibid., 123.

15. Ibid., 69. This is also worked out in terms of Christ being questioned by God, and rendering a faithful answer on our behalf at the cross. See T. F. Torrance, *Theology in Reconstruction*, 117–27.

16. T. F. Torrance, *Incarnation*, 255–56.

17. T. F. Torrance, *Atonement*, 154. "The ultimate or final judgment takes place only when God and man are ultimately or finally one in Jesus Christ." T. F. Torrance, *Incarnation*, 111.

18. T. F. Torrance, *Atonement*, 76–77, 121–22, 151.

19. Ibid., 161–63.

20. As we saw in chapter 4, an ontic union only would mean no cross and would truly be physical redemption.

man, "through the whole range of our dark enmity and misunderstanding, even to the ultimate point of God-forsakenness on the cross."[21]

The working out of this atonement as man is intimately bound up with Christ's vicarious confession on our behalf. As God, his confession is the judgment of death, but as man, as the Amen, the obedient answer within our flesh, he confesses the complete righteousness of God's judgment, "a confession actualized in obedient submission to the cross."[22] Thus, the vicarious confession of Christ as man reaches its summit at the cross. "From God's side the crucifixion is his righteous condemnation of our sin, but from man's side it is Christ's high priestly *amen* to the Father's judgment."[23] This confession assumes the full reality of the non-assumptus: "No confession of sin that did not reach down to the depths of our sinful existence, that did not reach acquiescence in the complete judgment of God upon our sin and death, would be true confession."[24]

This notion of agreement with the divine confession of judgment and condemnation is crucial here. Christ's confession is one "in which there is no resentment against God's righteousness,"[25] for "he makes our judgment of ourselves acquiesce in God's complete judgment."[26] He was very man "receiving and laying hold of God by submitting to the divine judgment,"[27] and, from within "Adam's rebellious existence," he acknowledges its justice and accepts the verdict.[28] He does all this with joy,[29] submitting our fallen humanity "freely and gladly" to the Father's judgment on the cross.[30] "From beginning to end there is not a murmur upon his lips, not a shadow over his gladness, not a stain upon his serenity."[31]

This glad obedience of Jesus within our sinful flesh takes place in the context of the increasing intensity of the conflict between God and man. This intensity culminates in the cross. "The discontinuity between humanity

---

21. T. F. Torrance, *Atonement*, 163.
22. Ibid., 90.
23. Ibid., 214.
24. Ibid., 90.
25. Ibid., 89. Not only is there no resentment, there is instead "entire confidence and trust in the heavenly Father." Ibid., 163.
26. Ibid., 116.
27. Ibid., 152.
28. T. F. Torrance, *Incarnation*, 73.
29. T. F. Torrance, *Atonement*, 151.
30. T. F. Torrance, *Incarnation*, 205.
31. Ibid., 111.

and God was . . . widened to an abysmal depth in the crucifixion."³² For Torrance, then, the cross is a kind of back validation of the non-assumptus. Speaking of the Word assuming our fallen flesh, he writes:

> There can be no doubt that the New Testament speaks of the flesh of Jesus as the concrete form of our human nature marked by Adam's fall, the human nature *which seen from the cross* is at enmity with God and needs to be reconciled to God . . . that is the amazing act of gracious condescension . . . that God the Son should assume our flesh . . . enter the situation where the Psalmist cried *Eli, Eli, lama sabachthani* . . .³³

The cross is the place humanity is exposed and unmasked. The "terrible deed" of the cross casts a dark shadow upon humanity and "exposes for the first time the real condition of mankind," enacting "the most terrible and scorching judgment on man that could possibly be made."³⁴ The very offer of absolute grace and forgiveness "implies a devastating disqualification" of man. "That disqualification, or judgment, reaches its height in the cross, where we have unmasked the meaning of sin and the depth of man's involvement in it."³⁵

It is at the cross where sin attacks, and attempts to destroy, the hypostatic union. For, while this union extends across the whole of Christ's life, Torrance can also say that "*on the cross*, the oneness of God and man in Christ is inserted into the midst of our being, into the midst of our sinful existence and history."³⁶ While the cross is God's "no" against us in judgment upon our sin, the resurrection is God's "yes" to us and "his affirmation of Jesus as Son of Man and all that he has done for us in our nature."³⁷ The resurrection is the sign that the hypostatic union held, and is now fully forged, in the face of "the strain imposed through the infliction of the righteous judgment of the Father upon our rebellious humanity which Christ has made his own."³⁸

---

32. T. F. Torrance, *Atonement*, 111. "The gulf between man and God is so complete that Christ on the cross had to cry 'My God! My God! Why hast Thou forsaken me?'" T. F. Torrance, *The Doctrine of Jesus Christ*, 158.

33. T. F. Torrance, *Incarnation*, 61. First set of italics mine.

34. T. F. Torrance, *The Doctrine of Jesus Christ*, 158.

35. T. F. Torrance, *Incarnation*, 246.

36. Ibid., 173. Italics mine.

37. T. F. Torrance, *Atonement*, 214–15.

38. Ibid., 216. While we are not exploring Torrance's doctrine of the resurrection here, let us make one brief comment germane to our thesis. Torrance uses the anhypostasia-enhypostasia couplet to understand the resurrection as both passive act of God (anhypostatic) and active human action (enhypostatic). See ibid., 205–6, 213–18; T. F.

Let us now take a closer look at the nature of the judgment enacted on the cross. We saw in the second chapter that the incarnation of the Word entailed the "assumption of refractory Israel into oneness with God" and led to an intensified judgment on Israel's self-will. Israel rejects the self-giving of God "in the crucifixion of the Messiah, and in so doing Israel shattered itself on the cross."[39] What took place on the cross revealed the inner mystery of Israel's elected role as man in "corporate enmity to God" and thus it "involved the reprobation of man's will to isolation from God."[40] Thus, there is a double rejection in the cross. "In the cross of Christ we have humanity's final rejection of God, and in that cross we have God's final rejection of humanity's sin."[41] Christ bears this divine rejection in his own person at the cross in such a way as to "slay the old sinful and perverted adamic existence."[42]

There are two salient points here. First, the judgment of the cross, like the condemning of sin in the flesh across the whole life of the Son, takes place upon our fallen humanity, and thus, it takes place in the ontological depths of that humanity. The personal and double-sided nature of sin requires this: "Because [the] perversion of mankind's inner attitude receives objective qualification in the opposition of God to it, the objectivity of that obstacle between God and humanity had to be removed by objective deed, *ontological act.*"[43] This is simply another way of stating that atonement takes place within the constitution of the incarnate mediator. This entails the fact that, in making atonement, Christ bears "not just upon his body, but upon his human mind and soul the righteous judgements of God."[44] For in his

---

Torrance, *Space, Time and Resurrection*, 51–56, 95. While we grant that Jesus speaks of raising himself up, if this is analogous to Torrance's conception of enhypostasia, it would seem to require that the dead human nature, or a human "person," be the actor. It can, we think, only be the Logos, the eternal Son, who raises himself up. The same can be said for the other end of the hypostatic union in the virginal conception of Christ. It is hard to see how that event can, in any manner, be a human enhypostatic action. Thus, the interlocked "twin signs" of the mystery of Christ, the virgin birth and the resurrection, seem to require a more "Alexandrian" accent to be made intelligible.

39. T. F. Torrance, *Incarnation*, 49. "Theologically, therefore, the complete destruction of Jerusalem and the temple in AD 70 had to follow upon the crucifixion of the Son of Man."

40. Ibid., 52.

41. T. F. Torrance, *Atonement*, 156. "The giving of himself in the cross when opposed by the will of man inevitably opposes that will of man and is its judgment." Ibid., 189.

42. Ibid., 132.

43. Ibid., 164. Italics mine.

44. T. F. Torrance, *The Mediation of Christ*, 85. "It is within his own person and life, in his own death, and as Calvin insists, not simply in the passion of his body, but in his *soul*, that reconciliation is wrought out through expiation of sin." T. F. Torrance,

soul, and thus within "our human nature and our human soul, complete agreement with the Father in his righteous condemnation of our sin" is wrought out.[45]

Second, for all of Torrance's criticisms of the "merely forensic," the atonement does have "profound forensic elements."[46] There is, in justification, a "forensic element . . . from which we cannot and dare not get away for that would mean God's repudiation of his law."[47] He can even speak of this forensic element in justification as "reckoning" or "imputation,"[48] and he is unafraid of the Anselmic language of "satisfaction."[49]

However, in contrast to the Old Testament cult of "symbolical substitution,"

> In the New Testament it is no more with symbolical actions that we are concerned, and that applies not only to cultic symbolism but to legal symbolism—it is not just a cultic or forensic transaction that has taken place, in which Jesus has symbolically taken our place, so that cultically and by legal transaction only our sins are taken away and laid on Christ and judged.[50]

With respect to cross, as elsewhere, the *goel*, or ontological, dimension is primary and integrates the other aspects of the atonement.

> This [incarnational atonement] by no means rules out the propriety of forensic, juridical or penal relations in a doctrine of the atonement, but they are intensified, deepened and refined in their import through what took place in the ontological depths of our Lord's atoning life and death.[51]

Atonement, 149.

45. T. F. Torrance, *Atonement*, 70.

46. T. F. Torrance, *The Mediation of Christ*, 85.

47. T. F. Torrance, *Atonement*, 116.

48. Ibid., 136. This is not, of course, taken in the same sense as it is in Federal Calvinism's bi-covenantal schema, but is seen to be a fruit of the eschatological tension between the already completed judgment in Christ and its future full disclosure.

49. Ibid., 123, 215. Torrance, though he can speak of Christ bearing the punishment for our sins, denies that this is penal substitution. "We cannot think of Christ being punished by the Father in our place and the New Testament nowhere uses the word *kolazō**, punish, of the relation between the Father and the Son." Ibid., 72. See T. F. Torrance, *The Doctrine of Jesus Christ*, 171.

50. T. F. Torrance, *Atonement*, 83.

51. T. F. Torrance, "The Atonement. The Singularity of Christ," 253. See T. F. Torrance, *Atonement*, 69.

The inadequacy of *purely* legal categories, for which Torrance everywhere argues, can be seen from another perspective. No one, he says, can be a responsible substitute for another because no one can truly "represent another *from within their guilt.*"[52]

> That is why the theology that deals only in forensic terms and speaks only of a purely objective atonement in that sense brings upon itself the suspicion of make-believe, and yet the biblical revelation speaks in the most astonishing terms of this substitutionary act of Christ. "He who knew no sin became sin for us, that we might be made the righteousness of God in him."[53]

Thus, the non-assumptus, in addition to requiring a subordination of forensic categories, also demands that we be personally represented from within our guilt. Jesus Christ, as the creator Logos, the personalizing person in whom all mankind consists, "is the only one who can represent all men and women from the innermost center and depth of human being."[54] Christ intervenes in our fallen flesh in such a way that

> there is a substitution where the guilty does not shelter behind the innocent, but such a substitution that the guilty is faced with the Light, that man is dragged out of his self-isolation and brought face to face with God in his compassion and holiness.[55]

This entails the "profound fact" that "Jesus Christ *actually* entered into our existence, and *actually* shouldered our sin."[56] Thus, Christ acts *for* us in such a way that we acted *in* him, and, indeed, died in him.[57] This brings us to the question of the extent of the atonement in Torrance's thought.

---

52. T. F. Torrance, *Atonement*, 125. This is related to Torrance's conception that the moral order itself needs to be set right, and thus cannot be the ground for a purely forensic substitution. "Gregory of Nyssa once pointed this out, when he showed that judged by the accepted moral criteria it would be wrong for one person to take the place of another or die in another's place, for no one can represent another within his moral responsibility, and no one therefore can be a responsible substitute for another from within his guilt." T. F. Torrance, "The Atonement. The Singularity of Christ," 252. This analysis rests on the notion that, in the fallen order, law itself, even the law of God, becomes an abstraction which masks and induces sin, and thus distorts the moral life. While this is surely correct, it does not tell against the law of God itself, as fulfilled in Christ, as a basis for forensic substitution.

53. T. F. Torrance, *Atonement*, 125–26.

54. Ibid., 126.

55. T. F. Torrance, *Conflict and Agreement in the Church: Order and Disorder*, 245; T. F. Torrance, *Incarnation*, 113.

56. T. F. Torrance, *Atonement*, 83.

57. Ibid., 83, 128, 152; T. F. Torrance, "Universalism of Election?," 316.

THE EXTENT OF THE ATONEMENT

Grasping Torrance on the extent of the atonement requires that we first briefly look at his understanding of election. Following Barth,[58] Torrance views election as a divine decision which becomes visible in our sinful history in the form of the hypostatic union in Jesus Christ.[59] There is, for Torrance, no eternal decree of God which is not identical with his Word.[60] This means that Jesus Christ *is* the election of God. "Election is the love of God enacted and inserted into history in the life, death, and resurrection of Jesus Christ, so that in the strictest sense Jesus Christ is the election of God."[61] Election, then, is the setting forth, the *prothesis*, of the mystery of Christ into our fallen humanity.

> Election means, therefore, that Christ assumes our flesh, assumes our fallen estate, assumes our judgment, assumes our reprobation, in order that we may participate in his glory, and share in the union of the Son with the Father.... In the supreme sense, Jesus Christ is himself the divine *prothesis*.[62]

This election which is Jesus Christ is both God's decision and man's election.[63] The relation between the divine and the human in election, thus,

---

58. The primary source being Barth, *CD*, II.2, 3–506. Torrance explicitly claims to be (broadly) following Barth on election: T. F. Torrance, "The Distinctive Character," 4–5. See Habets, "The Doctrine of Election," 340.

59. T. F. Torrance, *Scottish Theology: From John Knox to John McLeod Campbell*, 14, 172; Habets, "The Doctrine of Election," 336.

60. T. F. Torrance, *The School of Faith: The Catechisms of the Reformed Church*, lxxviii. Even Calvin receives mild censure at this point, for "particularly in his polemical works in defence of predestination ... there is a tendency ... toward abstracting the work of God in election from the work of Christ. At any rate there is no outright identification of the eternal decree of God with His eternal Word." The charge of "some form of determinism" is also leveled against "the Reformers and their followers" in T. F. Torrance, *The Doctrine of Jesus Christ*, 144. These caveats must be kept in mind when Luoma says "Torrance wants to make Calvin's doctrine of predestination sound more Christocentric than it does at first sight," or when Habets says "a weakness of Torrance's argument is his refusal to acknowledge this determinist element in Calvin's own theology." Luoma, *Incarnation and Physics*, 77; Habets, "The Doctrine of Election," 338.

61. T. F. Torrance, "Universalism of Election?," 315. Thus, for the key to our election, we are to look to the union of God and man in Christ, and not to some secret decree "behind the back of Jesus Christ, for that would be to split the act of God into two, and to divide Christ from God." See also T. F. Torrance, *Atonement*, 183; T. F. Torrance, *Theological Science*, 215; T. F. Torrance, "The Distinctive Character," 4–5; T. F. Torrance, *Incarnation*, 179.

62. T. F. Torrance, *Incarnation*, 178.

63. T. F. Torrance, *The Doctrine of Jesus Christ*, 144; T. F. Torrance, *Atonement*, 178.

contains the same "logic of grace" which we saw applied to the whole of God's action in Christ.[64] Thus, in accordance with the Chalcedonian adverbs, there can be no separation or division between the human and divine decisions in election.[65] Election enacted in our fallen flesh, election incarnate,[66] is governed by the anhypostasia-enhypostasia couplet and the mutuality between the terms. This, as we have indicated, coupled with Torrance's understanding of the creator Logos in conjunction with the couplet, means that both the incarnation and the atonement are universal in range.

> If incarnation and atonement cannot be separated, then Christ represents in his death all whom he represents in his incarnation.... Because he is the eternal Word or *Logos* in whom all humanity cohere, for him to take human nature upon himself means that all humanity is assumed by his incarnation; all humanity is bound up with him, he died for all humanity and all humanity died in him.[67]

The result is that all are elect in Christ,[68] all died in Christ, and all are judged in Christ.[69] At the cross, in particular, we see that *all* are both elected *and* damned in Christ.[70]

On the question of the extent of the atonement, then, Torrance is staking out a position in contrast to the twin errors of universalism on the one hand and limited atonement on the other.[71]

---

64. "In regard to election we have an analogy [between the divine decision and the human decision]—in the Person of Christ." T. F. Torrance, "Predestination in Christ," 127.

65. Ibid., 129–30.

66. "God's eternal election is nothing else than God's eternal love incarnate in his beloved Son, so that in him we have election incarnate." T. F. Torrance, *Atonement*, 183.

67. Ibid., 182. See T. F. Torrance, "The Atonement. The Singularity of Christ," 231, 245; T. F. Torrance, *Atonement*, 189. Also entailed here, with more emphasis on the anhypostatic ontological bond Christ has forged with all men, is the impossibility of annihilation. See T. F. Torrance, "Universalism of Election?," 317; Habets, "The Doctrine of Election," 350.

68. T. F. Torrance, "Universalism of Election?," 315, 318.

69. T. F. Torrance, "Predestination in Christ," 119.

70. Ibid., 119, 125. For this election and damnation in Barth, see Barth, *CD*, II.2, 340–506.

71. Torrance also opposes Arminianism, or any conception of an independent free-will. He can speak of a Christological confusion or separation of the human and divine with respect to election and predestination as yielding two main types of errors, the extremes of which are "a doctrine of irresistible grace and independent free-will." T. F. Torrance, "Predestination in Christ," 129–30. For his opposition to Arminianism and the mere "creation of the possibility of salvation" see T. F. Torrance, *Atonement*, 187;

> Thus it is argued, *a posteriori*, that if as a matter of fact some people believe in Christ and are saved and others reject Christ and are damned, then Christ must have died only for the believing and not for the unbelieving. But it is also argued, *a priori*, that if Christ died for all people, then all people must be and will be saved.[72]

The a posteriori reasoning of limited atonement rests, for Torrance, on a species of Nestorianism. Commenting with approval on what he takes to be the view of John Knox and the Scots Confession, Torrance writes:

> Nor is there any suggestion that this atoning sacrifice was offered only for some people and not for all, for that would imply that he who became incarnate was not God the Creator in whom all men and women live and move and have their being, and that Jesus Christ our Lord and Savior was not God and man in the one Person, but only an instrument in the hands of the Father for the salvation of a chosen few. In other words, a notion of limited atonement implies a Nestorian heresy in which Jesus Christ is not really God and man united in one Person.[73]

The invocation of the creator Logos here, yielding a Nestorian split in the work of Christ, tells us that Torrance thinks that advocates of limited atonement do not hold anhypostasia (ontological bond, work of God, Jesus as "man") and enhypostasia (personalizing person, work of man, Jesus as "a man") together properly. The result is that what Jesus does as God and what he does as man do not coincide.

> The indivisible oneness of God and man, Creator and creature, in the Person of the Lord Jesus Christ will not allow us to contemplate any disjunction between what Christ does in his divine nature and what he does in his human nature—to do that would be a form of Nestorian heresy.[74]

Habets, "The Doctrine of Election," 352. Thus, Torrance's view presents a fourth option which is neither universalism, limited atonement, or Arminian synergism. However, to focus on the non-assumptus, we shall restrict ourselves, as he often does, to the polarity of universalism and limited atonement.

72. T. F. Torrance, *Christian Theology and Scientific Culture*, 136. See T. F. Torrance, "The Atonement. The Singularity of Christ," 246.

73. T. F. Torrance, *Scottish Theology: From John Knox to John McLeod Campbell*, 19. Scots Confession IX is in view. See Cochrane, *Reformed Confessions*, 169–70.

74. T. F. Torrance, "The Atonement. The Singularity of Christ," 231. See T. F. Torrance, "Karl Barth and the Latin Heresy," 481.

More specifically, the work he does in his human nature is truncated with respect to the work he does in his divine nature as the creator Logos who has an onto-personal bond with all men. Noteworthy here is the relationship Torrance sees between this "Nestorianism" and his reworked understanding of impassibility, and thus, the non-assumptus. To assert that Christ suffered in his human nature only is a denial that it is "*God himself* who bears our sins" from within our fallen and condemned state. But, "we cannot divorce the action of Christ on the cross from the action of God. The concept of a limited atonement divides Christ's divinity from his humanity and thus rests upon a basic Nestorian heresy."[75] Advocates of limited atonement, then, can ground the work of Christ either in the will of God,[76] in which case, Torrance asserts, they have made it arbitrary, or in the nature of God as infinite, self-giving love, in which case the divine nature is attacked.[77]

Universalism, on the other hand, also rests on an anhypostasia-enhypostasia split. It absolutizes anhypostasia, which alone Torrance says would produce physical redemption, and creates an impersonal, non-enhypostatic, and thus deterministic, conception of atonement.[78] It fails to recognize that while in the cross we have election *and* damnation in the first place, in the "acute personalisation of the Cross toward men," we have election *or* damnation in the second place.[79] "And" is the general (anhypostatic) conception and "or" is the specific, personal, enhypostatic aspect of the cross as it encounters men. To deny this aspect of personal event means the "actual historical particularity of every choice as a free movement disappears, and necessity takes its place."[80]

---

75. T. F. Torrance, *Atonement*, 184–85. See T. F. Torrance, "The Atonement. The Singularity of Christ," 231–32, 245–46.

76. Or in an extrinsically construed (Nestorian) relation of wills between Christ and God.

77. T. F. Torrance, *Atonement*, 186–87. "The concept of a limited atonement thus rests upon a limitation of the very being of God as love, and a schizoid notion of the incarnation, i.e. upon a basic Nestorian heresy." T. F. Torrance, "The Atonement. The Singularity of Christ," 246.

78. "The failure to understand this [enhypostatic personal encounter] is the meaning of universalism. In the last resort universalism means an impersonal relation between God and man, and as such it is at heart deterministic." T. F. Torrance, "Predestination in Christ," 139.

79. T. F. Torrance, "Predestination in Christ," 126. Alternatively, this is judgment unto salvation in the first place (which in this context means in Christ himself) and judgment unto damnation or salvation in the second place (which in this context means in the personal decisions of men).

80. T. F. Torrance, "Universalism of Election?," 313.

216 The Unassumed Is the Unhealed

The respective charges Torrance levels above notwithstanding, limited atonement and universalism can be criticized jointly as failures to grasp the logic of grace displayed in Christ. In this regard, they share in two fundamental errors. First, they both fail to see that there is no logical-causal connection between the death of Christ and its application to men.

> Thus there is no necessary, timeless, and no formal-logical relation between the death of Jesus Christ on the Cross and the forgiveness of our sins. There is indeed a relation but it is only established by divine action and discerned through faith.[81]

The advocates of limited atonement and universalism both subject the cross "to the rationalism of human thought . . . for in both cases they have not yet bowed their reason before the cross of Christ."[82]

Behind this rationalistic denial of the ineffable logic of grace, particularly with respect to limited atonement,[83] lurks the non-assumptus. Against accusations leveled at Barth's embrace of the logic of grace, Torrance writes:

> It is just here that one discerns how deeply the Latin heresy, construing the Gospel in dualist and abstractive terms, is embedded in evangelical theology. Behind it there is evidently a rejection of the principle that the unassumed is the unhealed, and in particular a rejection of the truth that it is our alienated mind that the Son of God assumed in the incarnation in order to heal it.[84]

When Barth is charged with universalism, Torrance asks: "What is going on here? Is it just another form of the Latin heresy . . . ? Behind the charge of universalism against Barth there is a controlling frame of thought which operates with a notion of external logico-causal connections."[85] The role of the non-assumptus in generating this rationalism is prominent in the case of limited atonement since "the humanity of Christ is not regarded as

---

81. T. F. Torrance, *Theological Science*, 214–15. "What *logical* connection is there between the forgiveness of my sins in 1949 and the death of Jesus under Pontius Pilate?" T. F. Torrance, "Universalism of Election?," 311. "The connection between the atoning death of the Lord Jesus and the forgiveness of our sins is of an altogether ineffable kind which we may not and cannot reduce to a chain of this-worldly logico-causal relations." T. F. Torrance, "The Atonement. The Singularity of Christ," 246.

82. T. F. Torrance, *Atonement*, 187–88. For a similar charge, this time against liberals and evangelicals, see T. F. Torrance, "Karl Barth and the Latin Heresy," 480.

83. While universalism's denial of enhypostatic penetration into the depths of our personal alienation, and its consequent rationalistic determinism, also rests on a denial of the non-assumptus, Torrance tends to focus on the rationalism of the limited atonement position, especially in connection with the non-assumptus.

84. T. F. Torrance, "Karl Barth and the Latin Heresy," 480.

85. Ibid., 481.

having any inner ontological connection with those for whom he died, but is regarded only as an external instrument used by God as he wills."[86]

The second error which both limited atonement and universalism entail is a failure to come to grips with the irrationality of evil and sin, and thus, of reprobation. For universalism, if Christ died for all men, all must be saved. For advocates of limited atonement, if some are not saved, then Christ must not have died for them. Both parties are guilty of "systematising the illogical."

> Somehow evil posits itself and cannot be rationalised. The New Testament teaches that when it speaks of the *mystery of iniquity*, and of the *bottomless pit (abyssos)*. Evil is fundamentally discontinuity. No explanation involving continuity or coherence can ever approach the problem, for that would be to draw a line of continuity dialectically over discontinuity.[87]

While both limited atonement and universalism are guilty of rationalizing evil, this is a matter of great moment to Torrance's doctrine of the extent of the atonement because of its formal affinities with universalism.

Though he holds that there is an anhypostatic "and" (all are elect *and* judged in Christ), as well as an enhypostatic "or" (election *or* judgment) which obtains in the personal encounter of the cross with men, nonetheless, in Christ, who *is* the election, God has already decided (enhypostatic personal decision) for all men. No personal decision of man adds anything to his election in Christ.[88] In Christ, both ontically and personally, anhypostatically and enhypostatically, from within our fallen humanity, we have one who substitutes for us "at every point, where we human beings are called to have faith in the Father, to believe in him and trust in him."[89] Thus, Torrance can say:

> This ... reconciliation encounters me telling me that I am already reconciled to God in Christ, already died for, redeemed and forgiven. It tells me that already the great positive decision of God's reconciling love in my favour has been taken, and it can no more be undone than Jesus Christ can be undone, than the incarnation can be reversed or obliterated, or the cross made as if it had never taken place. . . . I am already included in the finished work and already part of Christ, for it was my nature,

---

86. T. F. Torrance, "Karl Barth and the Latin Heresy," 481.
87. T. F. Torrance, "Universalism of Election?," 313.
88. T. F. Torrance, "Predestination in Christ," 117. "No decision of his can add anything to the fact that God has chosen him already in Christ."
89. T. F. Torrance, *The Mediation of Christ*, 82.

my humanity, my flesh of sin, that he assumed and made one with himself in his one person.[90]

This "decision is not altered if man refuses it, but if someone goes to hell, they go because they dash themselves in judgment against an unalterable positive act of divine reconciliation."[91] The atonement, then, is universal in range. It is actual, and in no way potential, in accomplishment. Yet, Torrance rejects universalism as its logical corollary. He acknowledges, as we have seen, that the personal decision of men can, in effect, turn the "and" of the cross into an "or." But, he refuses to systematize this outcome. Thus, the continual appeal, in the face of the reality of reprobation and the rejection of the gospel, is to the abysmal irrationality of evil.[92]

ANALYSIS AND CRITIQUE

The Judgment of the Cross

Torrance's presentation of the cross contains a number of traditional features which, being common to the whole church, are unobjectionable. He grants the propriety, if not the full traditional sense, of forensic categories. He has a profound sense of the judgment enacted there and the depths into which Christ descended to procure redemption. His presentation of the personal, two-sided nature of sin and what that entails for the holiness of God and the condition of humanity is particularly helpful.

Yet, in light of the non-assumptus, three issues of relevance emerge. First, there is the nature of the humanity present at the cross. The discussion here dovetails with the issues surrounding the state of the post-virgin birth humanity that we looked at in chapter 3, as well as the state of the human will of Christ which we highlighted at the end of the last chapter. Humanity

---

90. T. F. Torrance, *Atonement*, 167. Alternatively, Torrance suggest we preach the gospel as follows: "He has believed for you, fulfilled your human response to God, even made your personal decision for you, so that he acknowledged you before God as one who has already responded to God in him, who has already believed in God through him, and whose personal decision is already implicated in Christ's self-offering to the Father. . . . Therefore, renounce yourself, take up your cross and follow Jesus as your Lord and Saviour." T. F. Torrance, *The Mediation of Christ*, 94.

91. T. F. Torrance, *Atonement*, 158.

92. See, for example, T. F. Torrance, *The Doctrine of Jesus Christ*, 95; T. F. Torrance, *The School of Faith: The Catechisms of the Reformed Church*, cxiii–cxiv; T. F. Torrance, *Christian Theology and Scientific Culture*, 87, 137; T. F. Torrance, *Scottish Theology: From John Knox to John McLeod Campbell*, 277; T. F. Torrance, "Predestination in Christ," 127, 142; T. F. Torrance, "Universalism of Election?," 313, 316–17; T. F. Torrance, *Atonement*, 157; Habets, "The Doctrine of Election," 350.

is depicted as involved in an increasing intensification of enmity which culminates at the cross. This enmity is personal and two-sided (God and man). Thus, it entails God being at variance with the center of the human person. At the supreme judgment of the cross, this humanity is decisively disqualified, unmasked, reprobated, and condemned. This is the final rejection of God by fallen man and the final rejection of man's sin by God. And all of this, given the non-assumptus and Torrance's theology of atonement, takes place in the ontological depths of the humanity Christ assumed from us. This raises, in a different light than we have looked at heretofore, questions about the state of Christ's humanity. How is it that *this* humanity, utterly reprobate and rejected, and not simply forensically, but ontically, was *definitively* healed and sanctified in the once for all assumption of the virgin birth? In terms of the human will and mind of Christ, we might ask how is it that he bent our wayward will back, and healed our alienated mind, through the whole course of his obedience, only to have the cross be the place of humanity's ultimate rejection of God? If definitive, once for all sanctification is difficult to account for here, progressive sanctification is equally so. Of course, salvation is by means of judgment for Torrance, and the process of "condemning sin in the flesh" extends across the whole life of Christ, but given his account of the cross, there seems to be *no* sanctification at all, indeed the opposite, until the work of the cross is completed.

Our second concern involves, again, the question of the human will of Christ. Here we focus on this will in the narrative of Christ's life as it culminates in the cross. Torrance's exposition of Christ's vicarious confession is one in which the Son, from within the depths of our sinful existence, offers a free, glad, and obedient Amen to the judgment of God on that same humanity. He acquiesces completely, and with delight, in the judgment which he bears in his very soul. None of this would be problematic if we were dealing with strictly forensic categories. The obedient humanity (or will) of Jesus would be receiving our sanctions as our legal covenant representative. But the non-assumptus demands a situation where the "guilty does not shelter behind the innocent," and confession is made from *within* our sin and guilt. This ontological situation appears to create the following anomaly at the cross. The humanity which Christ assumed, thus his will, is condemned. It is reprobated in its enmity and final rejection of God. Yet, there is also the presence of a fully obedient will which gladly agrees with and acquiesces in the judgment.

> From the beginning to the end of his life, he submitted our fallen humanity with our human will to the just and holy verdict of the

Father, freely and gladly yielding it to the Father's judgment, and was therefore obedient unto the death of the cross.[93]

We raised this issue with respect to the continuous historical life of Christ, but here the issue comes to its ontic culmination. The *same will* is exposed and unmasked in all its wickedness, *and* perfectly obedient and submissive. While we would not accuse Torrance of trithelitism (two human wills, plus the divine will), much of his account of Jesus' human obedience being personally *resisted*, of his obeying *where* we are disobedient, or *in the midst* of our impurity, casts a shadow which, particularly at the cross, begs for clarification.

Our third concern with the judgment of the cross lies with the relationship between its forensic and ontological aspects. We saw that he asserts the inadequacy of *merely* forensic categories. These are deepened and transformed by the more basic and integrative ontological substructure of incarnate atonement. A chief reason given for this inadequacy is that no one is qualified to represent another from within the depths of their personal guilt. Only the creator Logos, the personalizing person, can do this. And he does this enhypostatically (or noetically) from within the basic anhypostatic (or ontological) assumption of our flesh. However, as we have seen there simply is, even on Torrance's account, no enhypostatic assumption of our fallen humanity. He expressly states that Christ "sets aside that which divides us," namely our twisted, individual personalities, to assume what unites us, namely, our common nature. But this means that what the enhypostatic Son does, personally, and from within the depths of our guilt, must be construed, if not exclusively, at least more basically, in forensic categories. If this is coupled with our second concern above, where we saw that the ontological nature of what is transpiring in the human will of Christ was problematic, we can conclude as follows. Torrance's whole presentation of the cross, it appears, needs to move from a basically ontological one with forensic elements, in the direction of a more fundamentally forensic conception with profound ontological affinities to our humanity. That is, it needs to move in a more classical direction.[94] The role of the non-assumptus, however, precludes this.

---

93. T. F. Torrance, *Incarnation*, 205.

94. Here we add two observations. First, the "passive obedience" dimension of the cross, which is in view here, creates this anomalous situation with respect to the human will of Christ, and thus cries out for a more forensic conception. However, the active obedience, which Torrance says deals with our actual sins, would seem to require a similar move. How can Jesus' obedience deal with all acts of sin, as opposed to our sinful natures, except in some representative way? Put differently, the anomalous nature of the will of Christ, both throughout his life *and* at the cross, calls into question

The Extent of the Atonement

On the question of the extent of the atoning work of Christ, we shall focus first on Torrance's critique of limited atonement and then on his own view. First, the continual application of Nestorianism to limited atonement seems overdone. The view is traditionally held by people who repudiate Nestorianism. If one does not accept Torrance's conception of the anhypostatic assumption of human nature in its totality, or the argument that, because it is the creator Logos who became flesh incarnation and atonement must cohere in universal range, which is generally, if not exclusively, the case for advocates of limited atonement, then to accuse them of splitting incarnation and atonement, or the divine and human natures of Christ, is an exercise in question begging. For advocates of limited atonement, what Christ, *as mediator of salvation*, does in his human and divine natures is one, and yet distinguishable from other creational functions of the divine nature. Any view of *atonement*, including Torrance's view, which accepts the *extra Calvinisticum*, operates with some sort of a "split" at this point. Limited atonement may be open to criticism, but an elastic use of Nestorianism seems questionable. Torrance's concern that this either makes the will of God arbitrary or attacks his nature as love seems to us to provide more substantial grist for the advocates of limited atonement to consider.[95] Without gainsaying the legitimacy of Torrance's theological approach, the issue will have to be engaged on more exegetical grounds. While Torrance does say, of universalism, "there is not a shred of Biblical witness that can be adduced to support the impossibility of ultimate damnation. All the weight of Biblical teaching is on the other side,"[96] there is little or no engagement with the texts used in support of limited atonement.

On the question of limited atonement (and universalism) rationalizing the absurdity of evil, through logical-causal connections between the death of Christ and our salvation, we make two points. First, surely there is something profoundly true about the irrational nature of evil. However, to absolutize this would be a form of Manicheanism. Surely, it is not irrational to God? Why, then, if God has dealt with evil decisively, as Torrance

---

Torrance's ontological conception of active *and* passive obedience. Second, Torrance's repeated, and largely traditional, affirmations of the cosmic dimensions of redemption would also require a more forensic framework. Even granting that all things, visible and invisible, have an ontological relation to the creator Logos who has become flesh in Christ, they are, nevertheless, even on Torrance's elastic reading, not included in the hypostatic union. The cosmos can be healed without being "assumed."

95. Since the will of God, traditionally understood, is part of his nature this is really one concern and not two.

96. T. F. Torrance, "Universalism of Election?," 313.

repeatedly asserts he has done in Christ, does it not follow that it is, well, *dealt with*? Second, when Torrance says there is no logical relation between the death of Christ and my sins, he proves too much. For, when it comes to anhypostatic assumption, he regularly says that Jesus Christ assumed our fallen humanity, *therefore* (logical inference) our nature is healed, our sins are pardoned, etc. Yet, when it comes to enhypostatic insertion of this into the personal and social lives of men and women, no inferences are allowed. The connection here is ineffable. The imposition of "rigid categories" is forbidden in one direction only. This is another outworking of the split in Torrance's theology between anhypostasia and enhypostasia. In addition, as we indicated at the end of the last chapter, it shows that what happened enhypostatically *inside* the person of the mediator, does not cohere with its *ad extra* application.[97]

Turning to Torrance's own view of the extent to the atonement, the split we just mentioned becomes prominent. The combination of anhypostasia-enhypostasia *in Christ* means the atonement is universal, utterly efficacious, and permanently valid. No human decision can annul or undo it. Yet, when the atonement is inserted, enhypostatically, into the lives of human beings, it is contingent, and due to the mystery of iniquity, able to be rejected. Election is "and" in Christ (election AND damnation, election as judgment unto salvation), but "or" in its confrontation with men (election OR damnation, election as judgment unto damnation). But what then becomes of Christ's substituting for us *at every point*? Surely, we can grant that our decisions repose on his, but given the reality of human rejection, that will not procure the *total substitution* which Torrance advocates. Enhypostatic personal decision by men and women seems to invalidate the anhypostatic assumption and healing of their natures.

We conclude with two additional, and important, observations. The split between anhypostasia and enhypostasia in Torrance's theology is a direct result of the affirmation of the non-assumptus. This is a point often obscured or sublimated. Anhypostasia and enhypostasia, whatever one makes of their historical genesis, are used relatively harmlessly in numerous Christologies.[98] To assert that Christ had no personal existence before the incarnation (anhypostasia), and that he was given personal existence in the Son at the incarnation (enhypostasia) is commonplace. It surely raises questions, but it does not involve the problematics we have surveyed here and

---

97. We called this the "vortex" effect. Torrance speaks of the hypostatic union as, in some fashion, sweeping up time, language, rationality, and social relations into itself.

98. This is not to say that there is no need for clarification, but the problems that arise are often endemic to Christology qua Christology, and not to the non-assumptus specifically.

earlier (especially in the conclusion to chapter 4). It is the non-assumptus which lies under the problems here. Anhypostatic assumption *as Torrance conceives it*, as universal assumption of our fallen human nature, cannot be made to cohere with the enhypostatic uniqueness and singularity of the person of the incarnate Son, which, in the nature of the case, *sets aside*, our fallen personalities. The split is inevitable once the non-assumptus is affirmed, appeals to the personalizing person of the Logos notwithstanding. Finally, we observe, that, for the same reasons, the non-assumptus should be seen to lie under another major concern in Torrance scholarship, namely, the relationship between the carnal union and the spiritual union, or between Christ's action in our flesh and our response to the gospel. It is the failure to make the non-assumptus fully coherent which creates these problems, not vice versa. Thus, further progress on Torrance's doctrine of union with Christ, or his soteriology, depends on critical engagement with the non-assumptus.

7

CONCLUSION

T. F. TORRANCE, WE HAVE shown, has provided us with a Christology in which the non-assumptus is a pervasive, integral, and decisive feature. While we have not covered every aspect of his theology "downstream" from his Christology, we have touched on many of them including his bibliology, and various critical aspects of the relationship between what happens in Christ and what happens in believers, such as our birth in the Spirit, our baptism, our knowing, and our faith. "Behind," if you will, his Christology, we have covered what might be called his pre-Christology, his doctrine of the Word on the road to becoming flesh in the history of Israel. We have demonstrated that this aspect of his thought, while it is often acknowledged, needs to be seen as an utterly central and dominant feature. There is virtually no aspect of his theology "downstream" from his doctrine of the Trinity which is untouched by it.[1] Torrance has provided us with what might be called a fully worked out dogmatics of the non-assumptus. Anyone wishing to affirm it, or criticize it, needs to come to grips with its implications, and

---

1. There are exceptions, of course. There are aspects of Torrance's interaction with the sciences where it is not prominent. But even there, inasmuch as his Christologically formed epistemology drives his thought, the non-assumptus is not absent. One could, to choose another example, deal with his desire to reformulate natural theology without a great deal of attention to the non-assumptus. But again, if this is to be a prolegomenon to revealed theology, and the heart of revealed theology is Christology, the non-assumptus is not entirely irrelevant. While we have not covered his doctrine of the church, we have seen enough of his view of the Christian life to realize that everything rests on a second-order, pneumatic participation in what happened in Christ's assumption of our fallen flesh.

on that front Torrance's presentation and vigorous defense remain essential and stimulating.

While we have had occasion to criticize, sometimes sharply, the intelligibility of the concept, we have been moved and challenged by Torrance's passionate advocacy of the principle. His deep reverence for the Triune God, his warm love for Christ, his immense erudition coupled with childlike wonder—his sheer luminosity as a theologian—make him both a daunting and a delightful conversation partner.

We have sought to do two things. The first, as indicated, is to demonstrate the pervasive role of the non-assumptus. To accomplish this we began, in chapter 2, with an exposition of his Christological reading of Israel's history. In the mediation of revelation and reconciliation the Word penetrates into fallen Israel's social life as well as into her heart and mind. Here all the basic concepts concerning the non-assumptus which are deployed in Torrance's Christology proper are forged. Revelation and its interlocked relation with reconciliation, the Word's forging permanent structures of thought and speech in the midst of Israel, the conflict with the carnal mind, the covenanted way of response, the need for total substitution from within Israel as set forth in the cult, and finally in the Servant of the Lord, all show that the non-assumptus in Torrance's thought, like the Word himself, incubates in Israel as the womb of the incarnation.

We then turned in chapter 3 to Torrance's Christology proper and to the incarnation of the Word made flesh. We saw the non-assumptus to be critical in understanding his doctrine of the virgin birth of Christ into our humanity. Here, the once and for all union of God and sinful *sarx* is definitively accomplished. In chapter 4, we looked at the architectonic features of Torrance's Christology: the homoousion, the hypostatic union, and the anhypostasia-enhypostasia couplet. We demonstrated that, at every juncture, the non-assumptus is conjoined with, or underneath, the critical theological ideas; determining which brings forth and begets the others is virtually impossible. In the fifth chapter we looked at the continuous union of God and man in the historical life of Christ. Here we examined Christ's condemnation of sin in the flesh, and we saw how the non-assumptus works itself through all aspects of Christ's life as Torrance narrates it from the Gospels. In our concluding chapter, we looked at the cross of Christ. The judgment enacted at the cross, and the extent of the atonement, both depend on, and illumine, the non-assumptus. From Israel to the virgin birth, from Christ's baptism and temptations, through his teaching, confessing, praying, and healing, and unto the cross, the non-assumptus shapes the whole presentation vividly.

The second thing we have done is to criticize Torrance's theology of the non-assumptus. While we have made a number of criticisms, however, a few of them are crucial. First, there is the question of whether his exegetical conclusions, especially with regard to Romans 8:3, but not exclusively so, are anything more than probable. Second, we asserted that there does not seem to be a sufficient safeguarding of the sinlessness of Jesus. If God in Christ is continually condemning *sin*, and being *resisted* in that condemnation, throughout the life of Christ, then who (or what?) is resisting? If the enhypostatic personality of Jesus is identical to the Logos, then Jesus cannot have a fallen "personality." If this is so, then the intelligibility of a fallen human nature enhypostatically one with, and identical to, the Logos is called into question. Third, we showed that the status of this "fallen humanity" immediately after the virgin birth is ambiguous. The once for all sanctification of our flesh would seem to mean that, after the incarnation "in the narrow sense," Jesus assumes something akin to redeemed, but sub-eschatological humanity.

Turning to the most pertinent critiques, fourth, the human will of Jesus in his historical life does not seem to be a coherent entity. It is perfectly obedient, perpetually condemned, progressively sanctified, and increasingly resistant. This becomes palpable at the cross, where the same will is ontically condemned and fully obedient in its acquiescence to judgment. Fifth, the split between anhypostasia and enhypostasia, which we contended is actually caused by the non-assumptus, illumines the fact that what Jesus actually assumes is fallen human nature abstracted from fallen human persons. If what is not assumed is not healed, then it would appear that fallen persons are not healed (or are healed along more traditional "forensic" lines). Sixth, and finally, the *ad intra* and *ad extra* split between the way the hypostatic union works inside the person of the mediator, and the way it works extrinsic to the mediator, belies a fundamental problem with the basic conception. The net result, especially of these last three critiques, requires moving the whole of Christ's atoning work in a more forensic direction. Once that is granted, it is not at all clear that the non-assumptus, as narrated by Torrance, can be salvaged.

BIBLIOGRAPHY

Agnew, M. B. "The Concept of Sacrifice in the Eucharistic Theology of Donald M. Baillie, Thomas F. Torrance, and Jean-Jacques Von Allmen." Ph.D. diss. Washington, DC: Catholic University of America, 1972.

Anatolios, Khaled. *Athanasius: The Coherence of His Thought*. London: Routledge, 1998.

———. "The Soteriological Significance of Christ's Humanity in St. Athanasius." *St. Vladimir's Theological Quarterly* 40 (1996) 265–68.

Aulen, Gustaf. *Christus Victor: An Historical Study of the Three Main Types of the Idea of the Atonement*. Translated by A. G. Hebert. New York: Macmillan, 1969.

Barth, Karl. *Church Dogmatics*. Translated and edited by G. W Bromiley and T. F. Torrance. 4 vols. in 13 parts. Edinburgh: T. & T. Clark, 1957–81.

Berkhof, Louis. *Systematic Theology: New Combined Edition*. Grand Rapids: Eerdmans, 1996.

Berkouwer, G. C. *The Person of Christ*. Grand Rapids: Eerdmans, 1954.

Bevan, Andrew Maurice. "The Person of Christ and the Nature of Human Participation in the Theology of T. F. Torrance." Ph.D. diss., University of London, 2002.

Branick, Vincent P. "The Sinful Flesh of the Son of God (Romans 8:3): A Key Image in Pauline Theology." *Catholic Biblical Quarterly* 47 (1985) 246–62.

Bruce, A. B. *The Humiliation of Christ*. New York: Hodder & Stroughton, 1895.

Calvin, John. *The Gospel according to John 1–10*. 2 vols. Edited by David W. Torrance and Thomas S. Torrance. Translated by T. H. L. Parker. Calvin's New Testament Commentaries. Grand Rapids: Eerdmans, 1961.

———. *The Institutes of the Christian Religion*. 2 vols. Edited by John T. McNeill. Translated by Ford Lewis Battles. The Library of Christian Classics 20–21. Philadelphia: Westminster, 1960.

Camfield, F. W. "The Idea of Substitution in the Doctrine of the Atonement." *Scottish Journal of Theology* 1 (1948) 282–93.

Campbell, John McLeod. *The Nature of the Atonement*. Reprint. Eugene, OR: Wipf & Stock, 1999.

Cass, Peter I. M. "Christ Condemned Sin in the Flesh: A Study in the Soteriology of T. F. Torrance with Particular Reference to the Relationship between the Incarnation and Atonement and the Ontological and Forensic Metaphors and Their Ecumenical Significance." Ph.D. diss., Princeton Theological Seminary, 2008.

Cassidy, James J. "T. F. Torrance's Realistic Soteriological Objectivism and the Elimination of Dualisms: Union with Christ in Current Perspective." *Mid-America Journal of Theology* 19 (2008) 165–94.

The Church of Scotland. *The Biblical Doctrine of Baptism: A Study Document Issued by The Special Commission on Baptism of the Church of Scotland*. Edinburgh: The Saint Andrew Press, 1958.

———. *Interim Report of the Special Commission on Baptism*, 1955.

Cochrane, Arthur C., editor. *Reformed Confessions of the Sixteenth Century*. Louisville: Westminster John Knox, 2003.

Colyer, Elmer M. *How To Read T. F. Torrance: Understanding His Trinitarian and Scientific Theology*. Downers Grove, IL: InterVarsity, 2001.

———. "The Incarnate Saviour: T. F. Torrance on the Atonement." In *An Introduction to Torrance Theology*, edited by Gerrit Scott Dawson, 33–54. London: T. & T. Clark, 2007.

———. *The Nature of Doctrine in T. F. Torrance's Theology*. Reprint. Eugene, OR: Wipf & Stock, 2001.

———, editor. *The Promise of Trinitarian Theology: Theologians in Dialogue with T. F. Torrance*. Oxford: Rowman and Littlefield, 2001.

———. "Thomas F. Torrance on the Holy Spirit." *Word and World* 23.2 (2003) 160–67.

Cranfield, C. E. B. *Romans: A Shorter Commentary*. Grand Rapids: Eerdmans, 1985.

Crisp, Oliver. "Did Christ Have a Fallen Nature?" *International Journal of Systematic Theology* 6.3 (2004) 270–88.

———. *Divinity and Humanity*. Cambridge: Cambridge University Press, 2007.

———. *God Incarnate: Explorations in Christology*. London: T. & T. Clark, 2009.

———. *Revisioning Christology: Theology in the Reformed Tradition*. Aldershot, UK: Ashgate, 2011.

Davidson, Ivor J. "Pondering the Sinlessness of Jesus Christ: Moral Christologies and the Witness of Scripture." *International Journal of Systematic Theology* 10.4 (2008) 372–98.

———. "Theologizing the Human Jesus: An Ancient (and Modern) Approach to Christology Reassessed." *International Journal of Systematic Theology* 3.2 (2001) 129–53.

Davis, Leo Donald. *The First Seven Ecumenical Councils (325–787) Their History and Theology*. Collegeville, MN: Liturgical, 1983.

Dawson, Gerrit Scott. "Far as the Curse is Found: The Significance of Christ's Assuming a Fallen Human Nature in Torrance Theology." In *An Introduction to Torrance Theology*, edited by Gerrit Scott Dawson, 55–74. London: T. & T. Clark, 2007.

———, editor. *An Introduction to Torrance Theology*. London: T. & T. Clark, 2007.

Deddo, Gary. "The Holy Spirit in T. F. Torrance's Theology." In *The Promise of Trinitarian Theology: Theologians in Dialogue with T. F. Torrance*, edited by Elmer M. Colyer, 81–114. Oxford: Rowman and Littlefield, 2001.

Dorries, David William. "Nineteenth-Century British Christological Controversy, Centering on Edward Irving's Doctrine of Christ's Human Nature." Ph.D. diss., University of Aberdeen, 1987.

Gill, Timothy Charles. "The Doctrine of Revelation in the Theology of Thomas F. Torrance." Ph.D. diss., University of Leeds, 2007.

Gillman, Florence Morgan. "Another Look at Romans 8:3: In the Likeness of Sinful Flesh." *Catholic Biblical Quarterly* 49.4 (1987) 597–604.

Gorringe, T. J. "Not Assumed Is Not Healed: The Homoousion and Liberation Theology." *Scottish Journal of Theology* 38 (1985) 481–90.

Green, Joel B. *The Gospel of Luke*. NICNT. Grand Rapids: Eerdmans, 1997.

Grillmeier, Alois. *Christ in the Christian Tradition. Vol. 1. From the Apostolic Age to Chalcedon (AD 451)*. Translated by John Bowden. London: Mowbray, 1995.

Gunton, Colin. "Two Dogmas Revisited: Edward Irving's Christology." *Scottish Journal of Theology* 41 (1988) 359–76.

Guthridge, Joannes S.J. "The Christology of T. F. Torrance: Revelation and Reconciliation in Christ." Ph.D. diss., Pontificia Universita Gregoriana, Rome, 1967.

Habets, Michael. "The Danger of Vertigo: An Evaluation and Critique of Theosis in the Theology of Thomas Forsyth Torrance." Ph.D. diss., University of Otago, 2006.

———. "The Doctrine of Election in Evangelical Calvinism: T. F. Torrance as a Case Study." *Irish Theological Quarterly* 73 (2008) 334–54.

Hart, Trevor. "Anselm of Canterbury and J. McLeod Campbell: Where Opposites Meet?" *Evangelical Quarterly* 62 (1990) 311–33.

———. "Irenaeus, Recapitulation and Physical Redemption." In *Christ in Our Place: The Humanity of God in Christ for the Reconciliation of the World*, edited by Trevor Hart and Daniel Thimell, 152–81. Allison Park, PA.: Pickwick, 1989.

———. Review of *In the Likeness of Sinful Flesh: An Essay on the Humanity of Christ*, by Thomas Weinandy. *Scottish Journal of Theology* 49 (1996) 254–55.

———. "Sinlessness and Moral Responsibility: A Problem in Christology." *Scottish Journal of Theology* 48 (1995) 37–54.

Hendry, G. S. *The Gospel of the Incarnation*. London: SCM, 1959.

Heppe, Heinrich. *Reformed Dogmatics*. Translated by G. T Thompson. London: Allen & Unwin, 1950.

Heron, Alasdair. "Homoousios with the Father." In *The Incarnation: Ecumenical Studies in the Nicene-Constantinopolitan Creed*, edited by T. F. Torrance, 58–87. Edinburgh: Handsel, 1981.

———. "T. F. Torrance in Relation to Reformed Theology." In *The Promise of Trinitarian Theology: Theologians in Dialogue with T. F. Torrance*, edited by Elmer M. Colyer, 31–49. Oxford: Rowman and Littlefield, 2001.

Ho, Man Kei. *A Critical Study on T. F. Torrance's Theology of Incarnation*. Bern: Lang, 2008.

Houssiau, A. "The Virginal Birth of Christ." In *The Incarnation: Ecumenical Studies in the Nicene-Constantinopolitan Creed*, edited by T. F. Torrance, 111–26. Edinburgh: Handsel, 1981.

Irving, Edward. *Christ's Holiness in the Flesh*. Edinburgh: Lindsay, 1831.

———. *The Orthodox and Catholic Doctrine of Our Lord's Human Nature*. London: Baldwin and Cradock, 1830.

Johnson, Harry. *The Humanity of the Savior: A Biblical and Historical Study of the Human Nature of Christ in Relation to Original Sin, with Special Reference to Its Soteriological Significance*. London: Epworth, 1962.

Jungmann, J. A. *The Place of Jesus Christ in Liturgical Prayer*. Translated by A. Peeler. Staten Island, NY: Alba House, 1925.

Kang, Phee Seng. "The Concept of the Vicarious Humanity of Christ in the Theology of Thomas Forsyth Torrance." Ph.D. diss., University of Aberdeen, 1983.

Kapic, Kelly M. "The Son's Assumption of a Human Nature: A Call for Clarity." *International Journal of Systematic Theology* 3.2 (2001) 154–66.

Kelly, D. F. "The Realist Epistemology of Thomas F. Torrance." In *An Introduction to Torrance Theology*, edited by Gerrit Scott Dawson, 75–102. London: T. & T. Clark, 2007.

Kelly, J. N. D. *Early Christian Doctrines*. San Francisco: Harper and Row, 1978.
Kettler, Christian D. *The Vicarious Humanity of Christ and the Reality of Salvation*. Lanham, MD: University Press of America, 1991.
Kirby, Richard. "The Theological Definition of Cosmic Disorder in the Writings of Thomas Forsyth Torrance." Ph.D. diss., University of London, 1992.
Klinefelter, D. S. "God and Rationality: A Critique of the Theology of T. F. Torrance." *Journal of Religion* 53.1 (1973) 117–35.
Kruger, C. Baxter. "Participation in the Self-Knowledge of God: The Nature and Means of Our Knowledge of God in the Theology of T. F. Torrance." Ph.D. diss., University of Aberdeen, 1989.
Lee, Kye Won. *Living in Union with Christ: The Practical Theology of Thomas F. Torrance*. Issues in Systematic Theology, vol. 11. New York: Lang, 2003.
Lucas, Robert H. "The Whole Christ for the Whole Person: A Comparative and Critical Study of the Doctrine of Personhood in Hans Urs von Balthasar and the Doctrine of Sanctification in T. F. Torrance in Light of Their Trinitarian Theology." Ph.D. diss., University of Aberdeen, 1997.
Luoma, Tapio. *Incarnation and Physics: Natural Science in the Theology of Thomas F. Torrance*. American Academy of Religion Series. Oxford: Oxford University Press, 2002.
Mackintosh, H. R. *The Doctrine of the Person of Jesus Christ*. Edinburgh: T. & T. Clark, 1912.
Macleod, Donald. "Dr. T. F. Torrance and Scottish Theology: A Review Article." *Evangelical Quarterly* 72.1 (2000) 57–72.
———. *The Person of Christ*. Downers Grove, IL: InterVarsity, 1998.
Marley, Alan G. *T. F. Torrance: The Rejection of Dualism*. Edinburgh: Hansel, 1992.
McCall, Tom. "Ronald Theimann, Thomas Torrance and Epistemological Doctrines of Revelation." *International Journal of Systematic Theology* 6.2 (2004) 148–68.
McCormack, Bruce L. "For Us and Our Salvation: Incarnation and Atonement in the Reformed Tradition." *Greek Orthodox Theological Review* 43 (1998) 281–316.
McFarland, Ian A. "Fallen or Unfallen? Christ's Human Nature and the Ontology of Human Sinfulness." *International Journal of Systematic Theology* 10.4 (2008) 399–415.
McGrath, Alister E. *T. F. Torrance: An Intellectual Biography*. Edinburgh: T. & T. Clark, 1999.
McGuckin, John Anthony. *The Westminster Handbook to Patristic Theology*. Lousiville: Westminster John Knox, 2004.
Methodios, Archbishop. "The Homoousion." In *The Incarnation: Ecumenical Studies in the Nicene-Constantinopolitan Creed*, edited by T. F. Torrance, 1–15. Edinburgh: Handsel, 1981.
Meyendorff, John. "Christ's Humanity: The Pascal Mystery." *St. Vladimir's Seminary Quarterly* 31.1 (1987) 5–40.
Molnar, Paul D. *Thomas F. Torrance: Theologian of the Trinity*. Aldershot, UK: Ashgate, 2009.
Morrison, John Douglas. *Knowledge of the Self-Revealing God in the Thought of Thomas Forsyth Torrance*. Eugene, OR: Wipf & Stock, 1997.
Muller, Richard A. "The Barth Legacy: New Athanasius or Origen Redivivus? A Response to T. F. Torrance." *The Thomist* 54 (1990) 673–704.

Ott, Ludwig. *Fundamentals of Catholic Dogma*. 4th ed. Edited by James Canon Bastible. Translated by Patrick Lynch. Rockford: Tan, 1960.
Owen, H. P. "The Sinlessness of Jesus." In *Religion, Reason and the Self: Essays in Honor of Hywel D. Lewis*, edited by Stewart R. Sutherland and T. A. Roberts, 119–28. Cardiff: University of Wales Press, 1989.
Palma, Robert J. "Thomas F. Torrance's Reformed Theology." *Reformed Journal* 38.1 (1984) 2–46.
Purves, Andrew. "The Christology of T. F. Torrance." In *The Promise of Trinitarian Theology: Theologians in Dialogue with T. F. Torrance*, edited by Elmer M. Colyer, 51–80. Oxford: Rowman and Littlefield, 2001.
———. "Who is the Incarnate Saviour of the World?" In *An Introduction to Torrance Theology*, edited by Gerrit Scott Dawson, 23–32. London: T. & T. Clark, 2007.
Rankin, Duncan. "Carnal Union with Christ in the Theology of T. F. Torrance." Ph.D. diss., University of Edinburgh, 1998.
Redding, Graham. *Prayer and the Priesthood of Christ in the Reformed Tradition*. Edinburgh: T. & T. Clark, 2003.
Richardson, Kurt Anders. "Revelation, Scripture, and Mystical Apprehension of Divine Knowledge." In *The Promise of Trinitarian Theology: Theologians in Dialogue with T. F. Torrance*, edited by Elmer M. Colyer, 185–204. Oxford: Rowman and Littlefield, 2001.
Robertson, L. G. "The Relationship between Incarnation and Atonement in the Theology of T. F. Torrance." Th.M., Australian College of Theology, 1990.
Sarisky, Darren. "T. F. Torrance on Biblical Interpretation." *International Journal of Systematic Theology* 11.3 (2009) 332–46.
Scandrett, Joel Alan. "Suffering Servant, Wounded Word, Troubled Trinity: The Passion of God in the Theology of T. F. Torrance." Ph.D. diss. Madison, NJ: Drew University, 2006.
Shults, F. LeRon. "A Dubious Christological Formula from Leontius of Byzantium to Karl Barth." *Theological Studies* 57 (1996) 431–36.
Smail, Thomas A. *The Giving Gift: The Holy Spirit in Person*. London: Hodder and Stoughton, 1988.
Stamps, Robert J. *The Sacrament of the Word Made Flesh: The Eucharistic Theology of T. F. Torrance*. Edinburgh: Rutherford House, 2007.
Strachan, Gordon. *The Pentecostal Theology of Edward Irving*. London: Darton, Longman & Todd, 1973.
Tanner, Kathryn. *Christ the Key*. Cambridge: Cambridge University Press, 2010.
Thimell, Daniel, and Trevor Hart, editors. *Christ in Our Place: The Humanity of God in Christ for the Reconciliation of the World*. Allison Park, PA.: Pickwick, 1989.
Torrance, Iain R. *Christology After Chalcedon: Severus of Antioch and Sergius the Monophysite*. Eugene, OR: Wipf & Stock, 1998.
———. "Creation and Incarnation." *Greek Orthodox Theological Review* 43 (1998) 353–63.
Torrance, J. B. "The Contribution of John McLeod Campbell to Scottish Theology." *Scottish Journal of Theology* 31 (1973) 295–311.
———. "The Vicarious Humanity of Christ." In *The Incarnation: Ecumenical Studies in the Nicene-Constantinopolitan Creed*, edited by T. F. Torrance, 127–47. Edinburgh: Handsel, 1981.

Torrance, T. F., editor. *Belief in Science and in Christian Life: The Relevance of Michael Polanyi's Thought for Christian Faith and Life*. Reprint. Eugene, OR: Wipf & Stock, 1998.

———, editor. *The Incarnation: Ecumenical Studies on the Nicene-Constantinopolitan Creed*. Edinburgh: Handsel, 1981.

———, editor. *A Passion for Christ: The Vision That Ignites Ministry*. Edinburgh: Handsel, 1999.

———. "Alexandrian Theology." *Ekklesiastikos Pharos* 52 (1970) 185–89.

———. "Athanasius: A Reassessment of His Theology." *Abba Salama* 5 (1974) 171–87.

———. "The Atonement and the Oneness of the Church." *Scottish Journal of Theology* 7 (1954) 245–69.

———. *Atonement: The Person and Work of Christ*. Edited by Robert T. Walter. Milton Keynes, UK: Paternoster, 2009.

———. "The Atonement. The Singularity of Christ and the Finality of the Cross: The Atonement and the Moral Order." In *Universalism and the Doctrine of Hell*, edited by Nigel M. de S. Cameron, 225–56. Exeter, UK: Paternoster, 1992.

———. "The Atoning Obedience of Christ." *Moravian Theological Seminary Bulletin* (Fall 1959) 65–81.

———. *Calvin's Doctrine of Man*. London: Lutterworth, 1949.

———. *The Centrality of Christ: Devotions and Addresses at the General Assembly of the Church of Scotland, May, 1976*. Edinburgh: St. Andrew, 1976.

———. *The Christian Doctrine of God: One Being Three Persons*. Edinburgh: T. & T. Clark, 1996.

———. *The Christian Frame of Mind: Reason, Order and Openness in Theology and Natural Science*. Colorado Springs: Helmers & Howard, 1989.

———. *Christian Theology and Scientific Culture*. Oxford: Oxford University Press, 1981.

———. "Christian/Jewish Dialogue: Report of the Overseas Council of the Church of Scotland." In *The Witness of the Jews to God*, edited by D. W. Torrance, 139–50. Edinburgh: Handsel, 1982.

———. *Conflict and Agreement in the Church: Order and Disorder*. Vol. 1. Oxford: Oxford University Press, 1959.

———. *Conflict and Agreement in the Church: The Ministry and the Sacraments of the Gospel*. Vol. 2. Oxford: Oxford University Press, 1960.

———. "The Distinctive Character of the Reformed Tradition." In *Incarnational Ministry: The Presence of Christ in Church, Society, and Family*, edited by Christian D. Kettler and Todd H. Speidell, 2–15. Colorado Springs: Helmers & Howard, 1990.

———. *Divine and Contingent Order*. Edinburgh: T. & T. Clark, 1981.

———. *Divine Meaning: Studies in Patristic Hermeneutics*. Edinburgh: T. & T. Clark, 1995.

———. "The Divine Vocation and Destiny of Israel in World History." In *The Witness of the Jews to God*, edited by D. W. Torrance, 85–104. Edinburgh: Handsel, 1982.

———. *The Doctrine of Grace in the Apostolic Fathers*. Edinburgh: Oliver and Boyd, 1948.

———. "The Doctrine of Grace in the Old Testament." *Scottish Journal of Theology* 1 (1948) 55–65.

———. *The Doctrine of Jesus Christ*. Reprint. Eugene, OR: Wipf & Stock, 2002.

———. "The Doctrine of the Virgin Birth." *Scottish Bulletin of Evangelical Theology* 12.1 (1994) 9.
———. "Dramatic Proclamation of the Gospel: Homily on the Passion of Melito of Sardis." *Greek Orthodox Theological Review* 37 (1992) 147–63.
———. "The Evangelical Significance of the Homoousion: Sermon on John 5:17." *Abba Salama* 5 (1974) 165–68.
———. "The First-Born of All Creation." *Life and Work*, December 1976, 12–14.
———. *God and Rationality*. London: Oxford University Press, 1971.
———. "The Goodness and Dignity of Man in the Christian Tradition." *Modern Theology* 4 (1988) 309–22.
———. *The Ground and Grammar of Theology*. Charlottesville, VA: The University of Virginia Press, 1980.
———. "Hugh Ross Mackintosh: Theologian of the Cross." *Scottish Bulletin of Evangelical Theology* 5 (1987) 160–73.
———. "Incarnation and Atonement: Theosis and Henosis in the Light of Modern Scientific Rejection of Dualism." *Society of Ordained Scientists Bulletin* 7 (Spring 1992) 8–20.
———. *Incarnation: The Person and Life of Christ*. Edited by Robert T. Walter. Milton Keynes, UK: Paternoster, 2008.
———. "Introduction: Robert Bruce of Kinnaird." In *The Mystery of the Lord's Supper: Sermons on the Sacrament Preached in the Kirk of Edinburgh by Robert Bruce in A.D. 1589*, edited by T. F. Torrance, 13–36. London: James Clarke, 1958.
———. "Introduction." In *Theology and Church: The Shorter Writings 1920–1928*, by Karl Barth, 7–54. New York: Harper and Row, 1962.
———. "Israel and the Incarnation." *Interpretation* 10 (1956) 305–20.
———. "Israel: People of God—God, Destiny and Suffering." *Theological Renewal* 13 (1979) 2–14.
———. *Karl Barth: An Introduction to His Early Theology 1910–1931*. Edinburgh: T. & T. Clark, 1962.
———. "Karl Barth and Patristic Theology." In *Theology Beyond Christendom: Essays on the Centenary of the Birth of Karl Barth*, edited by John Thompson, 215–39. Allison Park, PA.: Pickwick, 1986.
———. "Karl Barth and the Latin Heresy." *Scottish Journal of Theology* 39 (1986) 461–82.
———. *Karl Barth: Biblical and Evangelical Theologian*. Edinburgh: T. & T. Clark, 1990.
———. "Karl Barth." *Scottish Journal of Theology* 22 (1969) 1–9.
———. "The Kerygmatic Proclamation of the Gospel: The Demonstration of the Apostolic Preaching of Irenaeus of Lyons." *Greek Orthodox Theological Review* 37 (1992) 105–21.
———. "The Legacy of Karl Barth (1886–1968)." *Scottish Journal of Theology* 39 (1986) 289–308.
———. *The Mediation of Christ*. Colorado Springs: Helmers and Howard, 1992.
———. "The Mission of the Church." *Scottish Journal of Theology* 19 (1966) 129–43.
———. "My Interaction with Karl Barth." In *How Karl Barth Changed My Mind*, edited by Donald K. McKim, 52–64. Grand Rapids: Eerdmans, 1986.
———. "The Place of Christology in Biblical and Dogmatic Theology." In *Essays in Christology for Karl Barth*, edited by T. H. L Parker, 13–37. London: Lutterworth, 1956.

———. "The Place of the Humanity of Christ in the Sacramental Life of the Church." *Church Service Society Annual* 26 (1956) 3–10.

———. *Preaching Christ Today: The Gospel and Scientific Thinking*. Grand Rapids: Eerdmans, 1994.

———. "Predestination in Christ." *The Evangelical Quarterly* 13.2 (1941) 108–41.

———. "The Problem of Natural Theology in the Thought of Karl Barth." *Religious Studies* 6 (1970) 121–35.

———. *Reality and Evangelical Theology: The Realism of Christian Revelation*. Downers Grove, IL: InterVarsity, 1982.

———. *Reality and Scientific Theology*. Reprint. Eugene, OR: Wipf & Stock, 2001.

———. "The Reconciliation of Mind." *TSF Bulletin* 10.3 (1987) 4–7.

———. "The Relation of the Incarnation to Space in Nicene Theology." In *The Ecumenical World of Orthodox Civilization III. Russia and Orthodoxy: Essays in Honor of Georges Florovsky*, edited by Andrew Blance, 43–70. The Hague: Mouton, 1973.

———. Review of *The Inspiration and Authority of the Bible*, by B. B. Warfield. *Scottish Journal of Theology* 7 (1954) 104–8.

———. *Royal Priesthood: A Theology of Ordained Ministry*. Edinburgh: T. & T. Clark, 1993.

———. "Salvation is of the Jews." *Evangelical Quarterly* 22 (1950) 164–73.

———. *The School of Faith: The Catechisms of the Reformed Church*. Reprint. Eugene, OR: Wipf & Stock, 1996.

———. *Scottish Theology: From John Knox to John McLeod Campbell*. Edinburgh: T. & T. Clark, 1996.

———. "The Soul and Person in Theological Perspective." In *Religion, Reason and the Self: Essays in Honor of Hywel D. Lewis*, edited by Stewart R. Sutherland, 103–18. Cardiff: University of Wales Press, 1989.

———. "The Soul and Person in Theological Perspective." In *Religion, Reason and The Self*, edited by Stewart R. Sutherland, 103–18. Cardiff: University of Wales Press, 1989.

———. *Space, Time and Incarnation*. Edinburgh: T. & T. Clark, 1969.

———. *Space, Time and Resurrection*. Edinburgh: Handsel, 1976.

———. "Theological Realism." In *The Philosophical Frontiers of Christian Theology*, edited by Brian Hebblethwaite and Stewart Sutherland, 169–96. Cambridge: Cambridge University Press, 1982.

———. *Theological Science*. Edinburgh: T. & T. Clark, 1969.

———. *Theology in Reconciliation: Essays Toward Evangelical and Catholic Unity in East and West*. Grand Rapids: Eerdmans, 1975.

———. *Theology in Reconstruction*. Grand Rapids: Eerdmans, 1965.

———. *Transformation and Convergence in the Frame of Knowledge: Explorations in the Interrelations of Scientific and Theological Enterprise*. Reprint. Eugene, OR: Wipf & Stock, 1998.

———. *The Trinitarian Faith*. Edinburgh: T. & T. Clark, 1991.

———. *Trinitarian Perspectives: Toward Doctrinal Agreement*. Edinburgh: T. & T. Clark, 1994.

———. "Truth and Authority: Theses on Truth." *Irish Theological Quarterly* 39 (1972) 215–42.

———. "The Truth of the Virgin Birth." *Herald Scotland*, 14 January 1994.

———. "Universalism of Election?" *Scottish Journal of Theology* 2 (1949) 310–18.
———. "What is the Church?" *Ecumenical Review* II (October 1958) 6–21.
———. *When Christ Comes and Comes Again*. Grand Rapids: Eerdmans, 1957.
Trook, Douglas A. "The Unified Christocentric Field: Toward a Time-Eternity Relativity Model for Theological Hermeneutics in the Onto-Relational Theology of Thomas F. Torrance." Ph.D. diss., Drew University, Madison, NJ, 1986.
Turner, H. E. W. *The Patristic Doctrine of Redemption: A Study in the Development of Doctrine during the First Five Centuries*. Reprint. Eugene, OR: Wipf & Stock, 2004.
Twombly, C. C. "The Nature of Christ's Humanity: A Study in Athanasius." *Patristic and Byzantine Review* 8.3 (1989) 227–41.
Walgrave, J. H. "Incarnation and Atonement." In *The Incarnation: Ecumenical Studies in the Nicene-Constantinopolitan Creed*, edited by T. F. Torrance, 148–76. Edinburgh: Handsel, 1981.
Walker, Robert T. "Editor's Introduction." In *Incarnation: The Person and Life of Christ*, by T. F. Torrance, xxi–lii. Milton Keynes, UK: Paternoster, 2008.
———. "Editor's Introduction." In *Atonement: The Person and Work of Christ*, by T. F. Torrance, xxxv–lxxxiv. Milton Keynes, UK: Paternoster, 2009.
Weinandy, Thomas G. *In the Likeness of Sinful Flesh: An Essay on the Humanity of Christ*. Edinburgh: T. & T. Clark, 1993.
Wiles, Maurice. *The Making of Christian Doctrine*. London: Cambridge University Press, 1967.
———. "The Nature of the Early Debate about Christ's Human Soul." *Journal of Ecclesiastical History* 16 (1965) 139–51.
———. *Working Papers in Doctrine*. London: SCM, 1976.
Yeung, J. H. "Being and Knowing: An Examination of T. F. Torrance's Christological Science." Ph.D. diss., University of London, 1993.

www.ingramcontent.com/pod-product-compliance
Lightning Source LLC
Chambersburg PA
CBHW051639230426
43669CB00013B/2361